Forgotten Families

of Hertfordshire and Bedfordshire

by

Evelyn Wright

The
Book
Castle

Also by Evelyn Wright:

Six Weeks is Forever
A Hertfordshire Family 1555 - 1923
St Michael's Woburn Sands - The Church, the Parish and the People
A Scottish Country Doctor 1818 - 1873

First published October 2003 by
The Book Castle
12 Church Street
Dunstable
Bedfordshire LU5 4RU

ISBN 1 903 747 39 2

Typeset by Heath Publications Bedfordshire
Printed by Antony Rowe Ltd.,
Chippenham, Wiltshire

Cover picture: Shephallbury, Stevenage about 1877

Contents

Illustrations

Illustrations on pages 15, 18, 20, 26, 32, 34, 38, 39, 42, 44, 46, 47, 61, 74, 76, 78, 82, 88, 140 are reproduced by permission of the Hertfordshire Archives and Local Studies. Illustrations on pages 4, 10, 28, 98, 111 are reproduced by permission of the Bedfordshire and Luton Archives and Records Service, on page 97 by permission of the Essex Record Office, and on page 133 by permission of the Suffolk Records Office.

Sources and Acknowledgements

The main sources of information have been the Victoria County Histories, the Heralds' Visitations (various editions) and the historical works of Sir Henry Chauncy (writing c.1700), Robert Clutterbuck (1815-27) and John Edwin Cussons (1870-81). Other books consulted include G M Trevelyan - English Social History; The Paston Letters ed. John Warrington; Tudor Food and Pastimes - F G Emmison; History of Bedfordshire - Joyce Godber; The History of Hitchin - Reginald Hine; The Wymondleys - Noel Farris; Austin's History of Luton; A Pilgrimage in Hertfordshire - H M Alderman; The Muster Books of North and East Hertfordshire ed. Ann J King; The Accounts of Thomas Green ed. Gillian Sheldrick; Clode's Early History of the Guild of Merchant Taylors; Liberty Loyalty Property - A G Davies.

I acknowledge with thanks the help of the Hertfordshire Archives and Local Studies; The Bedfordshire and Luton Archives and Records Service and the Essex and Suffolk Records Offices.

I am grateful to John Timpson for allowing me to quote from his Timpsons English Eccentrics and to Ann King for quotations from the introduction to the Hertfordshire Record Society publication mentioned above. I should also like to express my thanks to all who have allowed me to photograph their houses.

Thanks to the Harmer Family Association for their help in the early stages of my Harmer family research, and to Cynthia and Sue Cox, my fellow researchers (and distant cousins). Special thanks to Sue for her amazing skill and patience in deciphering and transcribing almost illegible 16th and 17th century wills and documents.

Finally I must record my gratitude to my husband John for his technical skill and expertise in designing the format of the book and particularly for the setting out of the family pedigrees.

Evelyn Wright
Aspley Heath, May 2003

Introduction

Let us now praise famous men, and our fathers that begat us
Such as did bear rule in their kingdoms ..... and were the glory
of their times.   Ecclesiasticus XLIV

This is a collection of stories about people once famous but now mainly forgotten, who lived in Hertfordshire and Bedfordshire many years ago. All of them were well-known in their day, and played a leading part in the life of the community. They formed an intriguing network across the two counties, the families marrying into each other generation after generation, and sometimes renewing links after a gap of nearly a hundred years.

The network extended into Suffolk and Essex and there it stopped. Even so, it is difficult to imagine how they kept in touch in the days when the only means of communication would have been a messenger on horseback! There would have been long and dangerous journeys to visit relatives as far apart as Hertford and Bury St Edmunds.

This book sets out not to praise these 'famous men' of the past, but rather to get to know them. They were all part of my own family, most of them direct ancestors. But we all have ancestors who lived through this period of history, and by finding out more about them we can bring them to life. We owe them so much - not least our very existence!

The quotation from Ecclesiasticus goes on to say "and some there be which have no memorial, who have perished as though they had never been." Some of the people mentioned in this book did have memorials. There are plaques and tombstones in many of our ancient churches, and sometimes almshouses, schools and colleges which they endowed still bear their names. For others there is no visible memorial. But we know that they still live on, each one a unique and indispensible part of this mysterious universe. Time is a strange dimension - difficult to comprehend. Time moves on, but it certainly does not wipe out what has gone before.

Many things change, but human nature remains the same. Although we lead very different lives we can still see our own characteristics in our ancient kinsmen, and can identify with their hopes and fears, their joys and sorrows. Above all we can enjoy their eccentricities!

These are people who lived here long ago, but whose past has in some way helped to shape our lives at the present day.

Chapter 1

The Bechers of Howbury Hall, Renhold

From the time they settled in Renhold around the year 1600, right through to the time when they sold the manor in 1781, the Bechers seem to have enjoyed a lifestyle rather more luxurious than most of their neighbours. During the earlier years we are told that Howbury Hall, in contrast to the manor owned by the Franklins nearby, was very elaborately furnished with curtains and chairs of satin and velvet, rich tapestries on the walls and a picture of Queen Elizabeth.

In fact there was probably an element of "keeping up with the Bechers" among the local gentry. This flamboyant behaviour was certainly carried over into the next century, when in 1730 we hear that Mrs Becher turned up at the Bedford Races in a Coach and Six!

This same Mrs Becher also entertained in grand style, her guest list including Sir George and Lady Byng, Lady Burgoyne, Sir Rowland Alston, Sir William Gostwick, and even the Duke of Bedford. Her dinner book, which has fortunately been preserved in the archives, is full of mouth-watering menus, though some items such as Roast Udder and Heart might not appeal to present day tastes. We can be sure, however, that it was all organically produced!

The Early Bechers

Sir William Becher bought Howbury Hall in 1624, but there is evidence in the Parish Registers that the family were in Renhold as early as 1603, so it seems likely that William moved there around the time of his marriage in 1595.

Sir William's grandfather was Henry Becher, a London Alderman, the son of a draper from Kent, who left all of his eleven sons an annuity of £200 apiece. Henry was the only son to have issue, so it seems that he inherited a fairly large fortune.

He married the daughter of Sir Nicholas Heron of Edcombe in Kent who would presumably bring with her a good dowry, so by the time William's father (also Henry) succeeded, the family fortunes would have been looking quite good. This Henry married the daughter and heir of John Kirk of Deptford, physician to the Queen, and his brother Edward was "Esquire to the Body" of the Queen. With all these Court connections it is not surprising that the furnishings of Howbury Hall included a picture of Queen Elizabeth. The link with the Royal household was extended even further when Sir William later married into the St John family of Bletsoe. (see footnote)

Howbury Hall

We can trace the history of Howbury Hall back to the 13th century when it was owned by John de Hoobury from whom it took its name. He acquired it from his wife, a member of the Beauchamp family, who owned most of the land in and around Bedford from the time of the Conquest.

Howbury Hall near Bedford

In the 14th century the manor was owned by the Piggot family, until they exchanged it with Elizabeth Latimer, their cousin, for the manor of Cardington. The Latimers, Nevills and Mowbrays, all closely related, owned the other manors of Renhold, and now they would all be united. The Piggot arms can be seen (if your eyesight is very good) on the south side of the tower of Renhold Church. The Gostwick family of Willington were the next owners, and it was from them that Sir William Becher bought the manor in 1624.

A Luxurious Lifestyle

When he settled into Howbury Hall, Sir William's large family of seven sons and four daughters were already growing up. He had married in 1595 Elizabeth, the daughter of Sir John St John of Bletsoe. It was during Sir William's lifetime that the house took on its luxurious style. We are told that they had court cupboards, cushions of crimson velvet embroidered with gold, a painted cloth 33 yards long with the story of the prodigal son, chairs of silk, velvet, satin and embroidery - and of course, the picture of Queen Elizabeth.

There were fires in most of the rooms and twice a year seventeen chimneys were swept at a cost of 17 shillings. A great deal of money was spent on clothes. The tailor's bill for William Becher for one year was £37 and items included doublets and cloaks, one trimmed with silver lace, and a hat with a pearled band. Hats were worn indoors for all formal occasions (except in the presence of the Sovereign) and also at meals. Gentlemen always wore their hats in church, and women were never seen with their heads uncovered.

In 1645 six yards of scarlet cloth at 42 shillings a yard were purchased for making a cloak. Then there were the buttons and buckles. Gold and silver buttons were available from Ralph Smith the draper, who was mayor of Bedford in 1676. Most of the Becher family clothes came from London, but gloves were bought in Northampton.

The bills for food were also quite substantial, although it must be remembered that the household would be very large. Sir William had eleven children and presumably a large staff living in. There was a bill for £100 one year for meat, presumably bought from the Home Farm, and £30 was spent on bread, cakes and flour from the local baker.

Compared with the bill for food, the bill for staff wages was very low. Sir William's man cook had £8 a year, Lady Becher's maid had £4 and Nan the washmaid had £2 10s. But even these wages were above the statutory maximum wage which was laid down each year at the Quarter Sessions, the general rate for a washmaid being only £2.

Two generations later we read of the expenses for the second Sir William, knighted at the time of the Restoration. When he and his second wife with their 8 children and various relatives were living at Howbury Hall, a year's supply of beef cost £62, with £37 for other meat. Sugar, spice, soap and "other small things" sent from London cost £40. Sir William paid Mr Zouch £10 for his wife's portrait in 1665, and he gave her various presents of jewellery, and also a yearly allowance for her own use. The accounts show money spent on Valentines, but to whom they were sent we do not know.

Sir Oliver Becher, a Proud and Affectionate Father

Many of the family details in the archives were recorded by Oliver, the eldest son and heir of the first Sir William, who would have taken over the manor when his father died in 1640. His mother, Elizabeth St John, lived on until 1658, but probably moved out to the Dower House. Although there would have been plenty of room in the manor house it was usual for the widow to move out, to make way for the new Lady of the Manor.

Oliver was born in 1608, and in 1627 he married Elizabeth, daughter of Sir William Tate of Delapré near Northampton. They had ten children and Oliver was obviously a very proud and affectionate father. He makes three detailed lists in his records - one simply giving the names and dates of birth of each of the children, to which he later added notes about their marriages and families. The second list gives the exact day and time of their birth - for example: "William Becher was borne the 24th of Aprill 1628 being Thursday, about 4 of the clock in the morning." This was the eldest son, later to become the second Sir William, and Member of Parliament for Bedford in 1667.

The other children were Oliver 1629, Edward 1630, Elizabeth 1631, John 1633, Francis 1634, Mary 1635, Judith 1636, St John 1637 (sometimes written phonetically as Sinjion) and Katherine 1640.

The third list gives the godparents of all the children, and there are many distinguished names among them. They include Zouch Tate Esq, My Lord St

John, Sir John Hurst, My Lady Chernock, My Lord Rochford and Sir Beauchamp St John. The St John family were godparents on many occasions, as the children's grandmother was of course Elizabeth St John, and there was soon to be another link with the family.

The three eldest children, we are told, were born at Fotheringay - presumably the home of the maternal grandparents, but all the rest were born at Howbury Hall. We are told that little Edward Becher, being five years old, died at Delapré on the 13th December 1635 and was buried at Hardingstone Church.

The Next Generation

When Oliver Becher (the father) died he was succeeded by his eldest son William who was married to another member of the St John family - Frances, the eldest daughter and co-heir of Oliver Lord St John, son of the Earl of Bolingbroke. Having produced two children - Anabella and St John, she died just before William received his knighthood.

William remarried two years later. His second wife, the widow of Mr Hillersden of Elstow, was the daughter of Mr Huxley of Edmonton. We hear a great deal about this Lady Becher. It was she who had her portrait painted, and who received gifts of pendants and other jewellery from her husband. She also helped to re-organise the garden at Howbury Hall with 200 rose trees. She produced four more children for Sir William, and it was her son William who inherited from his father. St John, the eldest son of the first marriage had already died without issue.

Sir William died in 1694 and was buried in the chancel of Renhold Church. His widow Lady Becher went to live in Bow where she died in 1704. She came back to Bedfordshire to be buried beside her first husband at Elstow.

William, the next Lord of the Manor of Howbury Hall, was married to Mary Denis of Kempston in 1697. They had a son William, but poor Mary died just 6 weeks after the birth, at the age of 24. William remarried in 1699. His wife was Jane Clarke and it was Jane who became well known as the writer of the Dinner Book. They had two daughters. Jane Rachell was born in 1700, and one of her godmothers is recorded as the Countess of Bristol, suggesting a link with the Hervey family. Their second daughter Mary was born two years later, but she died of convulsions at the age of six months. She too had some distinguished godparents - The Earl of Bolingbroke, Lady Crouch and Lady Franklin.

The eldest son, William, whose birth cost Mary Denis her life, inherited the estate. He married a Miss Clarke in 1751 and died without issue. His widow enjoyed the estate until her death in 1766.

After this we hear little more about the family, but we know that Edward Becher was Lord Mayor of London in 1727 and that members of the family lived on at Renhold even after the estate was sold.

The Tenants and their Peculiarities

Apart from the family details one of the most interesting items in the archives is the list of tenants, with remarks about their characters which are very revealing. They were obviously meant to be confidential because they are listed by numbers and are not on the same page as the names themselves. (The Vicars at this time were not always quite so careful. They sometimes wrote remarks about the personal life or character of their parishioners in the Burial Registers).

We are told that one family is industrious but sick, and another "good young people likely to do well". There is also "a good farmer and industrious wife, but ill-matched notwithstanding". A young bricklayer is "likely to retrieve his father's hopes" and we learn that the blacksmith will do well if he can with so large a family. Another entry states "Schoolmaster and of course learned and virtuous". Of course!! Another tenant is "a good farmer and an honest fellow, very kind to his housekeeper".

There are not many adverse remarks, but the writer does describe one as a "notorious Fidler and an idle thoughtless young man". Another is "industrious and thriving but an odd boy".

Fishing in the Ouse - from Robin's Brook to Gadsey Corner

One item in the records which may interest local residents is the entry about the fishing rights. "The Becher Royalty for free fishing in the River Ouse and Back Brook is from Robin's Brook Goldington to Gadsey Corner, a mile in length." This is mentioned in a Deed dated 24 March 1650.

Over the years several members of the Becher family were Justices of the Peace or Members of Parliament. The country gentleman usually represented his own home constituency and, we are told, often won the seat by bribery.

Parliamentary Elections - Bribery and Corruption!

There was sometimes outright bribery with large sums of money changing hands, or perhaps pressure from the landlord to the tenant. The 3rd Duke of Bedford, we read, declared that he knew the election of 1727 was to be bought and that he would buy it even if it was 4 guineas a vote. Sir William Gostwick of Willington, one of the county members for 1698-1713, fought seven elections and at the end of his Parliamentary career he was in debt to the extent of £26,500. A few years later his grandson and heir was obliged to sell the estates and leave the country.

As we know, Sir William Becher was the Member for Bedford soon after the Restoration, and there is no evidence that he had to resort to bribery. But the guest lists for the famous dinner parties described in Mrs Becher's Dinner Book certainly included more gentlemen than ladies, perhaps suggesting a 'political' reason for inviting them.

Mrs Becher's Dinner Book

Mrs Becher's Dinner Book is perhaps the most fascinating item in the Becher archives and has become well-known as a valuable piece of social history. In addition to the guests listed earlier, we also find Mr Hillersden and Mr Ferrer, both of whom were Members for Bedford Town.

There is also Parson Laurence, Parson Bolton, Mr Chester, Mr Osborn, Mr Howland, Major and Mrs Aspin, Lady Manax, Sir Samuel Ongle, Brother and Sister Hanbury, Captain Elloways and Cousin St John. Frequent guests were members of the various families into which the Bechers had married, and of course of the Becher family itself.

The first menu to be recorded is dated Nov. 1st 1709, and to give an idea of the general pattern this one is quoted in full:

A Soup
A Fish
a calves head Hashed   a custard Puding   3 fowles & a tongue & rice
_____

2nd Snipes and Larks
stewed oysters   custard cheesecakes   a coller of Eele
& roasted apples
2 neats tongues   4 partrages & 5 boned pidgeons   A Scorseneroe Pye
a jole of Sturgeon
_____

3rd with Sweetmeats
dryed cumfits   dryed sweetmeats
& pastatiahs
Jellys
peaches   pears
Cheese
_____

november ye 1st 1709   & a rump of Beef roasted
at the side table

Other items on the menus include Hogee Pogee (perhaps an 18th century version of Lancashire Hot Pot), Hanch of Venison, Buttock of Beef, Loyn of mutton, rabbits, Pigg, Green Goose and Lampery. A favourite vegetable was the Heartychoke, and we also hear of tansy, turneps, carrots, and cabbedg, but no mention of brussels sprouts!

When the Duke of Bedford came to dinner the menu included 3 turkeys and 6 lobsters. The guest list on that occasion included Gostwick, Orlebar, Bell and Hillersden, presumably without their wives, and just Mrs Howland and Mrs Nelthrup to represent the ladies. There is no mention of the Duchess of Bedford.

This Mrs Becher was quite an outstanding character. She was Jane Clarke, daughter of Sir George Clarke of Watford and maternally descended from the 1st Earl of Bridgwater. She, like the Bechers, was also related to the St John family of Bletsoe.

Captain Becher and Becher's Brook

It was almost certainly this Mrs Becher who arrived at the Bedford races in a coach and six. These races were first held on Cow Meadow in 1730, and soon became a regular event.

A hundred years later the Becher name appears again in connection with the steeplechase, described as "the bastard sport of hurdle racing to please the ladies". The race held on March 8th 1830 was said to be the first organised steeplechase ever run in England. It started on the hill where Harlington Church stands and the winning post was the obelisk in Wrest Park. Captain Becher, riding Tatler, was one of those taking part. His name is now best remembered by its association with the Grand National course at Aintree - and the famous Becher's Brook. Captain Becher was also involved with setting up the steeplechase headquarters at the Turf Hotel in St Albans.

When Sir William's grandson William died without issue in 1751 the next heir was John, the grandson of Sir William's younger son John, and he was succeeded by Richard who sold Howbury Hall in 1781 to Nathaniel Polhill, a Tobacco Merchant and Banker of Southwark. Richard, we are told, was leaving the Kingdom for the East Indies, where he would no doubt set up a business with the £17,500 he received for the manor.

The present Howbury Hall is a rebuilding of the early 18th century house which was almost completely destroyed by a disastrous fire in 1849.

Members of the Becher family continued to live on in the area after the manor was sold, but they gradually faded from the limelight. The name however will be remembered and the family certainly left their mark on the parish.

Communion silver was given to the church by both Elizabeth and William Becher in 1675 and 1684, and the Becher arms are on the flagon and patten. A later communion cup has the initials E.B. and the date 1734.

In 1723 William Becher left £600 for purchase of land to provide an income for maintaining a schoolmaster, and of course, Becher's Brook has entered and become established in the racing vocabulary of the 21st century.

The family also left its mark in the valuable accounts and household details now safely preserved in the Bedfordshire Records Office, just waiting for the rare occasions when they can be brought to light. On these occasions the family comes to life once more, as we picture the people who lived and loved, worked and played in our familiar villages so many years ago.

* * * * * * *

Footnote: The St Johns and the Royal Connections

The St. John family of Bletsoe Castle was related to the Royal Family through Lady Margaret Beaufort - born in 1441. She was the only child of Margaret Beauchamp and John Beaufort. But this was Margaret Beauchamp's second marriage. She was married first to Sir Oliver St. John, and therefore Lady Margaret was half-sister to the St. John children, and was brought up with them at Bletsoe Castle.

In 1455 Lady Margaret married Edmund Tudor, the half-brother of Henry VI. Their only son, Henry Tudor, later became Henry VII. His son, Prince Henry (Henry VIII) spent long periods at Bletsoe with his grandmother and his cousins, one of whom, Sir Oliver St. John, became guardian to the young princesses, Mary and Elizabeth, both of whom were later to be Queen.

Bletsoe Castle about 1820

Chapter 2

The Bull Family of Hertford

In a handsome timbered house in St. Andrew's Street Hertford, towards the end of January 1603, a baby girl was born. Her name was Rebecka, and she was named after her mother, Rebecka Piggot of Tewin. Her father was Henry Bull, one of the Chief Burgesses of Hertford.

The birth of a new baby was always a cause for rejoicing, but at this time the thoughts of Henry Bull and his friends were occupied with graver matters. The great Elizabethan age was coming to an end, and already King James VI of Scotland was preparing to travel south to take his place as James I of England.

Queen Elizabeth died on 24th March 1603 and the whole country mourned the loss of one of the greatest monarchs it had ever known. For the people of Hertfordshire it was almost like a personal bereavement. Elizabeth had spent much of her early life at the Royal Palace in Hatfield, whence she had been summoned in November 1558 to return to London as Queen of England. Throughout her reign she was a frequent visitor to the county, staying with her cousin Henry Cary at Hunsdon, and with William Cecil in his magnificent house at Theobalds.

Royal Visits to Hertfordshire

There were state visits too, in 1561 and again in 1581, when, during an outbreak of plague in London, her parliament met in Hertford. But from now on things would be very different. The new king would visit the stately homes of Hertfordshire, but his preference was really for the flat open countryside on Royston Heath, where he could indulge his passion for hunting and horse-riding. He did, however, much admire Cecil's great house at Theobalds and persuaded him to exchange it for the old brick palace of Hatfield.

Meanwhile, in the family home in St Andrew's Street, the new baby was flourishing. There had been four previous children, two by Henry's first wife Cecily, who died giving birth to their second child in 1593. The baby, their first son, died a few weeks later. Henry remarried in 1596 and the following year they had Alice, who also died in infancy. The next baby, the son and heir, fortunately survived. They called him Richard after his grandfather, and also after the little brother who died. Young Rebecka, Henry's fifth child, was probably strong and vigorous from the moment she was born. She was to grow up to become one of the most dominant characters in our family history and lived to a grand old age. She married George Harmer of Weston and lived for another thirty years after his death in 1665. As a widow she helped to run the family estate, and took a keen interest in the lives of her children and grandchildren, travelling long distances to visit them, even at an advanced age.

Bullsmill and Benwick Hall

Although she was born and brought up in the town house in Hertford, Rebecka probably spent part of her childhood at Benwick Hall, a beautiful house on the banks of the River Beane at Stapleford, which had been the country home of her grandparents and great grandparents for over a hundred years. There is now no trace of the old house, but for many years the water-mill remained, giving its name to the hamlet of Bullsmill, which still serves as a reminder of the family who lived there 400 years ago.

The pedigree in the Visitations takes us back to Rebecka's great-great-grandparents, Richard Bull of London and Hellen Skipwith of St Albans. When he left London, Richard may have lived for a while in St. Albans. He certainly owned land in Hertfordshire in 1483, when it is recorded that the manor of Halfhyde or Westmill was in the possession of Richard Bull.

The Knighton Connection

When Richard died, his property went to his son Charles who was married to Jane Knighton of Bayford. By this time the family was well and truly established in Hertford, where Charles owned a great deal of property which was later described in his son Richard's will. The Bull family were very closely associated with the Knightons, who in turn had strong links with many Suffolk families, including the Underhills, Caldebecks, Stutevilles, Turnors, Hunts and Brownes.

Charles Bull was married to Jane Knighton, and his sister Alice married Jane's brother Thomas Knighton, so their children were closer than most cousins. Two of these cousins went on to marry into the Hunt family of Hunts Hall in Ashen, on the Suffolk-Essex borders, after which the Hunt cousins married each other! Thus the Bulls, Knightons and Hunts were related in many directions.

When Charles Bull died his son Richard inherited most of the property. Richard, like his two Knighton cousins, had married into the Hunt family. His wife is described as 'Alice Hunt of Stanford', Stanford being a hamlet adjoining the parish of Southill in Bedfordshire. Alice was almost certainly the sister of Richard Hunt who married Ann Knighton. We know that members of Richard's family held the manor of Stanford, which was very close to Northill and Ickwell where the Barnardiston, Piggot and Fyshe families were living.

Richard Bull, Bailiff of Hertford

Richard Bull was closely involved in the civic life of Hertford, and in 1578 was elected Bailiff. (This office was later known as Mayor, but until 1605 the official title was Bailiff). As one of the Chief Burgesses, Richard would have been responsible for making ready the Castle to receive the official guests, including the Queen and her retinue, when parliament met in Hertford in 1581.

It was perhaps because of their experience in writing reports and keeping records that the pedigrees which both Richard and Henry Bull prepared for the Heralds' visits were so much more detailed than many of the others. In the 1572 Visitations, Richard very kindly tells us that 'Henry Bull is five years old' and 'Richard Bull is seven weeks old.' Little details like this are particularly moving, making our distant ancestors seem much closer.

As it happens, we also have a record of Henry's baptism in the St Andrew's parish registers, and the dates do not quite agree. Henry was growing up faster than his father realised, and was seven years old, not five. But father was not mistaken about the age of the baby who was probably still keeping him awake at night! The recorded 'seven weeks' seems to be quite correct.

Richard Bull, the father, died in 1585 and his burial is recorded in the St Andrew's parish registers:

> 15 Sept. Mr. Richard Bull, gent. and sometime one of the Burgesses of Hertford.

Richard left a detailed will, and most of his estates went to his elder son Henry. The will is interesting as it includes several place names which still exist in Hertford today.

> ... The capital messuage wherein I now dwell in the parish of St Andrews, and that tenement thereunto belonging adjoining in the occupation of Rafe Lee with all the houses, backsides and other appurtenances thereunto belonging ... two messuages or tenements in the....occupations of Richard Crowche and Thomas Wrattinge in the said town of Hertford nigh unto the mill, with all the houses, edifices, buildings and other appurtenances thereunto belonging ... a messuage or tenement situate at the west end of the town of Hertford ... now in the occupation of Anthony Garland or his assignes, and all houses, edifices, buildings, orchards, grounds, meadows, pastures, feedings and other profits and hereditaments appertaining to the said messuage and the two pightels at the said town's end now in the tenure of Robert Hitchcock, and one pightell lying in Blakemore and another pightel adjoining unto Castle Mead and that close or croft called Rafes Close adjoining nigh unto the

> common meadow called Hartham ... also my four messuages or
> tenements now in the several tenures or occupations of Leonard
> Halford, John Prinsdiche, William Ford and Cuthbert Stevenson,
> situate and being in the said town of Hertford, with all the edifices,
> buildings, orchards, backsides and other hereditaments to the same
> pertaining.

This sounds like quite a large slice of Hertford, which would have been very
much smaller than it is today. To those who know Hertford well, some of the
place names may still be familiar. There may even be descendants of the Lees,
Crowches, Wrattings, Garlands, Hitchcocks, Halfords, Prinsdiches, Fords or
Stevensons still living in the town. In addition to the property in Hertford,
Richard also mentions Benwick Hall (described as Bouwiche Hall in the erratic
spelling of the day):

> My messuage or tenement called Bouwiche Hall situate in the
> parish of Stapleford ... with all lands, tenements, meadows,
> pastures, feedings, woods, groves, springs, fishings and other
> effects thereunto belonging and lying in the parish of Stapleford
> and Bengeo ... and all my lands tenements etc ... known by the
> name of Bakers or by any other name whatsoever in the said parish
> of Stapleford and Bengeo (except my messuage and tenement in
> the tenure of George King) and those grounds holden of the manor
> of Russells ..., and all that messuage or tenement called Baldwins
> in Waterford ...

Having disposed of his estates, Richard bequeaths £50 to his ten-year-old
daughter Alice to be paid at the age of twenty-one or on the day of her
marriage. Alice also receives a bed with blankets, pillows, bolsters and
coverlets - all great luxuries at this time. Richard also inherits a bed with
similar bedding, but he is not to have this until he reaches the age of 24. (He is
only 13 at this time.) Richard leaves only £5 to his married daughter Elizabeth,
who has probably already received a good dowry. Although Henry is 20 years
old he is included in his father's instruction to his wife Alice to 'have a care to
the well bringing up of my two sons Henry and Richard, and my daughter Alice
in godly learning in the fear of God.'

Henry Bull, Chief Burgess and Justice of the Peace

Henry Bull not only inherited his father's property, but also his interest in local
government. In addition to his position as Chief Burgess, he was also a Justice
of the Peace, and in 1600 he was Bailiff (Mayor) of Hertford at the early age of
thirty-five.

It is likely that the various generations of the Bull family spent the early part of their adult lives at Benwick Hall, where their young children could grow up and play in the pleasant woods and meadows of Stapleford. Later, as their administrative duties became more numerous, they would have moved back to the town house in Hertford.

Henry was probably born at Benwick Hall but we know that his father was later living in Hertford, so we can assume that Henry spent his formative years in the town, witnessing the pomp and pageantry in which his father would be taking a prominent part. Henry would have been 13 years old when his father served his year as Bailiff, and at the age of 16 he would have witnessed all the grandeur of the occasion when the Queen and her parliament assembled in Hertford.

HARTFORD

Henry himself was very much a townsman, and probably never went back to live at Benwick Hall. It was Henry or possibly his son Richard who finally sold the family home. By the end of the 17th century Benwick Hall had passed to the Goldesborough family, from whom it went to the Wilsons. Between 1795 and 1803 it was the home of Thomas Blore the topographer, who during this time collected a vast mass of material referring to the topography and antiquities of the county, which was afterwards used by Clutterbuck in his history.

With Benwick Hall went the manor of Russells, partly in Stapleford and partly in Bengeo and Hertford. Besides the general right of common, Benwick Hall had attached to it two acres in Brocket's Bush. All this belonged to Henry Bull and was later acquired by the Wilson family. Benwick Hall and Russells finally went to a certain Richard Emmot who pulled down the house and built a 'dog kennel' in its place. But now even that is gone. It seems likely that Henry also sold much of the Hertford property, because it does not appear in his will, although he may already have handed it over to Richard before he died.

Henry Bull died in 1637 and his will is interesting but again slightly puzzling. He not only leaves the usual bequest to the poor of his own parish of St Andrew's Hertford, but there is also a bequest to the poor of the parish of Harston in Cambridgeshire. We have no knowledge of any connections with this parish, though Little Bradley, the home of his Knighton ancestors, is not far away.

Henry leaves to his younger son Edward a house and land on the Heath in the parish of St. Andrews, which is in the occupation of John Rogers. To Richard he leaves part of a farm called Rowney, lying in the parishes of Great Munden, Little Munden and Sacombe. He names the various pieces of land as Redding Field, Redding Grove, and Collier's End. This was purchased from Henry's niece and nephew, Helen and William Butler (presumably the children of Beckingham Butler of Tewin Bury). He still owes £250 to his niece Helen and states that if Richard fails to discharge this debt, then the property will go to Edward - plus the debt!

Henry then turns to matters nearer home. To his son Richard he bequeaths 'my great presse standing in the chamber wherein I usually lodge, and the brewing copper, brewing vessell and all other ymplements belonging to the brewhouse.' Richard inherits the house and all that remains in it, and Henry particularly reminds his executors not to allow the house to be stripped bare before Richard gets it. He says that Richard will receive the specific bequests and also 'whatever else my executors shall think good to leave in my dwelling house for comeliness'.

The Gold Ring with the Death's Head

Henry's daughters Cecily and Elizabeth receive money and a share of the goods and chattels, but Rebecka is not mentioned at all. The executors were his brother Richard and his son Edward, and for their pains he gives to his brother a 'gold ring with the death's head' and to his son Edward 'the old silver ball called mother's ball'.

It is interesting to speculate where the gold ring and the silver ball are today. Are they lost in the earth, melted down, or tucked away in an old jewel box in some dusty attic?

Henry's will is dated 29th November 1637, but according to the St. Andrew's parish registers he was then already dead. On this occasion we must believe the will, and assume that the clerk at St. Andrew's had got his records in a muddle. The records state that Mr. Henry Bull was buried on October 3rd, and that his wife Rebecka was buried a week earlier, on 26th September. It seems likely that the year is correct and that Rebecka and Henry both died within a few weeks of each other towards the end of the year 1637.

There are still a few unsolved mysteries in the history of the Bull family. In 1615 we find that Henry Bull and a certain John Cason were in possession of the mansion house and manor of Brent Pelham. This is surprising because the Pelhams were near the Essex borders, away from the usual Bull territory. Whether Henry was related to the Casons, or was just a friend or business partner we have not discovered, but it seems likely that there were family connections, possibly through the Mannocks of Stoke-by-Nayland in Suffolk.

Susan Oxenbridge, "a proper comely Lady"

Chauncy in his delightful conversational manner, tells us all about the Cason family. Edward Cason, son of Thomas of Steeple Morden in Cambridgeshire, was one of the Masters of the Bench in the Middle Temple. He made a Learned Reading there in 8 James I (1611) and later married Jane, daughter of Sir Henry Boteler of Hatfield Woodhall. Their son, Sir Henry Cason, married Susan Oxenbridge, by whom she had issue Edward and John, who with Henry Bull inherited the manor of Brent Pelham.

We soon discover why Chauncy was so interested in this family. He had a deep admiration for Susan Oxenbridge! When Henry Cason died, Susan married Sir Thomas Cecil, son of Robert Cecil, 1st Earl of Salisbury. Chauncy continues with an enthusiastic account of the lady in question:

> And not long after, Sir Thomas Cecill died; his lady surviving; she was a proper comely Lady, endowed with a most rare and pregnant wit, a florid and ready Tongue, very sharp, but witty in her Repartees; her common Discourse did much exceed the ordinary Capacity of her Sex; and she dying at a great Age.

Chauncy was of course writing in the early 18th century, long before the rules of sexism had been invented!

The manor of Brent Pelham previously belonged to Edward Newport and his son John, a well-known royalist. John was married to Katherine, daughter of Sir Francis Mannock of Gifford's Hall in Stoke-by-Nayland. The Mannocks were related to the Chapmans and to the Dacres family of Cheshunt, and all were part of the family network.

With all these connections there is bound to be a story here, but the details remain a mystery.

Another unidentified character is Major Richard Bull of Marwell, near Southampton. He too married into the Dacres family of Cheshunt, who were related to Trevor Roper (Lord Dacre) and to the Hydes of Throcking. The name Richard Bull suggests he was a fairly close relation, and could well have been Rebecka's uncle (Henry's brother).

A certain William Bull, Clk. M.A. is listed as Rector of St Andrew's, Hertford in 1633. He took over from Edward Baynes who is said to have 'resigned', but was in fact turned out by the House of Commons. The connection with St. Andrew's suggests that William was a relative, but we have not yet placed him on the family tree.

Finally, going forward into the 18th century, we come across two sculptors, Thomas and Richard Bull. They were based in London, but did a great deal of work in the Hertfordshire churches, including Redbourn where we know there were family connections.

So with Major Richard Bull in the army, the Reverend William Bull in the church, and a couple of freelance sculptors, we have a good mix of professions. But in the closer family we shall always think of Richard and Henry Bull as caring land-owners and conscientious public servants, giving much of their lives to their duties as Burgess or Mayor of Hertford.

The Old St Andrew's Church, Hertford

Chapter 3

The Capells of Little Hadham Hall
and the Hertfordshire Militia

Sir William Capell was born at Stoke-by-Nayland in Suffolk, but probably spent most of his life in London as a city merchant. His links with Hertfordshire began in 1510, when he bought the manor of Walkern, although there is no indication that he ever lived there.

He was a Sheriff of London in 1489, and was twice Lord Mayor - in 1503 and again in 1509. He was knighted by Henry VII and according to the Heralds' Visitations "lyeth buryed in a stately chapple by him bilte in St. Bartholomew's church by ye Exchange". He was married to Margaret, daughter of Sir Thomas Arundell, and they had a son Giles, who is described simply as "Sir Giles Capell of Hadham". We are told that he was buried beside his father at St Bartholomew's, so there was as yet no strong link with Hertfordshire.

Two generations later, however, the family seems to be well settled in the county. Sir Henry Capell was living at Little Hadham Hall and was recorded as Muster Captain, or Captain of Array, for Hertfordshire. In 1585 he also served as High Sheriff for the county.

At the same time the Capell family had estates at Abbess Roding and Rookwood (or Clovills) in Essex, which seem to have been acquired through two marriages to the daughters of Sir Weston Browne - a neighbour of the Petres of Ingatestone Hall. (see Chapter 13)

Four generations of Capells, all the eldest sons called Gamaliel, lived at Abbess Roding, until in 1700 it was sold or mortgaged to John Howland of Streatham, whose daughter Elizabeth carried the estate in marriage to Wriothesley Russell, Duke of Bedford.

Sir Henry Capell, Muster Captain

Meanwhile, in Little Hadham, the Capells were making their mark. The office of Muster Captain was a very prestigious one, and Sir Henry Capell was responsible for recruiting and training his band of able men to form part of the County Militia.

At this time there was no regular army and the country relied on the County Militia, selected from various bands of men between the ages of 16 and 60, who were required to do four days training a year under the command of the local Muster Captain. These Captains had to be men of substance, for they were expected to provide most of the armour, arms and ammunition at their own expense.

Henry Capell at this time was a very wealthy man, employing thirty-nine male servants, including some classed as 'gentlemen' in their own right. These would have been the sons of neighbouring noble families, following an accepted educational process. Having been to university and before going on to Inns of Court, they would spend a period in another household, learning a range of estate management skills to prepare them for their future position in the world.

Most of the Hertfordshire Muster Captains and Commissioners were related to each other, and many were related to the Queen herself through the Boleyn family. It has been suggested that these men were specially chosen because this relationship would ensure their loyalty to the Queen. This may or may not have been the case. As we know, families could be very fickle and unpredictable - especially in matters of religion and politics.

Little Hadham Hall

The names of the Captains included Knollys, Hunsdon, Cary, Sadlier, Brocket, Hervey, Pulter and of course Capell. The latter family was one of the few who did not have a direct relationship with the queen, but Henry Capell's successor, Edward Pulter, was definitely part of the royal lineage. He was married to Mary Lytton of Knebworth, who was connected with the Carys and Boleyns. His sister Ann was married to Henry Boteler, whose nephew married Catherine Knollys, the great-granddaughter of Thomas and Elizabeth Boleyn. The Pulters were also related to the Capells. Sir Henry Capell's granddaughter Penelope was married to Litton Pulter, son of Edward Pulter and his wife Mary Lytton (or Litton) of Knebworth.

The Muster Books

The Muster Books for North and East Hertfordshire - the Hundreds of Edwinstree and Odsey - were carefully preserved in the Capell family archives, and are now kept in the County Records Office. They are beautifully written in a clear and scholastic hand, probably by a professional scribe living in the Capell household at Little Hadham. They give us a great many interesting details, not only about the organisation of the militia, but also about the inhabitants of the various Hertfordshire towns and villages between 1580 and 1605.

Some of the names are listed under headings according to their status in the community. The first heading reads "Hable men for Service" and probably lists those most suitable for selection if a group of soldiers were needed urgently. Next comes "Farmers their sonnes and servants". This would be the yeomen farmers, a very respected and responsible group of men, who usually made up a large proportion of those finally called upon to serve if needed. Then there were the "Artificers and their sonnes and servants" and last of all "Pyoners and labourers".

Under another group of headings we have men listed according to the various arms which they bore. There was the Caliver Section, the Corselets, Muskets, Pikes, Bills and occasionally Bows, though these appear mainly at the beginning of the period, and were used less and less as the years went by.

Tall, Well-built Men and Corselet Armour

It is interesting to read the descriptions of the type of man chosen for each section (though if a man happened to have a weapon of his own he would probably have been allowed to use it). We are told that the Corselet Section consisted of "tall, well-built men who wore corselet armour ... the role for a courageous man." This is good to know, because our ancestor John Harmer of Rushden and his son Edward both belonged to the Corselet Section.

They carried swords, daggers and pikes and were trained in sixteen postures of drill - three standing, five marching and eight charging. They formed ranks to protect the musket and caliver men, regrouping quickly when necessary and forming an impenetrable circle.

John and Edward were each responsible for arming one other man. William Lane was furnished with John Harmer's caliver (a kind of musket) and John Wood was armed by Edward Harmer. John Harmer also provided one of the three riding horses for the Rushden militia.

In addition to all this John Harmer was obliged to pay the £25 levy which all the wealthy gentlemen were required to pay at the time of the Armada.

The Spanish Armada

In 1587, when the Armada crisis was looming, Henry Capell's man rode to London on his own horse to make an official purchase of ammunition. Every detail is recorded in the Muster Book. He stayed in London for six nights, at the cost of a shilling a night, plus ten and a half pence for the horse to be fed and stabled. He went to Rotherhithe and back on the ferry, before returning with the ammunition (presumably carried by horse and cart). This was to be carefully stored for use if the country were invaded, and not used for any other purpose.

In each village a special room or outbuilding was set aside for the storing of the arms. Often they were kept in the parish church in the tall cupboards which had once held the ceremonial banners and crosses which were no longer in use since the Reformation. The cupboards were now put to much better use (some people considered) for the storing of pikes and lances!

The various items were to be inspected and cleaned regularly. Scouring with sand was recommended for the cleaning, but this was not a very good idea as it encouraged even more rusting. After a few years many ammunition collections were nothing more than a heap of rusty metal.

One collection of armour which has survived can still be seen in its chamber above the porch of Mendlesham church in Suffolk, where it has been waiting 'ready for use' ever since the days of the Armada.

The Militia sets off for Tilbury

In 1588 a band of selected men from the Hertfordshire Militia set out for Tilbury to join with the militia from all over the country to resist the expected Spanish invasion. Once the soldiers crossed the county border they were entitled to a maintenance allowance, but during the 40-mile march through Hertfordshire the Muster Captain had to beg or buy (out of his own pocket) their nightly board and lodging.

Certain inns along the route had been licensed as suitable places to stop for rest and refreshment, and the soldiers were not allowed to stop at any other hostelry. Some of the inn-keepers (mainly women) are named in the Muster Books. It was their duty to make sure the men did not drink to excess, or indulge in any other behaviour which might affect their physical fitness. We are told that the Hertfordshire troops were a particularly well-disciplined band of men, quite unlike the 'rabble' which Shakespeare describes in some of his plays.

Each parish was required to provide not only men and weapons, but at least one riding horse or cart horse, and we are told that the carters had to use great skill in managing their teams of unmatched horses who were not accustomed to working together.

When the militia travelled to Tilbury each cart was pulled by four harnessed horses (with a fifth to carry the carter), and two or three relief horses. The journey took between two and three days. A second carter had the task of taking the horses to the blacksmith when they needed to be shod. Relief horses would have to be provided for extra pulling and braking on steep hills - especially the Thundridge-Wadesmill hill.

The Early Warning System

The Muster Books provide us with details of the ingenious early warning system - the chain of beacons across the country. They came under the supervision of the Muster Captains and the manning and maintenance was one of their most important duties. They were guarded by specially trained and trustworthy beacon keepers, and there were severe penalties for unauthorised firing.

Ann King, in her introduction to the Hertfordshire Record Society Publication about the Hertfordshire Militia, tells us:

> Beacons blazing along the south coast of England had presented an awesome sight which alarmed the French in 1545 when they attempted invasion. No doubt they had a similar effect on the Spanish as they approached England in July 1588. In a warning system unique to England each coastal site consisted of three beacons. Vigilant beacon keepers watched for distant unknown ships and cautiously lit the first of their beacons only when ships presented a threat. The second was lit when vessels were identified as foreign and potentially dangerous, and all three would blaze only if the enemy prepared to come ashore.

> In coastal counties constables were particularly mindful of Privy Council orders to have trained men ready for service at an hour's notice when a group of three blazing beacons was identified. The next rank of beacons inland comprised beacons in pairs. When the watchers saw a coastal site had two beacons ablaze, they lit their first one. The other one was fired when a coastal group of three were all alight. Only then did the inland beacons flash a warning across the length and breadth of England. This system also ensured that inland troops went in the right direction to support the front line men at the coast.

> Beacons usually consisted of a metal basket surmounting a tall pole with a ladder to put against it for ease in filling with

combustible material. A good steady burn with a bright flame was required for two hours. For mistakenly firing a beacon the penalty was heavy and so watchers carefully checked the location of distant fires. Responsibility for beacon management fell on local men of substance, yeomen farmers and the like, those who would not accept bribes or be lax in their vigilance.

In Hertfordshire there were only four beacon sites: on the tower of St Peter's Church in St Albans, on Hertford Heath, at Graveley and Therfield. Just beyond the county's southern boundary was Monkton Hadley, and westwards were two key beacons at Pegsdon and Ivinghoe. Therfield could receive the signal from either of them, or from Hertford Heath. However it is unlikely all beacons were fired in 1588. The Spanish fleet sailed up the channel and then made for Calais where Drake's fire ships were awaiting them. Most of the Spanish ships were destroyed, and the survivors were driven into the North Sea. As a precaution some beacon watchers were not stood down until October of that year.

Therfield Beacon

Therfield beacon site is on top of a 500 ft high north-facing chalk escarpment, giving a view over a vast expanse of the Cambridgeshire fens and lowlands and beyond. The beacon flame could have been seen for many miles across Hertfordshire and Bedfordshire and in an arc to Suffolk.

A house thought to be the Beacon Keeper's still remains in the area. High in the eaves of this house are small watchers' windows each looking towards another beacon site. It is said that the old sill of the window facing the Hertford Heath beacon had faint directional lines incised in it.

In the Muster Book for 1596 we find a memorandum stating that the cost for watching the beacon for 6 weeks would be 14s. per week. This memorandum was signed by Arthur Capell, the son of Henry, who had obviously taken over the role once filled by his father.

Edward Pulter of Cottered and Wymondley

But we know that for 22 years, from the time when Henry Capell resigned (or died), the Hertfordshire Muster Captain was Edward Pulter of Cottered and Wymondley. As we have seen, he was related by marriage to Henry Capell, and had probably acted as an assistant or deputy for many years before he took over the leadership. It was Edward Pulter who led the 'select band' to Tilbury in 1588. Like Henry Capell, he received no pay for this public service, and willingly gave his time and money as one of the duties which went with privilege and wealth. We are told however that he was (understandably) a little resentful when asked to pay the extra £25 for the defence of the country in 1588. He had already paid out much more than that in time and money for the defence of his kingdom.

Arthur Capell, who followed Edward Pulter as Muster Captain around 1596, was now the father-in-law of Edward's son Litton Pulter, so the two were closely connected by family ties in addition to their shared civic duties. By the time Arthur took over, the threat of war had receded, but the militia remained in readiness for any emergency right up to the 19th century.

Arthur, Lord Capell, "murdered for his loyalty to the King"

Arthur was married to Mary, the daughter of Lord Grey of Pirgo. He was succeeded by his son Sir Henry Capell, and then by his grandson Arthur.

In 1641 Arthur was Member of Parliament for Hertfordshire, but in 1649 he was tried for treason. He was a supporter of the Royalist cause, had taken part in the Second Civil War, and had been captured at the siege of Colchester. Only a few of the prisoners were tried for treason, and it is said that Cromwell spoke so much of his friendship for Lord Capell that those present thought that he would be found innocent. However, Cromwell also said that Capell's qualities were such that, while he lived, he would always be a danger to the Commonwealth. Capell was found guilty and executed.

Here we have an example of a man whose character and ability were admired by both the opposing sides and who was executed as much for his good qualities as for his conflicting loyalties.

In the church at Little Hadham there is the following inscription:

> Hereunder lieth interred the Body of Arthur Lord Capell
> Baron of Hadham, who was murdered for his loyalty to the King
> Charles the First, March 9th 1648 [ie 1649]

At the Restoration his son, Sir Arthur Capell, was created Earl of Essex and the family honour was restored. We know that he was still at Hadham Hall in 1665, but we hear of few Capell connections in later years.

The Capells of Hadham Hall should always be remembered, however, for their courage and integrity and for generous and devoted service to the Hertfordshire Militia and to their country.

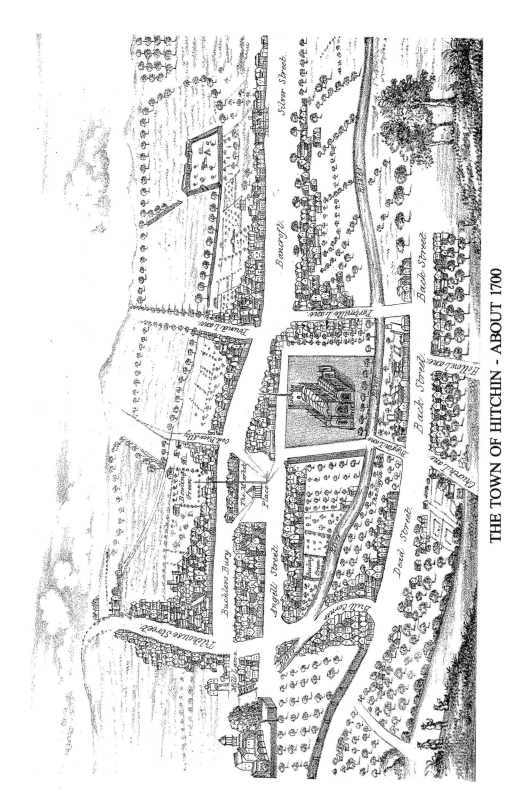

THE TOWN OF HITCHIN - ABOUT 1700

DRAWN ON STONE BY J DRAPENTIER FROM THE ORIGINAL ENGRAVING BY C L TYLER

Chapter 4

The Chapmans of Hitchin
and the Nodes family of Shephallbury

In the early 16th century Hugh Chapman of Cambridge married Ann, the only daughter of John Mardock of Mardocks Manor near Ware in Hertfordshire. The Mardocks had been a wealthy family and were entitled to bear arms, but we know little about them and they seem to have left no mark on the history of the area. With Ann's marriage the Mardock name died out, but there still remains a farmhouse bearing the name, to remind us of the family who lived there long ago.

The Mardock estate descended through the Chapman family for two more generations, but Thomas, a younger son, inherited only a few small properties in Hitchin, including Western House (now 35 Tilehouse Street). Around 1550 he married Joan, the daughter of George Nodes of Shephallbury.

George Nodes had been Sergeant of the Buckhounds to Henry VIII, and had acquired the manor of Shephallbury in 1541, probably as a gift from his royal master. He had no sons, so his two daughters, Jane and Joan, might have expected to inherit the property, except that their father had decided that it was to descend "in male tail". He left the whole lot to their cousin Charles, and the two girls were obviously not amused!

Western House, Tilehouse Street, Hitchin

The birthplace of George Chapman
Poet, Playwright and Translator

Later the two sons-in-law, William Kympton and Thomas Chapman, claimed a right to the property, but did not succeed. Jane Kympton, the elder daughter, did eventually inherit a "messuage" called Copidhall, originally part of the manor, but Joan Chapman seems to have inherited nothing. Thomas and Joan had three sons and three daughters, one of whom, Elizabeth, married Thomas Piggott of Tewin Water.

When Thomas Chapman died in 1589 he left a detailed and interesting will. He named all his children, and he even named his grandchildren - a very useful thing to do from the point of view of his descendants when researching the family history. To his two elder sons, Thomas and John, he left various properties, and to each of his grandchildren the sum of 40 shillings. To his youngest son, George, he left one hundred pounds - and five silver spoons!

Had it not been for this legacy one of John Keats's most famous poems might never have been written. The poem, of course, is "On first looking into Chapman's Homer". Although Chapman himself was a well-respected playwright, poet and scholar, he is now best remembered because of Keats's poem.

George Chapman, Elizabethan Playwright and Poet

George studied either at Oxford or Cambridge - or possibly both - and for a time earned his living as a schoolmaster. But as soon as he received his legacy he was off to London.

He belonged to the group of Elizabethan poets and playwrights which included Ben Jonson, Edmund Spenser, Christopher Marlowe and William Shakespeare. He worked closely with his friend Ben Jonson, and they collaborated in several plays including Eastward Hoe in 1605. Eastward Hoe gives a vivid picture of old London, which is said to have inspired Hogarth's famous engravings. But the play caused offence to the newly crowned King James I because of satirical references to the Scots. This landed them in the Fleet prison, and Ben Jonson wrote to his patron the Earl of Salisbury for help:

George Chapman
From the engraving by William Pass

> I am here, my most honoured lord, unexamined and unheard, committed to a vile prison, and with me a gentleman, whose name may have come to your lordship's notice, Mr. George Chapman, a learned and honest man ...

The same year Chapman was in trouble again for unfortunate references to the French queen in his play 'The Conspiracie and the Tragedie of Charles, Duke of Byron'. But it was not in George's nature to stir up trouble, and many contemporary writers remarked that his personal character stood very high. He was described as 'of most reverent aspect, religious and temperate'. His plays were well received, and one entitled 'All Fools' was described by Swinburne as 'one of the most faultless examples of high comedy in the whole rich field of Elizabethan drama'.

While his plays showed a witty and lively mind, it was in his poetry that his genius was most widely acclaimed. It was much admired by later critics such as Lamb and Coleridge, while in his own day Shakespeare describes him as '.. a spirit by spirits taught to write above a mortal'.

Chapman's Translation of Homer

But the main work of Chapman's life was his translation of Homer, in which he claimed to be inspired by the spirit of Homer himself. It took him 26 years, and when he had finished he wrote, 'The work that I was born to do is done.'

He would have been gratified to know what effect it had on one of the greatest poets of the 19th century. Keats came upon a borrowed copy, and remained out of bed all night to read it, such was its vitality and force. He shouted with delight when some passage of special energy pleased him, and straight away he wrote his famous sonnet declaring that he had never experienced the full force of Homer's genius until he heard Chapman 'speak out loud and bold':

> Then felt I like some watcher of the skies
> When a new planet swims into his ken.

Chapman had many friends both in London and in his home town of Hitchin, where he was a familiar figure walking the cobbled streets or wandering in the surrounding countryside when he returned home to visit his family.

But he never lived in Hitchin again. His life was in London, where he had several distinguished patrons, including Prince Henry. The prince had promised him a pension while he was working on his translation of Homer, but unfortunately died long before it was completed.

Another of Chapman's patrons was Sir Henry Fanshawe of Ware Park who had been one of Prince Henry's confidants. When he had finished the first twelve books of the Odyssey in 1614, Chapman sent a presentation copy to Sir Henry, with the following inscription - 'For my righte worthie Knighte, my exceeding noble friende, Sir Henry Fanshawe, a poore Homericall new yeare's gift.'

But the money forthcoming from his various patrons was not enough to live on, and although he made a certain amount from his plays, and published books of poetry, he spent the latter years of his life in poverty. When he died in 1634 he was buried in the churchyard of St Giles in the Fields. A monument was erected over his grave, designed by his beloved friend Inigo Jones. The monument still stands, but the inscription has been changed. The original, which was in Latin, is translated thus:

> D.O.M. Here lies George Chapman, a Christian Philosopher and Homerical poet. He lived 77 years and died 12 of May 1634, for whose worth and memory to posterity Inigo Jones, Architect to the King, for ancient friendship made this.

In more recent times T S Eliot referred to him as 'potentially the greatest artist of the Elizabethan dramatists.'

John Chapman, Rector of Willian

It has been asked why George Chapman's wealthy brother Thomas did not help him when he was in dire poverty, but perhaps the family did not appreciate the situation. Unlike many poets, Chapman was famous in his own lifetime. His plays were being produced in London, and several books of poetry were published, but fame did not necessarily bring fortune. His brother John, who was a parson, would certainly have helped had he known that his brother was near to starvation. John was the Rector of Willian for one year 1606 - 07. In spite of this short incumbency, there is a memorial to him in Willian church, possibly because of the reflected glory of his famous brother. The communion silver in Hitchin church also holds a reminder of the family. On the patten is the inscription 'the gift of Anne Chapman, widow of John Chapman late rector of Willian.'

All the Chapman family were generous to the poor, (though not to their own brother!). Thomas in 1595 set aside £10 'to be laid out in barley and converted into malt, the yearly income thereof to redound to the use of the poor of Hitchin.'

Both John and Thomas had sons, several of whom went into the church. In 1668 Thomas Chapman, Clerk, of Little Wymondley, settled an annual rent charge of five shillings on a house in Stevenage, the amount to be distributed among the poor in bread on St Andrew's Day by the Vicar and churchwardens.

There is a brass in Walkern church to Edward Chapman, another of George Chapman's nephews. George himself never married, though he fell in love several times, and wrote poems in praise of womanly beauty. But the Chapman name lived on for many years in Hitchin, the literary tradition being perpetuated by a descendant who founded the firm of Chapman and Hall, publishers of such well-known authors as Dickens, Trollope and Mrs Gaskell.

All of Thomas Chapman's three daughters were married by the time he made his will in 1581, (he died 8 years later). They are named as Margaret

Chambers, Joan Monk, and Elizabeth Piggot, and to each of them he leaves £10 and two silver spoons.

The Monk Family of Hitchin

The Monks were evidently a well-known Hitchin family, for in his 'History of Hitchin', Reginald Hine specifically mentions them, when he tells how the Parish Registers can give a moving story of the life of the local inhabitants. He writes:

> ... in their pages one may gravely and profitably study the rise and fall of families, the havoc of plague and civil war, the whims and oddities of nomenclature, the occupations and immoralities of the people, the peculiarities of the incumbents, the carelessness of the scribe and the deadly working of the worm ... You can grieve to see the rich and flourishing family of Monk gradually decline from their timbered mansions in Bancroft into the Dead Street slums ... You come with delight and refreshment upon such names as Katherine Jolleyfellow, Greediana Tarboys and Affabel Battel.

We do not know if Joan Monk and her husband lived in one of the timbered mansions of Bancroft, or whether the family fortunes had even then begun to decline. But we do know that her sister Elizabeth Piggot, in her will of 1616, leaves Joan some of her clothing, though this does not necessarily mean that she was poor.

Thomas Chapman, the Poet's Father, buried at Hitchin

In his will Thomas Chapman asks to be buried at Hitchin near his wife Joan who, he records, died in 1566. This tells us that George would have lost his mother when he was only seven years old. Perhaps it was his older sister Elizabeth, our ancestor, who looked after him in his early motherless years, and as they walked together in the beautiful countryside around Hitchin, helped to nurture in her brother that love of beauty which was later to find expression in his life's work in the realms of poetry and literature.

The Nodes Family of Shephallbury

The family of Joan Nodes, George Chapman's mother, continued to live at Shephallbury for many generations. Charles, who inherited the property from his uncle George, married Elizabeth Mitchell of Codicote, and named his eldest son after his uncle (as indeed he should!). This second George of Shephallbury married Helen, the daughter of Edward Docwra of Brotherhood House, Hitchin, and one of their daughters, Helen Nodes, married William Boteler, son and heir of Thomas Boteler of Biddenham and Harrold Hall in Bedfordshire.

Joyce Godber refers to this George Nodes in her 'History of Bedfordshire'. Speaking of the sadness of families divided by the Civil War (1642-49) she writes 'George Nodes of Hertfordshire in 1642 was glad to see his Boteler grandchildren; "I am old and crazy [ill] and I doubt whether I shall see them again. We think the times more dangerous now than ever they were - I pray God amend them".' The Boteler grandchildren would have been Thomas, William, Helen and Ann, the children of Helen and William Boteler who lived at Harrold Hall in Bedfordshire.

The Nodes family were still at Shephallbury in the 18th century. The accounts of Thomas Green, a music teacher and instrument tuner, show that he was visiting Shephallbury several times a year between 1752 and 1764 to tune a harp, a spinet, and a harpsichord for Mrs Nodes. In the 19th century Shephallbury was owned by the Heathcote family, who were direct descendants of George Nodes through the female line, having presumably inherited in spite of the 'male tail'. The old manor house was replaced in 1865 by a new Gothic style building adjoining the site of the original house. In 1806 the Heathcotes also bought the Manor of Wymondley, which included the Priory and Wymondley Bury. In 1609 this property had belonged to Thomas Piggot and his wife Elizabeth Chapman, who was a granddaughter of George Nodes of Shephallbury. Thus, although they may not have realised it, the Heathcotes were acquiring a property which had been in their family 250 years earlier.

Shephallbury - built in 1865 to replace the original manor house

Going back even further, the manor of Wymondley had previously belonged to the Argenteins and Alingtons from the time of the Norman Conquest. David de Argentein was a Norman who served under William the Conqueror, and his son John is thought to have built Great Wymondley Castle - of which only the earthworks now remain, to the east of the parish church. The Argenteins and their descendants the Alingtons were Cupbearers to the King - and both were part of the family network. But that is another story!

Chapter 5

The Coningsby, Elwes, Fyshe and Barre Families
of North Mymms and Ayot Mountfitchet

While most of the land-owning families in Hertfordshire and Bedfordshire were related to each other by marriage, there seems to have been a particularly close link between the Coningsby, Fyshe, Harmer, Hyde and Boteler families.

From the early 15th century the Fyshe (or Fish) family had held the manor of Ayot Mountfitchet, later known as Ayot St Lawrence, or Great Ayot. The Hertfordshire historian Cussons, writing around 1870, tells us "Though the parish was and is known by the name of Great Ayot, it contains 360 acres less than the adjoining parish of Ayot St Peter, or Little Ayot".

At the time of the Conquest there was just one manor, known as Aiete, and it was not until nearly three centuries later that the distinction was made. There was apparently 'some little uncertainty' how much of Aiete constituted the present manor of Ayot St Lawrence and how much Ayot St Peter. The Mountfitchet name, according to Chauncy, appeared at the time of Henry II when one of his courtiers, Richard Mountfitchet, was lord of the manor.

Clandestine Marriages

The parish of Ayot St Peter in the 17th century may have been carrying out 'clandestine' marriages. The priests in charge of various churches (mainly in London) were unscrupulous enough to waive the rules in order to obtain the often substantial fees which were demanded.

We were puzzled when the parish records showed that on two separate occasions members of the family living in Wymondley and Weston, had been married at Ayot St Peter. Then we discovered that another couple, Frances Harmer and James Oldham of Weston, were married at St James's Duke Place in London.

Then we found, in the Saul & Markwell guide to genealogy, a statement which suddenly seemed to make sense of the whole situation. The information was as follows:

> From 1660 so-called clandestine marriages (ie without banns or licence) took place, especially in London, at Fleet Prison Chapel,

at 'marriage houses' in the Liberties of the Fleet etc. Some 40,000 marriages took place at St James's Duke Place between 1664 and 1694.

Since Frances and James were definitely marrying without Father's consent, and since both the other brides had good reason to wish to keep the marriage a secret, we can now assume that the priest at Ayot St Peter was obligingly marrying desperate young couples in his quiet Hertfordshire church!

The information about St James's Duke Place is particularly interesting as a piece of family history, because Frances Harmer was married in 1683, and therefore formed part of the statistics quoted in the guide book.

The parish of Ayot St Lawrence, on the other hand, is perhaps best remembered today as the home of George Bernard Shaw. A member of our family remembers seeing him, as a very old gentleman, riding round the village on his tricycle. His memory has been preserved by the name 'Shaw's Corner', which now appears on the map.

Shaw's Corner, Ayot St Lawrence

Lawrence de Ayot and the Barre Family

Going back to the 14th century, the manor of Ayot came to the Barre family by the marriage of Richard Pembrugge to the daughter of Lawrence de Ayot. Their daughter, Hawise Pembrugge, married Thomas Barre and their son, Sir Thomas Barre, was Sheriff of Hertfordshire in 1415, and Member of Parliament in 1420. He was also Surveyor of the King's hay, for which service he received 40 marks a year, plus 3 tuns of red wine. In 1394 he accompanied the King to Ireland, and was required to serve him and ride with him when called upon. He outlived his wife and son and died on 30th December 1421. He and his wife Elizabeth are buried in the church of Ayot St Lawrence. He was almost certainly the ancestor of Milliscent Barre who married Thomas Fairclough of Weston around 1540.

His grandson, Sir John Barre, married Indonea, daughter of John Hotolf, who brought with her the manors of Knebworth and Panshanger. Here the story becomes very long and involved and the various manors were linked and inherited by many well-known names, including Sir Thomas Bourchier, Sir William Parr and Sir William Say.

Nicholas Bristow, Clarke of the Jewells to Queen Elizabeth

There were also links with the Bristow and Brocket families. Nicholas Bristow of Ayot St Lawrence was 'Clarke of the Jewells' to Queen Elizabeth. His father and grandfather had also served in this way throughout the reigns of Henry VIII, Edward VI and Queen Mary. Members of the Bristow family married into the Harmer, Hyde and Boteler families. Nicholas was buried at Ayot St Lawrence.

The Brocket family of Brocket Hall, Wheathampstead, was connected with the Lyttons, Spencers, Perients and Mordaunts. In the 16th century Sir John Brocket lived at Markyate Cell - later home to the Fanshawes and Lady Kathleen Ferrers, the 'Wicked Lady'. John was married to Mary Snagge, whose family built the old manor house at Marston Moreteyne in Bedfordshire.

The manor of Knebworth went finally to the Lyttons, who were closely related to the Fairclough and Hervey families. Panshanger passed to Nicholas Throckmorton, then to Edmund Skeggs and Sir Gervase Elwes, before going to the Lord Chancellor Earl Cowper in 1719.

The Elwes Family, Notable Eccentrics

The link with the Elwes family is interesting. They were closely related to the Hydes and the Soames, and lived for a time at Throcking Hall. They were also related to the Herveys of Ickworth Hall, through the marriage of Gervase Elwes to Isabella Hervey.

Gervase and Isabella had a son, Sir Harvey Elwes, who lived at Stoke-by-Clare in Suffolk, and is mentioned in 'Timpson's English Eccentrics'. He was certainly one of the most eccentric members of the family, though there were many others. Timpson's book also includes the Reverend John Alington of Letchworth Hall and Lord Salisbury of Hatfield, who liked to ride round St James's Park on a tricycle - an unusual form of transport for a Prime Minister!

Sir Harvey Elwes and his nephew John were known as the Misers of Ashen. Sir Harvey was a very rich man, owning most of the land in Clare and also in Ashen, just across the Essex border. He kept his annual expenditure down to £100 a year, and that included the wages, such as they were, of his three servants. He never bought new clothes; instead he kept a chest of old suits which belonged to his grandfather, and wore each suit until it fell to pieces. He lived entirely on partridges which he shot himself, plus one boiled potato a day.

His nephew John, a regular visitor to Stoke College (the family home at Stoke-by-Clare), at first seemed to be a perfectly normal young man, but he respected his uncle's lifestyle and gradually developed his own peculiar habits. On the ride from London, instead of stopping at inns for refreshment he carried two boiled eggs, and if he was thirsty he drank from a stream alongside his horse.

When Sir Harvey died, his nephew, now Sir John Elwes, inherited the whole of his estate, and also inherited a large fortune from his mother. Gradually he became even more mean and eccentric than his uncle. John Timpson tells us:

> Astonishingly, John Elwes was elected to Parliament and spent twelve years as an MP, but he had no interest in politics, never made a speech, and sat on whichever side of the House seemed convenient at the time. In spite of mixing with politicians, who are not usually noted for their frugality, he did not alter his own parsimonious habits. His shoes were never cleaned in case the friction wore them out. He rode on the grass verge to save wear and tear on the horseshoes, and made wide detours to avoid paying at the toll-gates. For clothing he delved into Sir Harvey's old chest in the attic; his one luxury was a wig he found in a hedge, topped by a hat he removed from a scarecrow.

> His meals became steadily more gruesome. The meat was so mouldy it moved on the plate; he is said to have supped off a moorhen that had been gnawed by a rat, and he was thrilled to bits when he caught a pike which had an undigested fish in its stomach. 'This is really killing two birds with one stone' he exulted.

> One biographer records that he broke both legs in an accident and would only allow the doctor to put a splint on one, saying he could copy it on the other leg and thus halve the bill. ....

> But there was another side to his character too. He was a rider of great skill and courage; as a magistrate he was renowned for his fairness and integrity, and surprisingly in someone who was so ludicrous in his meanness, he retained a remarkable sense of humour. When he was out shooting and one of the other guns, a hopeless shot, put two pellets in his cheek, causing considerable pain, Elwes merely commented wryly: 'My dear sir, I give you joy on your improvement - I knew you would hit something by-an-by'. But no doubt he made sure who paid the doctor . . .

> John Elwes' eccentric lifestyle and revolting diet seemed to do him no harm at all. He lived until the age of seventy-six, and remained remarkably fit until his peaceful death in 1789. He left a house at Stoke full of rotten floor-boards, cracked windows, peeling paint

and sagging doors on broken hinges, and a garden which was a desolate wilderness. He also left the equivalent in today's figures of about twenty million pounds.

The Fyshe Family of Ayot

The Fyshe family came to Ayot around 1400, but it is not clear whether they inherited or bought the manor. In 1508 Thomas Fyshe married Elizabeth Hyde of Throcking, and in the next generation there were marriages to Margaret Barnardiston of Northill and also to members of the Perient, Pulter and Blundell families. The Barnardiston marriage brought estates in Southill and Northill and the family lived for a time at Ickwell Bury and the Old House at Ickwell. It was this branch of the family who in 1634 had no male heir. Mary, the only daughter, married Richard Palmer and, for the sake of the inheritance, the name was changed to Fish Palmer.

In the next generation there were branches of the Fyshe family at Biggleswade and also in various parts of Hertfordshire, including Hatfield and North Mymms. Around 1590 Leonard Fyshe of Ayot married Emma Graves (the sister of Cecily Graves, the first wife of Henry Bull of Hertford). Their grandson, Leonard Fyshe of Hatfield and North Mymms, married Rebecka Harmer, the daughter of Thomas Harmer and Rebecka Bull of Weston, thus re-establishing a link which had existed, but not been renewed, for five generations. Rebecka and Leonard were fourth cousins, both being the great great great grandchildren of George Hyde of Throcking.

Leonard Fyshe of Hatfield and North Mymms

Leonard Fyshe seems to have been a wealthy man, and he acquired or inherited the manor of Potterells, which was part of the Coningsby estate at North Mymms. He died very suddenly, only a few years after the marriage, leaving Rebecka with two young children - Mary aged seven and six-year-old Leonard. There is a memorial to Leonard (Captain Leonard Fyshe) in the churchyard at Hatfield.

Leonard left a nuncupative will (a will dictated by the dying person in the presence of several witnesses) which of course was very short, with no significant information. However, there was a detailed inventory attached to the will, from which we learn quite a lot about the life-style of Leonard and Rebecka, and about the manor house at Potterells. It was a three-storey house with at least eight bedrooms and extensive living rooms, including the main hall, two parlours and a 'shovelboard' room. The contents of the home included fifteen beds with all the bedding, three court cupboards and numerous chairs, curtains, cushions, chests and tables. (Transcript of inventory on page 156)

Soon after this the Hervey family seem to have acquired the manor of Potterells, so it is possible that Rebecka, Leonard's widow, was for some reason unable to afford to live in this rather grand house. However, we hear later that her daughter Mary Fyshe married Roger Coningsby of North Mymms Park and that she 'inherited' Potterells which was once her childhood home.

The Manors of North Mymms

In addition to Potterells there were three or possibly four other manors associated with North Mymms. There was the manor of Piggots (mentioned in another chapter) and this manor house was later used as a guest house to North Mymms Park. Then there was Brookmans, which took its name from a certain John Brookman who held the manor in 1400. We hear that he acquired it from Nicholas de Mymm, and it was then known by the name of Mymmeshall - obviously the origin of the present name of North Mymms. The third manor was More Hall, sometimes known as Gobions,

Brookmans, Herts

and attached to it was another small manor called Leggats. In 1500 More Hall was the home of Sir John More, father of the famous Sir Thomas More who is said to have written his 'Utopia' here.

After the trial and execution of Sir Thomas More in 1535 the property was confiscated. Edward VI in 1550 granted it to his sister Princess Elizabeth (later to be Queen Elizabeth), but it finally went back to Sir Thomas More's grandson and was held for a time by the Roper family.

Sir Thomas More's daughter Margaret had married William Roper of Canterbury, the brother of Agnes Roper who married George Hyde of Throcking, whose daughter Elizabeth later married Thomas Fyshe of Ayot Mountfitchet!!

The Coningsbys of North Mymms

The main manor of North Mymms was for many generations the home of the Coningsby family. Sir Humphrey Coningsby was Lord Chief Justice under Henry VIII and his son John was High Sheriff of Hertfordshire in 1547. John was married to Elizabeth Frowick, who was the granddaughter of Sir Robert Knollys - who once owned the manor of Potterells.

In the next generation Sir Henry Coningsby and his sister Ann both married into the Boteler family of Watton Woodhall. Ann married Sir Philip Boteler, and Elizabeth Boteler married Sir Henry Coningsby. Ann and Philip had a son, another Sir Philip Boteler, who later married into the Knollys family. Sir Henry Coningsby and his wife Elizabeth also had a son, Sir Ralph Coningsby, and it was Sir Ralph who, in 1601, built the grand brick mansion known as North Mymms Park, to replace the old manor house, which apparently stood a little more to the east, near the church.

North Mymms Park

On the front of the house above the portico are the Coningsby arms, three rabbits (or coneys). The arms are very similar to those of the Coney family of St Albans, except that the Coney family have four coneys instead of three. Although we do not hear much about the Coneys, we find that the family connections still go on and on! Sir Ralph Coningsby's daughter married Henry Coney of St Albans, and their daughter Frances married into the Harmer family.

Sir Ralph Coningsby, the builder of North Mymms Park, was Treasurer to Queen Elizabeth and Sheriff of Hertfordshire in 1596, but it was their son Sir Thomas Coningsby who was perhaps the most well-known member of the family because of his distinguished political career.

Sir Thomas Coningsby, Seven Years in the Tower

Thomas was born in 1591, and was the High Sheriff in 1638 and again in 1642. He was an ardent supporter of Charles I and was arrested by the Parliamentarians at St. Albans in 1643 and imprisoned in the Tower for seven years. Meanwhile, all his property at North Mymms was confiscated, and his wife Martha and their four little children, Harry, Ralph, Thomas and Elizabeth, had to leave their home and take refuge with royalist relations. At the

Restoration, the property was returned to the family, but Thomas, who had suffered greatly during his long imprisonment, never really recovered, and died four years later. His son Harry sold the estate to the Hyde family of Aldbury.

Harry, who later became Sir Harry Coningsby, is recorded in 'Who was Who'. He was well-known as a translator and writer and he wrote an account of his father's sad career.

In the British Museum is the manuscript of a letter dated 30th March 1665, addressed to Sir Thomas Hyde, the son of the purchaser of North Mymms, requesting him to 'allow this little booke a little roome in the house which was so nearly associated with the glorious and honest deportment of my most dear father'.

According to 'Who was Who', Sir Harry was the only son of Thomas, but there were in fact two other sons, Ralph and Thomas. Ralph probably died in childhood, but we know that Thomas married and had a son Roger. This was the Roger Coningsby mentioned earlier who married Mary Fyshe and lived at Potterells.

The reference to Thomas Hyde gives a final twist to the complicated maze of family relationships. The Hydes (related to Sir Thomas More through the Roper family, and also to the Boteler, Harmer and Fyshe families) had now taken over the manor which for so long had belonged to the Coningsbys. So North Mymms did not really pass out of the family. It was still home to one of the same network of families who played an important part in the history of 17th century Hertfordshire.

Chapter 6

The Docwras of Hitchin, Putteridge, and Lilley

The Docwra family was descended from Peter Docwra of Docwra Hall near Kendal in Westmorland (Cumbria). They first appear in Hertfordshire at the beginning of the 16th century, when Thomas Docwra is recorded as the last Prior of the Knights of St John of Jerusalem in Hitchin. He lived at Brotherhood House, one of the timbered mansions of Bancroft.

A generation later, Thomas's nephew John Docwra acquired the manor of Putteridge. He bought it from Sir Edward Darrell who held it by a yearly rent of one pound of pepper and one pound of cummin.

John married into the Rotherham family of Someries Manor at Luton, and when he died, Putteridge, and no doubt some of the Rotherham wealth, went to his eldest son Thomas. Thomas Docwra later came to be regarded as one of the most distinguished and learned Hertfordshire gentlemen of his time.

Thomas Docwra, a Distinguished and Learned Gentleman

Thomas was educated at Grays Inn, became Justice of the Peace in 1559 and was Sheriff of Hertfordshire in 1580. He was appointed Clerk to the Receiver General of the Duchy of Lancaster, and later succeeded to the office of Receiver General.

Thomas was not only influential, but also extremely wealthy. In addition to the manor of Putteridge he also inherited the Brotherhood House property from his great-uncle Thomas and soon afterwards he bought the manor of Lilley. He died in his house at Putteridge, but he and his wife are both buried in Lilley, where there is a monument on the north side of the chancel. The monument shows various coats of arms, including Docwra, Brocket, Haspedine, St George, Hales, Periam and St John. There are lengthy inscriptions which give details of Thomas's life and achievements, and also commemorate his son Thomas who died in 1620:

> Here under lieth the Body of Thomas Docwra the elder, Esq; Lord
> of the Town, and Patron of this Church, descended of the ancient
> Family of the Docwra's of Docwra Hall in Kendal in the County
> of Westmorland, Nephew and Heir unto the Right Honourable Sir
> Thomas Docwra, Last Grand Prior of the Knights of St John of

Jerusalem: He had to Wife Mildred Hales of an ancient family in Kent, a grave and vertuous Matron with whom he lived 52 years, having been Justice of the Peace forty years, and High Sheriff of the Shire, Anno 23 Eliz. Beloved and reverenced of all for his Gravity, Wisdom, Piety, Justice and Hospitality. He died in his House at Putteridge, by him built, in the 84th year of his Age, Anno Dom. 1602 Leaving four Sons and two Daughters

Thomas Docwra his eldest Son, by his Study in the University, Inns of Court, and France, attain'd unto good knowledge and experience; his first Wife was Helen Daughter of George Horsey, Esq; and of his Wife the Daughter of the Right Honourable Sir Ralph Sadlier, Kt. by whom he left only one Daughter, married to Sir Henry Pakenham, Kt. his second was Jane one of the Daughters and Heirs of Sir William Periam, Kt. Lord Chief Baron of the

One of the timbered mansions of Bancroft

Exchequer, with whom he lived two and twenty years, and left issue Periam and Henry; Anne, Elizabeth, Jane and Mary. He was Justice of the Peace and High Sheriff for this County, an. 3 Jac. He was not ambitious of Honours or Titles but contenting himself with his Estate, whereof he lived plentifully, was worthily esteemed for his Wisdom, Judgement, Moderation and Liberal House-keeping. In the 92nd year of his age, he did Meekly and Christianly render his Soul unto God at Putteridge aforesaid, 6th. Martii an. Dom. 1620. And was here interred.

A Prevention of Forgetfulness

This is the Tomb of him who gave content,
By shunning that to which the most are bent.
He did not stoop to vain ambitions lure,
But deem'd his own more happy and more sure:
And thus my due and last farewel I take,
Bound to protect his State and Children for his sake.

Another inscription repeats some of the details about the first Thomas but adds a list of the names of his children still living: Thomas, Ralph, John, Edward, Frances and Ellen. From other sources we learn something of the history of these sons and daughters.

The Next Generation

We know that Ralph inherited property at Fulbourne near Cambridge and that Edward was living at Brotherhood House in Hitchin, probably renting it from his brother who had inherited it when Great-Uncle Thomas died.

Hitchin Priory
Thomas Docwra was the last Prior of the Knights of St John of Jerusalem

Frances Docwra married Peter Taverner of Hexton, thus linking the Docwras with the Nedhams of Wymondley Priory, the Harmers of Weston, the Wingates of Lockleys Manor at Welwyn and the Stones and Soames of Segenhoe in Bedfordshire. In his will proved in 1602, Thomas (the elder) mentions his grandson John Taverner. He leaves him all his books, urging him to concentrate on his studies and make good use of them. John certainly fulfilled his grandfather's wishes because he later became a Professor at Gresham College in London.

Ellen, (or Helen) Docwra married Jasper Horsey who was High Sheriff of Hertfordshire in 1572.

Thomas Docwra the Younger, Steward of the Manor of Hitchin

Thomas, the eldest son and heir, was twice married. His first wife was Ellen Horsey, the sister of Jasper, and by her he had one daughter who married Sir Henry Pakenham. His second wife was Jane, a widow, daughter of Sir William Periam, Chief Baron of the Exchequer, who bore him two sons and four daughters.

About 1611 Thomas bought another property - the manor of Pirton. Whether he lived there or at the house at Putteridge we do not know, but we are told that Jane - who outlived her husband, died at Pirton, where there is a memorial in the church. Thomas, as we know, was buried beside his parents at Lilley.

Thomas was Steward of the vast manor of Hitchin, a position which he obtained through the influence of his first wife's grandfather Sir Ralph Sadlier, who had himself held the Stewardship for many years previously.

Reginald Hine, in his 'History of Hitchin', tells us that Sir Ralph Sadlier took his duties very seriously, and spent his whole life in the service of the State. As an old man he was thankful to hand over these responsibilities, which had included 'the thankless task of keeping Mary Queen of Scots in watch and ward'. Referring to his office as Steward of the Manor of Hitchin, Hine suggests that his successor, Thomas Docwra, was not quite so conscientious. He did 'hold court' occasionally, in 1590, 1591, 1592 and 1597, but 'there is reason to think it more for the sake of the dinner than from any sense of duty'.

'Holding Court' for the sake of the Dinner!

At one of the courts Docwra collected £8-0s-8d in fines rents and fees, but of this no less than £2-11s-8d was spent on the dinner. The three course meal included venison, beef, mutton, rabbits, geese, capons, larks and pigeons, with 'Warden Pyes and fruit for pudding, all washed down with two gallons of wine and about as much beer as would flood out the river Hiz'.

The River Hiz
from Bridge Street, Hitchin

It is clear, says Hine, that Docwra neglected his duties as Steward, for in 1604 Sir Robert Cecil, the Lord Lieutenant, had to request him to hold a court 'to preserve order and to prevent disturbance of the deputy-bailiffs in their office'.

Two of the offences which were tried at the court were 'taking in a stranger to dwell without the consent of the Churchwardens'; and 'buying up poultry before the market bell be rung'. Other cases included 'putting horses in the fields before all the harvest be home'; and building a pigeon house. (It was an infringement of the Lord's privilege to build a pigeon house. Only the Lord or gentlemen with a certain status were allowed to have pigeons 'which eat other men's corn').

Perhaps Thomas Docwra neglected his duties as Steward because he had taken on too many commitments. He had taken over from his father as Receiver General to the Duchy of Lancaster, and was also Member of Parliament for Clitheroe, one of the Duchy boroughs. His obituary on the monument in Lilley Church does not seem to mention this. It also states "He was not ambitious of Honours or Titles, contenting himself with his Estate". This we find difficult to believe! Perhaps in his final years - he lived to be 91 - he may have been content to sit at home and enjoy his house and garden, but he had certainly enjoyed his share of titles and honours in his earlier days.

Thomas's eldest son Periam made a very good marriage. His wife was Martha St John, the sister of Oliver St John of Bletsoe, the Earl of Bolingbroke. This linked the family closely with the Bechers of Howbury Hall and with the Herveys of Thurleigh, the Piggots, and the Faircloughs of Fairclough Hall at Weston.

Mr Penne's Walnut Tree at Codicote

An interesting incident involving a member of the Docwra family took place in 1627 and is recorded by Chauncy. There seems to have been a great interest in a certain walnut tree belonging to Mr Penne of Scissevernes Manor in Codicote. Edward Wingate of Lockleys and Jasper Docwra of Hallwoods made the following declarations:

> 'Edward Wingate, Esq. one of the Justices of the Peace for this County, did certifie under his Hand, Anno 1627, that there was a great Walnut Tree, grew on Scissevernes Greene, in this Parish, which was of that great extent that the Branches thereof cover'd 76 Poles of Ground: it fell with Age, and the weight of the Boughs cleft the Body of the Tree in the Middle to the Ground. Mr Penn (who was Lord of the Manor) sold so much of it to a Gunstock-maker of London as he would carry thither for ten pounds which he paid, and sawed out in Planks of two inches thick, and half as much as filled nineteen Carts and Waggons. Mr Penn had thirty Loads more which the Man left with the roots and branches; with the end of one root he wainscoted a fair Room,

made a Portall and many Chairs and Stools of the remainder; and Mr Penn averred to my self and others, that he had divers times been offered fifty pounds for this Tree.'

'Jasper Docwra born in Hallwoods in Codicote, doth averre that in the year 1622 he measured the circumference of Mr Penns Walnut Tree, he being then 15 years old, and it was eight of his Fathomes of both arms in compasse round the Body.'

We do not know exactly where Jasper Docwra fits into the Docwra pedigree, but he presumably took his name from one of his Horsey uncles. We know that he was the son of Francis Docwra and Susan Penne, and the grandson of Thomas Penne who held the manors of Hallwoods and Scissevernes.

Sir John Docwra, a Supporter of the Jacobite Cause

There is another reference to the Docwra family in the Sessions Records for 1689, though again we cannot tell exactly where Sir John fits into our pedigree. "Mr George Needham maketh oath that Sir John Docwra said that King William was no King and that the parliament now sitting was no parliament, and that there would be no parliament till King James should get his throne at Whitehall again."

This of course was the year after James II fled to France, after his second wife Mary of Modena, a Roman Catholic, had given birth to a son James Edward. James Edward would have been heir to the throne, displacing the previous heir, Mary, the daughter of King James' first wife, the Protestant Anne Hyde. We learn from this little episode that Sir John Docwra was a Jacobite - a strong supporter of the Stuart family, and probably involved in the efforts to bring the young heir James Edward Stuart (later known as the Old Pretender) back to England. James Edward's son was the famous Bonnie Prince Charlie - the Young Pretender.

Ridgmont and Segenhoe in Bedfordshire

One more glimpse into the life of the 17th or early 18th century Docwras comes quite unexpectedly in the Parish Registers of Ridgmont in Bedfordshire. It concerns an affidavit made to the curate of Ridgmont and Crawley by Mrs Dorothy Docwra, widow and relict of Thomas Docwra, late of Putteridge, Herts. It states that she wishes to give everything to her two nieces Dorothy and Catherine Stone of Ridgmont, spinsters, except one great china bowl which she leaves to her granddaughter Isabella Warburton. She desires to be buried privately in the vault at Lilley beside her dear husband.

Dorothy Docwra was the great-granddaughter of William Stone who was Lord of the Manor of Segenhoe and Brogborough in the 16th century. His daughter

Ann was married to Sir Stephen Soame of Suffolk and Hertfordshire (Hyde Hall) who was Lord Mayor of London in 1598.

Finally there is one more member of the Docwra family whose name has gone down in history because of a brilliant idea which came to him in 1683. He was the man who devised a new penny postal system for London. His idea was never taken up by the authorities, and it was over 100 years before Sir Rowland Hill managed to get his own scheme accepted.

The Docwra name still occurs in the area today, and because it is somewhat unusual we can be almost certain that these are the descendants of the family whose lives and achievements were commemorated in the church at Lilley back in the 17th century.

"THE BIGGIN," HITCHIN.

The Biggin, one of the ancient Monastic buildings of Hitchin
dating back to the 14th century

Holy Trinity Church Weston

Weston was the home of the Fairclough and Harmer families for many generations. Inside the church, on the chancel wall, is a memorial to John Fairclough and his wife Ann Spencer. Beneath the floor is the Harmer vault, where several generations of the family were buried, although no memorial slabs remain - perhaps they suffered the same fate as those in Throcking Church! (see Chapter 9)

Chapter 7

The Faircloughs and early Harmers of Weston

Tuesday 5th August 1555 was the wedding day of Thomas Harmer and Elizabeth Fairclough. Elizabeth was the daughter of Thomas Fairclough of Fairclough Hall in Weston, where the family had lived for more than 100 years. Thomas Harmer also came from an old Hertfordshire family, with roots in Bedfordshire going back to the 13th century. At the time of his marriage he was Lord of the Manor of Newberry, which was one of the manors of Weston.

Weston, situated a few miles to the south-east of the town of Baldock, consisted at this time of four, or possibly five, separate manors, and included all of the present parish of Weston together with certain lands which are now in Baldock, Gravely and Clothall.

Laurence Fairclough, Esquire to King Henry VI

Fairclough Hall was the home of the Fairclough family from the reign of King Henry VI and probably earlier. The pedigree in the Heralds' Visitations shows that Sir Laurence Fairclough, with his wife Elizabeth, was there in 1468 and that his father Sir Ralph Fairclough was living there before him. Laurence would have been the 'marshall of the King's hall' mentioned in 1476, and an earlier Laurence, who was the King's esquire in 1437, would have been his grandfather. It was probably this Sir Laurence who built the original Fairclough Hall. The present house dates from the 17th century and was built on or near the site of the earlier manor house.

Links with the Barre, Spencer, and Hervey Families

Elizabeth's father, Thomas Fairclough, was married to Milliscent Barre. We are told that she was sole heir to her father, but unfortunately we do not know his name. However, it is almost certain that he was a member of the Barre family of Knebworth and Ayot, descended from Laurance de Ayot back in the 13th century.

Elizabeth had one brother, John, who was married to Ann Spencer of Cople, and his memorial remains in Weston church. Their son Thomas married Mary Hervey of Thurleigh, a descendant of the early Harmer family who held the manor of Thurleigh in the 13th century. Mary's sister, Elizabeth Hervey, was later very worried about Mary, whom she refers to in her will as "my sister

Fairclough". The bequest states: "to my sister Fairclough and her children, John, Litton, Elizabeth and Mary, £6 each for life". This gives us an indication that all is not well with the Fairclough family fortunes, and by the time young John inherited the estate things were even worse.

The Sale of Fairclough Hall to William Hale

There are papers in the archives which confirm that the situation was serious. One document relates to a debt of £1200 owed by John Fairclough to Rowland Hale. This was an enormous sum of money in 1660 and there was no way it could be repaid. A few years later, John was obliged to forfeit the estate which had been the home of his family for at least eight generations. It was sold to William Hale, who already held the manor of Weston and was acquiring vast estates throughout Hertfordshire and Bedfordshire. Members of the Fairclough family stayed on as tenants for several more generations. They continued to marry into wealthy families and some no doubt inherited estates elsewhere.

But the Fairclough name in Weston was gradually dying out, and by the 19th century even the name of Fairclough Hall had gone - replaced by 'Halls Green Farm'. Fortunately the old name has now been revived, keeping alive the memory of its earliest inhabitants.

The Wedding of Thomas and Elizabeth

On the wedding day in 1555 we can imagine the excitement at Fairclough Hall. In the dining hall the maids would be putting the finishing touches to the festive table, while in the kitchen the men were bringing in yet more logs to stoke the

enormous fire blazing in the open hearth. The smell of newly baked bread and roasting meat would bring a mouth-watering anticipation of pleasures soon to come, for everyone - guests, family and servants alike - would sit down together for the wedding feast, the only distinction of rank being the position at the table - above or below the salt. Some of the wedding guests would have been

Fairclough Hall, Weston

arriving over the past few days, for travelling was difficult, and anyone coming from a distance would set off in good time and enjoy the hospitality of the house for a day or two before the ceremony. There may have been relatives from Bedfordshire and more distant parts of Hertfordshire, but the guests would also include friends from the neighbouring manor houses - the Kymptons from Howells, the Wilsons of Walkern and Willian, the Clarkes of Benington, and perhaps the Nedhams from Little Wymondley Priory. The Pomfrets of Baldock may also have been invited and there would no doubt have been members of the Barre family - relations of Elizabeth's mother Milliscent.

A Wedding Feast at Ingatestone Hall

We have no record of the wedding feast at Fairclough Hall, but in a similar establishment, at Ingatestone Hall in Essex, Sir William Petre was keeping a detailed record of all his household expenditure. His step-daughter, Catherine Tyrrell, was married in June 1552, and the description of the feast can give us some idea of the kind of food which was being prepared for Thomas and Elizabeth and their guests.

On the eve of Catherine Tyrrell's wedding the dinner consisted of: 4 lings; 5 couple haberdins; 16 mackerels; 2 congers, one boiled and one baked; 15 couple soles; a thornback; 2 pikes; 4 mullets; 40 flounders; 3 dishes of butter (4½ lbs); a lead of cheese (56 lbs) and a score of eggs.

On the following day the dinner included a whole ox and a quarter, 4 veals, 6 lambs, 2 kids, 2 bucks, 22 geese, 2 cygnets, 24 capons boiled and roasted, 7 pheasants, 16 rabbits, 2 dozen chickens, 6 'brewers' (a kind of snipe), 7 partridge, and 5 dozen quails.

We are not told how many guests, servants and villagers sat down to the feast, but it must surely have been a vast number. For supper on the wedding day they consumed 5 muttons, 4 lambs, 1 kid, 1 buck, 16 capons, 3 pheasants, 3 dozen chickens, 36 rabbits, 20 pairs of pigeons, 4 peachickens and 2 dozen quails.

In addition to the meat, fish and fowl there would have been bread but probably no vegetables. In Tudor times vegetables tended to be used in soups and salads but not often eaten with the meat. A great variety of herbs and spices would have been used.

The Petre accounts mention mace, cloves, saffron, ginger, cinnamon, pepper and caraways. The herbs are not listed, because these would have been brought in straight from the kitchen garden.

The acater also made some unusual purchases that week - 'an hundred marchpane bread - 6d, a quarter gold - 16d, 1lb turnsole for jellies - 2s'. Marchpane was a confection of sugar and almonds, similar to marzipan, while the gold was real gold-leaf, used for gilding some of the sweetmeats, including the gingerbread and probably the marchpanes. The 'turnsole' refers to linen rags steeped in the juice of the turnsole plant, which were put into the hot liquid when making jellies, in order to give the violet or purple colouring.

Six Hundred Eggs and Eight Gallons of Cream

There is no record of the puddings and desserts which were provided for the wedding feast at Ingatestone Hall, but the list of provisions for the week includes 6 hundred eggs and 8 gallons of cream, suggesting that vast quantities of syllabub and custard were being made for the occasion. The sweet dishes at this time were often very elaborate, for the cooks were highly skilled, and cooking was a work of art. Many of the country house cooks received their training in the great kitchens of the royal palaces.

One speciality, known as a 'subtlety', was made from finely spun sugar, perhaps in the shape of a swan, or something appropriate to the occasion. It is all too easy, when thinking of our 16th century ancestors, who ate with fingers rather than forks, from heavy pewter dishes and platters, to imagine that their food was equally plain and simple. But this was certainly not the case on festive occasions.

Life in a Tudor Country House

When all the festivities at Fairclough Hall were over, Thomas and Elizabeth would have returned to Thomas's family home at Dane End. Thomas was now Lord of the Manor, because his father John had died a few years earlier. But his mother and younger sister would still be living in the family home, and Elizabeth would now be trained by her mother-in-law to become an efficient Lady of the Manor.

A great deal of information about life in a Tudor country house can be found in the 'Paston Letters'. The Paston family of Norfolk (who were related to several branches of our family in the 'network') left a large collection of letters extending over several generations. From these letters the social historian Trevelyan draws a picture of the woman's role in the running of the country house. He writes:

> When once a lady was married, she entered on a sphere of activity, influence and even authority. The Paston letters tell the tale of several generations of matrons by no means slaves to their husbands, but rather their counsellors and trusted lieutenants. They seem utterly devoted to their lords' interests, to which their numerous children must be sacrificed ... Their letters show them taking part in the legal and business interests of the family, as well as the purely domestic sphere where they ruled supreme. To organise the feeding and clothing of the inhabitants of one or more manor houses was in itself a task for life, requiring the same sort of administrative ability as ladies in our day so often devote to public work or professional employment. The household require-

ments could not in those days be met by hasty shopping. Everything that could not be supplied by the estate must be ordered months beforehand - wines of France, sugar grown in the Mediterranean, spices, pepper, oranges, dates and the better kinds of cloth ... As to home produce, the preparation, curing and storing of the meal, meat and game off the estate and the fish from the ponds, besides the command of the dairy, the brew house and the kitchen with its fire of logs roaring up the great chimney, were all under the supervision of the lady Chatelaine. Much of the clothing too ... was spun and woven, cut out and made up in the house or the neighbourhood under the lady's orders.

Family Life at Dane End

The Harmer family, as we read in another chapter, were almost certainly descended from John Harmer who owned estates in Marston Moreteyne and Thurleigh in the 13th century. They first appear in Hertfordshire in the early 16th century, when they held lands in Rushden, Clothall and Graveley. Later they acquired Newberry Manor, partly in Graveley and partly in Weston, and with it came the old manor house known as Dane End.

In 1557 Thomas and Elizabeth had their first child, a little girl called Lucie, and two years later there was another daughter, Elizabeth, followed by Joanne in 1561 and Ann in 1563. At last, in October 1565, Elizabeth gave birth to their first son. He was named Thomas after his father and also after his Fairclough grandfather, and there would have been great rejoicing at the safe arrival of the son and heir.

In November 1567 a second son was born. He was baptised John, and was later known as John of Baldock. When he died in 1613 he left a very detailed will which has provided a great deal of interest and information for later generations.

The next child was another daughter Mylicente, born in 1569, followed by Bridgette in 1572 and finally George in 1577. Both Thomas and Elizabeth lived to see their sons married, and the birth of at least thirteen grandchildren - (Thomas had 9 children and John of Baldock had 4). Thomas died in 1608, and Elizabeth lived on for another eight years. In her old age, the death of her son John of Baldock, at the age of 46, must have brought great sadness.

John of Baldock

'John of Baldock' the second son of Thomas and Elizabeth, was married early in 1592, a few months before his older brother Thomas. His wife was Ann Pomford (or Pomfret) whose father Thomas is listed as one of the freeholders of the parish of Baldock in 1561. Another Thomas Pomfret, Rector of Luton Parish Church from 1660-1705, and his son John, Rector of Maulden and a well-known local poet, almost certainly belonged to the same family.

John's will was probably written in his own hand, just a month before he died in 1613. It frequently happens that the writers of these 17th century wills obviously knew that they were about to die, and yet they still managed to write long and complicated wills.

It must have been with great relief that John signed his name and added his seal. His brother-in-law Thomas Pomford and his cousin John Cawdell added their names as witnesses, and James Sloane made his mark. Did Thomas Pomford know that John had left him all his 'best apparel' in his will, and did he find himself looking with interest at the fine woollen cloth of the doublet, with its silver buttons and lace trimmings?

John's wife Agnes and his three daughters Ann - aged 20, Joan 14, and Elizabeth only 10 years old, are named in the will, but sadly their only son Thomas, who would have been 16, is not mentioned, so we assume he died in early childhood. Instead John names his nephews Thomas and Joseph, the sons of his older brother Thomas, to be his heirs if it should happen that none of his daughters managed to produce 'an heir of her body lawfully begotten'. The will refers to lands, houses and tenements in Weston, Willian, Clothall and Munden, as well as the house and land in Baldock.

Exactly where John's house was situated we do not know, but it is possible that one of the 16th century houses still standing in Baldock today could be the one where John Harmer lived and died nearly 400 years ago.

John Harmer's House at Baldock

It was obviously a house of some importance, for we read of the gatehouse, the hall and the 'parlour next the hall', as well as the kitchen, brewhouse and cellars. All the rooms had 'lofts' above, and if, as seems likely, it was an early Elizabethan hall house, the upper storey would have been added quite recently, probably by John himself. Until it became the custom to build chimneys on an outside wall the fire would be in the centre of the hall, and the smoke would find its way out through a hole in the roof. With the coming of chimneys it was possible to have an upper floor and lots of extra rooms, but they were not necessarily used as bedrooms. It took time to get used to the idea of moving the beds upstairs, and the upper rooms were lofts or store rooms rather than bedchambers. John still had his bed in the parlour downstairs. We know that there were 13 acres of land, gardens and orchards surrounding the house, so it was probably one of the manor houses which was originally part of his father's estate in Weston.

Although he was a comparatively wealthy man, John's personal possessions were few by today's standards. Silver was the main symbol of wealth, and the most frequently mentioned items in wills of this period were silver spoons. No silver was mentioned in John's will, but the inventory lists four silver spoons, which were valued at twenty four shillings (see Inventory pages 152-155).

Pewter Platters and Silver Spoons

The Reverend William Harrison, writing about 1570, records a change in his own lifetime from wooden platters (treens) to pewter, and from wooden spoons to silver or tin. The age of forks was yet to come.

This was a time of many changes. John's inventory includes at least six beds with bolsters, pillows, mattresses and feather beds. There were also valences, curtains, coverlets and blankets. But two generations earlier most people, even the nobility and gentry, had no such luxuries. Harrison writes:

> If it were so that our fathers, or the good man of the house, had a mattress or a flockbed and thereto a sack of chaff to rest his head upon he thought himself to be as well lodged as the lord of the town, that peradventure lay seldom in a bed of down or whole feathers. Pillows were thought meet only for women in childbed. As for servants, if they had any sheet above them it was well, for seldom had they any under their bodies to keep them from the pricking straws that ran oft through the canvas of the pallet and razed their hardened hides.

In the house at Baldock it seems likely that even the servants had sheets both above and below their bodies, for John seems to have been particularly well equipped in this department. The inventory reads:

> In the loft over the hall. Item - thirty paire of sheetes.

They were valued at £10, a very considerable sum of money at this time, and more than a labourer would earn in a year. There were also 'nine pairs of pillowbeares, fower cloathes and other childbeed lynen.' No doubt Agnes, like most ladies of the manor, looked after the sick and needy in the parish. When any poor woman of Baldock went into labour, Agnes would be there with a supply of bed-linen, and other small luxuries for the mother and baby. The next item reads:

> Item - fyve dossen of table napkins, xi table cloathes and three drinking cloathes.

All this sounds like rather a lot of table and bed linen, even for a large household, but perhaps Agnes liked collecting fine linen and looked upon it as an investment. Certainly it would be passed down through many generations.

John's will was typical of its time. It was the custom to leave one's clothes to friends and relatives - also feather beds and mattresses, valences, blankets and pillows.

Since very few items were washable, and dry-cleaning was a thing of the future, it is questionable just how welcome some of these bequests might be! It is to Thomas Pomford, whom he describes as 'my welbe loved frende and brothere in lawe' that John leaves his best cloak and all his best apparel.

To his eldest daughter Ann he leaves some of the lands in Munden Magna and also:

> ... the bede and bedsteede standing in the lowe plor [parlour] next the hall with all the furniture thereto belonginge and my best valence... and curtains and the table and one trunck standinge in my beste lofte and my grateste brasse pott.

Ten-year-old Elizabeth, with her mother, has been named as joint executrix of her father's will, and is to inherit half of his property.

But Agnes herself died four years later, and Elizabeth, still only fourteen years old, became the sole owner of the house and land at Baldock and all the other lands, goods and chattels which had not been specifically bequeathed to her older sisters.

John's Concern for his Daughter Joan

John seems to have been slightly worried about his middle daughter Joan, fearing perhaps a runaway marriage or an escape to the bright lights of London. This was the great age of the playhouse and the theatre, with Ben Jonson and William Shakespeare delighting their audiences night after night with thrilling dramas and heart-rending tragedies.

Life in the quiet town of Baldock must have seemed, by contrast, extremely dull and boring. John states in his will that if, before the age of 18, Joan goes away from home without her mother's consent, then her Uncle Thomas shall collect the income from her property and pay her an allowance as he thinks fit.

But it seems that all was well and by the time Agnes was writing her will in 1617, both Joan and Ann were married into well-known local families. Joan had obviously behaved herself, because she had the special privilege of inheriting her mother's feather bed. Agnes writes:

> I give to my daughter Joan, the wife of James Maple, the feather bede and boulster where on I now lye, and one coverlet and the bede above, and two joined stooles and a little table standing in the lofte and three pewter dishes and one ketle called the soope ketle.

The Maple Family

James Maple was almost certainly a kinsman or ancestor of the Maples who became well-known as upholsterers and furniture makers, setting up business in Tottenham Court Road in the 19th century. From the same family came Sir John Blundell Maple, Member of Parliament for Dulwich from 1887, and also renowned as a cricketer, who helped to provide a cricket and recreation ground for St Albans in 1892.

Agnes's will illustrates a trend which appears frequently in later wills - that of borrowing and lending money within the family. A gentleman's income would come almost entirely from his rents, and if payment was delayed, there would be a serious cash flow problem. Sometimes a debt outstanding from one member of the family was bequeathed to another, in payment of money owed to this other person. Thus the burden of recovering and repaying a debt was passed on. The will continues:

> Whereas Richard Welles of Baldock oweth me by bounde [bond]
> twentie poundes, my will is that tenn poundes thereof be paid to
> my brothere Thomas Pomford, for the satisfaccon of a debte which
> he claymeth was the goodes of my mother Pomfords late deceased
> if the same be due ... and the same debt of XXs I give unto James
> Maple my son in law for and towards the payment of a certain debt
> I now owe him ...

Both John and Agnes follow the usual custom of leaving money to the poor. John leaves 'fortie shillings of good englishe money' to be given to 40 poor people on the day of his funeral, and Agnes, four years later, leaves 20 shillings. No doubt the poor people of the parish always looked forward to funerals!

Elizabeth Fairclough, the widow of Thomas Harmer, died three years after the death of her son John of Baldock. With her death, and the departure of the Fairclough family from their old home, the Fairclough dynasty of Weston came to an end. But their descendants lived on through the Harmer family for many years to come, and Fairclough Hall still remains today as a reminder of this ancient Hertfordshire family.

Dane End - the Harmer family home for 300 years.

The present building with its 18th century facade incorporates part of the original manor house. The old granary, which once formed part of the courtyard, also remains. The newly built 'mansion house' mentioned in the Marriage Settlement of 1601 was sold off with part of Newberry Manor in 1620. It is thought that the house was pulled down by Thomas Puckering soon after he acquired the manor.

Chapter 8

The Harmers of Dane End, Weston

Thomas Harmer, the eldest son and heir of Thomas Harmer and Elizabeth Fairclough, was married in 1592, a few months after his brother John of Baldock. As we read in another chapter, Thomas's wife was Jane Kympton from the neighbouring manor of Howells. The following year Jane gave birth to George, who was baptised in Weston church on 9th December 1593. During the next five years they had two daughters, Susan and Ann, and two more sons, Joseph and Thomas.

We hear little about the domestic life of Thomas and Jane, and unfortunately the only reference in the archives to Thomas Harmer is not a flattering one. Thomas, as the son of the Lord of the Manor, would have been a well-respected member of the local community. He was a church-warden, and as such responsible for looking after the needs of the poor, the maintenance of the highways and the censuring of wrong-doers. It is unfortunate therefore that the only record we have of his character shows him in a somewhat different light.

Thomas Harmer, an Angry Young Man

The Quarter Session Records are one of the few sources of information at this time but they do give a rather one-sided view. Accusations are made and investigated but we are not told of the background or even the verdict. There may have been particular reasons for the anger and indignation which caused Thomas Harmer to act as he did in 1592. The accusation was as follows:

> Whereas from time immemorial there was a common way ...... in a field in Weston, on 18th December 1592, Thomas Harmer the younger, by force and armes, knowingly and designedly stopped up and debarred ye commen gappe with a great and very deep ditch and a quick set hedge.

In 1594 Thomas was in trouble again, when, being taxed for the maintenance of the gaol and prisoners at Hertford Castle, he 'forcibly tore up the bill of assessment and furthermore erased his name out of the bill of the collection on behalf of the poor.' One of the Justices who would have heard his case would have been Henry Bull of Hertford, his son George's future father-in-law. But Henry Bull evidently did not think too badly of Thomas Harmer, otherwise he would never have allowed his daughter Rebecka to marry into the family!

Sadly in 1598 Jane died giving birth to their third son. The young family would almost certainly have been living at Dane End with Thomas and Elizabeth, and Elizabeth would no doubt have taken charge of her motherless grandchildren. George would have been only five years old, Susan and Ann four and three, and Joseph just a toddler. The new baby, Thomas, was baptised in Weston church on the same day that his mother was buried.

A New Mansion House at Dane End

In 1601 Thomas, the widower, married Elizabeth Clarke, the daughter of George Clarke of Benington. We have a copy of the Marriage Settlement for Thomas Harmer and Elizabeth Clarke, an agreement drawn up by the two fathers to ensure that Elizabeth and her future children would be well provided for. From this document we discover, amongst other things, that Thomas (the elder) had recently built a new 'mansion house' at Dane End, and the old home had now taken on the status of a farm house. But when Newberry Manor was sold in 1620 the mansion house went with it, and the Harmers returned to the old family home. The present Dane End farmhouse, a listed building, is recorded as being of 17th century origin with later additions and alterations, so it is not clear how this fits in with the historical facts.

Thomas and Elizabeth had their first child in 1602, and she was named Elizabeth after her mother and her grandmother. In 1604 they had another daughter, Mary, followed by John in 1606 and finally Benjamin in 1608. Benjamin is often mentioned as the heir, but presumably he inherited the property which came to Thomas through the Clarke family. It was George, the eldest son of the first marriage, who inherited what was left of the Harmer estates.

The Harmer family had now come upon hard times, and in 1620 Thomas sold Newberry manor to Sir Thomas Puckering, who had already acquired Weston manor. Thomas kept back part of the land including Newberry Wood, the name acting as a reminder of the old family estate for many years to come. There were also other lands which Thomas was able to pass on to his son George, and a detailed account of George's inheritance is given in the Inquisition Post Mortem carried out after Thomas's death in 1625.

The Inquisition Post Mortem

The term 'Inquisition Post Mortem' occurs frequently in old records. When a landowner died, the Crown often took an interest and made enquiries as to how the property had come into the owner's possession, hoping that some of it might possibly revert to the Crown. The Harmer properties were evidently quite complicated, and had to go before three different courts before they could be sorted out. The existing document gives us an interesting account of the property which Thomas still owned at the time of his death, which included:

> .. a capital messuage .. Dane Ende .. containing in all 240 acres in Weston juxta Baldock and Walkerne parcel of the manor of Lannock, 4 acres of wood called Newberry with appurtenances in Weston, one other messuage and 60 acres of land with appurtenances in Weston, 32 acres of land with appurtenances in Clothall and divers lands, tenements and heraditaments in Clothall and Norton.

Whether George was allowed to keep all this property, or whether some was forfeited to the Crown we are not told, but he seems to have lived very comfortably and was later able to provide suitable dowries to marry his daughters to wealthy husbands.

The Humberstones of Walkern

We hear nothing more of Thomas's sons Joseph and Thomas (except that they were mentioned in John of Baldock's will) but we know that his daughter Ann was married to John Payne. We also know that Elizabeth married Thomas Humberstone in 1621 and they lived at Tile Kiln Farm in Weston.

The Humberstones were a well-known local family, Lords of the Manor of Walkern. In the Walkern church archives is a report of an incident which took place on Easter Sunday 1637, when Thomas Humberstone and Elizabeth refused to go up to the altar rail for communion and insisted on kneeling in their own pew in the chancel. Bearing in mind Thomas Harmer's past record, we can conclude that Elizabeth had inherited some of her father's characteristics!

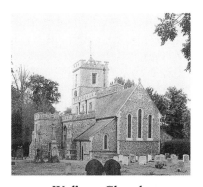

Walkern Church

Thomas's will survives, and though it is short is does give one intriguing piece of information. It begins:

> In the name of God, Amen. I, Thomas Harmer of North Hawe, gent, in the countie of Hertford ...

What was Thomas Harmer doing in North Hawe? Until now, we have never come across any of the family living in this part of Hertfordshire, although we later find members of the family at North Mymms Park and Potterells. It remains a mystery. Thomas asks that his body may be decently and orderly buried in the chancel of the parish church at Weston. Whether or not this request was carried out we do not know, for there is no memorial to Thomas Harmer in Weston Church. The church however has been much altered and rebuilt, so there may once have been a monument which has now disappeared.

A Generous Bequest to the Poor

Thomas leaves the very large sum of £200 to his youngest son Benjamin, and £3 to Elizabeth, but to each of his other children he leaves just twelve pence, a token amount to indicate that they had not been omitted inadvertently. They had probably already received their inheritance when Thomas moved away from Weston. Thomas is generous to the poor of the parish (in spite of refusing as a young man to pay his subscription!). The usual amount to be left to the poor seems to have been 40 shillings, but Thomas's will states:

> To the poore of the Parrish and Towne of Weston where I was
> borne, the somme of six poundes of lawfull English monye.

If, as suggested, we multiply by 100 to get a rough equivalent in present-day values, it would mean that the poor of Weston benefited on this occasion by about £600.

Thomas's heir, George Harmer, was married to Rebecka Bull of Hertford in 1623, and he came into his inheritance two years later. But it seems likely that Thomas had already handed over the Weston property before he retired to North Hawe, probably at the time of George's marriage.

Rebecka Bull was an autocratic and strong-minded young lady, well aware of her distinguished ancestors. However, it was to be a long and apparently happy marriage. They had six children, and Rebecka was a devoted mother and grandmother.

The first child, Rebecka, was born in 1625, followed three years later by John, the future heir to the estate. The next year they had a second son, George, who eventually went to live in Ireland. Then came Thomas, who married Ann Tooke of Essendon. Edward, the third son, was married to Elizabeth Flindell of Ayot St Lawrence. There was one more son, William, and also a second daughter, Mary, who married Robert Offley of Hertford. Robert was the son of Edmund Offley, a Burgess of Hertford, and the grandson of Sir Thomas Offley who was Lord Mayor of London in 1556.

George died in 1655 at the age of 62. He lived to see his elder daughter Rebecka married to Leonard Fyshe, who was already related to the family through the Hyde ancestors. George, like his father, requested that his body should be decently buried at Weston, either in the church or the chancel as his executors should think fit. Once again no memorial remains, but this is probably due to the fact that the church was extensively 'restored' during the Victorian period.

The Problem of the Younger Sons

George's will gives useful information about the family. His first concern is for his two youngest sons, Edward and William, to each of whom he leaves £120, of which £20 is to apprentice them to a 'good trade or exercise'. The remaining £100 they each receive at the age of twenty-one, and until this time they also have a £6 a year allowance for their maintenance. It was always a problem to know what to do with younger sons. Some would go into the army or the church, or perhaps study law at the Inner Temple or Gray's Inn, while others would be apprenticed to some useful craft or trade. Trevelyan, in his English Social History, remarks on this as a particularly English trend:

> The younger son of the Tudor gentleman was not permitted to hang idle about the manor-house, a drain on the family income, like the impoverished nobles of the continent who were too proud to work ...

George's younger daughter Mary is to receive £150 at the age of twenty-one with an additional maintenance allowance of £7 a year (surprisingly a pound more than her brothers). To his son Thomas he bequeaths £100, of which £50 is to be paid on the feast of the Annunciation immediately following his death, and the other £50 two years later. Young George is to have £50, but not until the year 1658 (three years hence).

It is likely that Thomas and George had already received houses and land from the estate. Rebecka also had probably already received her share of the inheritance at the time of her marriage.

Next we come across another example of a trend we have noticed before - that of transferring a debt from one member of the family to another. George's son-in-law Fyshe (young Rebecka's husband) owes £120 to George's daughter Mary, and she is to transfer this debt to John, who will be paying her allowance.

The debt, if and when he could recover it, would help to reimburse him for the money he was paying out. Presumably John, as the heir, would now be responsible for keeping his mother, his unmarried sister, and all the dependent members of the family.

Rebecka takes her son John to Court

The dowry which a wife would bring to her husband's family at the time of her marriage was intended partly to make sure that her children were well provided for, and partly to ensure that if she was left a widow she would receive a suitable allowance from the family estate. This would include a dower house and one third of the family income. Thus, while his mother was alive, the young Lord would be required to pay out a third of his income, which could be quite a burden, especially if the old lady lived on well beyond her three score years and ten! This situation seems to have caused quite a few problems to poor John, because his mother Rebecka lived on for another thirty years after George's death. Rebecka was later to take her son John to court for not paying her Thirds, but eventually she 'forgave him' the debt, and treated him very generously in her will.

The Nedhams of Little Wymondley Priory

Around 1655 John Harmer married Mary Nedham of Little Wymondley Priory, and they went on to produce a large family. Mary died in 1675, soon after the birth of their twelfth child, Dorseus. John would then have been forty-eight years old. He had eleven living children, ranging from eighteen-year-old Frances to the recently born Dorseus. It would have been understand-able if at this stage John had looked for another wife, to help run his home and care for the children. But this was not the case. His second marriage did not take place until twenty-two years later!

It would have been a hard time for the older girls, Frances and Barbara, who with the help of the servants looked after their younger brothers and sisters. For a few years their grandmother Rebecka would have been alive to give help and support, but she was now an old lady, probably living in Hertford, so the young family would have had to manage mainly on their own.

Quite soon came the time when Frances would expect to be married to some wealthy young squire. Girls were often married at sixteen or seventeen, and if they reached the age of twenty without finding a husband, there was cause for concern. Perhaps John could not afford to provide a suitable dowry, or perhaps he simply wanted to keep Frances at home to run the house.

A Clandestine Marriage

By the age of twenty-five Frances was getting desperate, and decided to take matters into her own hands. In August 1683 she ran away to London with a certain James Oldham, and they were married at St James's Duke Place. We hear no more of Frances, except that she is mentioned in her father's will, so he obviously forgave her. He left her only £5 (equivalent to £500 today), but this was quite usual for a married daughter, who would have already received a dowry of some kind. Frances was to receive the £5 only if she came personally to demand it. This was to make sure that she really did receive it herself, and that it did not disappear into someone else's pocket.

The second daughter, Barbara, perhaps also seeing visions of lonely spinster-hood looming on the horizon, found her own way of dealing with the situation. Not a clandestine marriage this time, but an illegitimate baby! Her daughter Joanna was baptised at Weston on 2nd May 1697. Later that year, on November 1st, Barbara was married at Ayot St Peter to Thomas Stanton, presumably the father of her child. Again John remembers her in his will, and leaves her £5 to be paid at the rate of 4 shillings a year. It would therefore be twenty-five years before she received the final payment, by which time she would be seventy-six years old (if she lived that long).

Edward and William Stanton, Talented Sculptors

It seems that John provided Barbara and her husband with a cottage on the estate, because in his will he mentions three cottages, one of which is occupied by Thomas Stanton. These cottages sound very pleasant, with orchards, buildings and four acres of pasture land, so Barbara and her family probably lived very comfortably, even if it was not a 'mansion house', which she might have expected if she had been provided with a good dowry and a wealthy husband. We know nothing of Thomas Stanton or his family, but Nicholas Pevsner, in his 'Buildings of England', makes frequent references to Edward and William Stanton who were very talented sculptors, and whose work can be seen in many Hertfordshire churches. It is possible that Thomas Stanton was a member of the same family.

The Warren Family

Less than a year after Barbara's marriage to Thomas Stanton, John himself decided to embark on a second marriage. His new wife was Ann Warren, a distant cousin of his first wife Mary Nedham. The marriage took place on August 2nd 1698 at Ayot St Peter, where Barbara had been married the previous year. It may be significant that Ayot St Peter at this time was performing marriages from all over the county, for those who for some reason did not wish to be married in their own parish.

We get the impression that these marriages were carried out quietly, perhaps even secretly, and the situation later presented to family and friends as a 'fait accompli'. The fact that Barbara had an illegitimate daughter, and John was a seventy-year-old widower with eleven grown-up children, may account for the fact that in both cases a quiet wedding seemed more appropriate.

The following year John and Ann had their first child - a daughter Elizabeth, baptised at Aston in May 1699. Sadly the baby died the following year and was buried at Weston in March 1700/01. By this time Ann was expecting her second baby, and in July 1701 a son, John, was born.

It is surprising that John the father, being the sort of person he so obviously was, had not already given his name to one of the sons of his first marriage, but apparently not. This son was to become his heir, which again is rather surprising, when he already had five sons from his first marriage. It may be that these older sons were to inherit considerable wealth from their mother's family - possibly one of the reasons why two of them, Eustace and Nedham, had been given Nedham names.

The next child, born in 1703, was another daughter - again named Elizabeth, which seems to suggest that this was the name of Ann's mother. This Elizabeth also seems to have died, because she is not mentioned in her father's will. In 1705 there was a second son, Joseph, and in 1706 a third son George. Finally John and Ann had another daughter, Phyllis, who was born in May 1711. John was now eighty three years old, and he died a few months later, after a full and very eventful life. He was buried at Weston, probably in the family vault, but again no memorial remains.

The change from Julian to Gregorian Calendar

John's will was made in September 1711 and proved in January 1711. This sounds odd but we have to remember that the Julian calendar was still in use, and the new year began on March 25. It was not until 1752 that the Gregorian calendar took over, and the beginning of the year was moved to January 1st.

All of John's children were provided with houses and land, but the largest bequests went to the four surviving children of his second marriage - John, Joseph, George and Phyllis, who each received £100, to be paid at the age of twenty one. There was also an extra £20 for each of the boys, to apprentice them to a good trade. John was included in this bequest, even though he was to inherit all his father's property in Weston and Walkern.

Newberry Wood is specifically mentioned in the will, also a pasture called Duffads near the tile kiln. John's widow Ann has the three cottages for her life-time, after which they also go to John. These three cottages were still known as 'Harmer's Row' right up to the beginning of the present century. Newberry Wood later became known as Harmer's Wood, and another meadow, part of the old Dane End Farm, was known as Harmer's Close, names which are still in use today.

In addition to the rents from the cottages, Ann is to have an income of £5 a year, to be paid to her by her son John at the rate of £1-5s every quarter. It is to be hoped that young John behaved better than his father, and paid up without being taken to court!

John has now brought us into the 18th century. The age of the Tudors and Stuarts is coming to an end, and from here on there will be rapid changes in the economic and social history of the country. King William has been succeeded by his sister-in-law Queen Anne, and although the Jacobites are still hopeful, neither James Edward Stuart (the Old Pretender) nor his son, Bonnie Prince Charlie, will ever occupy the British throne.

The Yeoman Farmers

For the Harmer family too it is the end of an era. It is apparent from John's will that he is still a wealthy man - the £500 in bequests alone would be equivalent to at least £50,000 today. But it is also apparent that he is now splitting up the estate. Much of the property has been sold, and the proceeds divided amongst his children. Although young John is the heir, and will have Dane End farmhouse and probably a good sized farm in Weston, he will now have to earn his living. He will no longer be a 'gentleman' living on the income from his estates, but will join the ranks of that very worthy section of society - the yeoman farmers.

From now on we find no more details in the history books, and for this reason we know less about the 18th and 19th century Harmers than about their Tudor and Stuart ancestors.

Dane End, Weston

Dane End remained in the family until the 19th century, after which some of the descendants acquired farms elsewhere while others, following John's advice, became apprenticed to a 'good trade'. Two generations became wheelwrights in Weston, but by the end of the 19th century the Harmers of Weston had disappeared. However, the name lives on - Harmer's Wood, Harmer's Close, and the nearby village of Harmer Green, are all reminders of the family who lived here in Hertfordshire for at least eight generations.

Hyde Hall, Sandon

The present house is on the site of the mansion built by William Hyde for his son
Leonard around 1565

The ancient moat with some of the original 16th century farm buildings

Chapter 9

The Hydes of Throcking

Towards the end of the 14th century a certain William Hyde, citizen and grocer of London, decided, like so many other wealthy London merchants, to buy a country estate in Hertfordshire. In 1398 he purchased from the Botelers and the de Argenteins the manor of Throcking, which was to become the home of the Hyde family for the next 300 years.

There were during this time two other Hyde families who came from the same Dorset roots and bore the same arms. The Hydes of Aldbury appeared on the scene when John Hyde bought the manor in 1544. A century later came the Hydes, Earls of Clarendon. Edward Hyde was Lord Chancellor and a close friend of Charles II. It was his daughter Anne Hyde who became the first wife of James II and mother of Mary and Anne, who in turn succeeded to the throne.

But it was the Hydes of Throcking who formed part of the network of families which included most of the landed gentry of Hertfordshire. They held the manors of Throcking, Sandon and Rushden, with other properties in the surrounding villages. George Hyde who died in 1553 left bequests to the poor of Sandon, Baldock, Norton, Leyston, Aspenden, Cottered, Rushden and Wheathampstead. There were also bequests to the poor of Barnet and Hadley, Isleham in Cambridgeshire and Potton in Bedfordshire.

William Hyde, a Grocer of London

The pedigree drawn up from the Heralds' Visitations and from the various wills which have survived, begins with William Hyde the London grocer. The term 'grocer' is slightly misleading because over the years it has become very specialised, and we tend to think of the local corner shop or perhaps the supermarket. But the term originally referred to a wholesale dealer - a "grosser", and William was probably a very wealthy merchant.

We know nothing more about William, except that he bought the manor of Throcking, and nothing about his son Laurence who succeeded him, except that he had two sons. The elder son George in due course succeeded his father, while Ralph, the younger son, became Rector of Throcking in 1472. Things now become rather confusing because of all the Georges and Leonards and Williams. If only our ancestors had used a wider variety of names - how much easier it would have been! But so far all is clear. In the next generation, Leonard, George's elder son, is Lord of the Manor while George, the younger son, having succeeded his uncle Ralph, is safely tucked away in the Rectory.

The Manor of Hyde Hall, Sandon

It was during Leonard's lordship that the manor of Sandon, later known as Hyde Hall, was added to the family estates. With it came the smaller manor of Daniels, which traditionally went to the younger sons. No doubt they would have been happy to inherit this lovely house with its moated garden and views across the rolling Hertfordshire countryside. The house was rebuilt in the 17th century and extended 200 years later, but much of the original building still remains.

The manor of Daniels (or Danyells) at Sandon
A 17th century rebuilding of an earlier manor house, extended in the 19th century

The old manor house at Sandon was rebuilt two generations later by William Hyde, and became known as Hyde Hall. But before this could happen there was to be a strange twist in the line of inheritance, involving the death of the young heir - yet another Leonard - as we shall see later. The present Hyde Hall is an 18th century rebuilding of the house built by William is 1565, but some of the outbuildings are the originals. The old moat is there too with a family of ducks, who may even be descendants of those who were there 400 years ago!

The first Leonard, having acquired the manor of Sandon towards the end of his life, died in 1509 and asked to be buried "in the church of the blessed Trynite of Throkkyng". He leaves money for the church in "Clothiall" and for the chapel of St John Baptist in Buntingford, and also allocates 40 marks for the repairing of the steeple of Throcking Church and for hanging a bell there. He seems to have had a supply of lead stored away somewhere, because he states that all such lead as he has, can be used as far as the 40 marks and the lead may extend. The value of the mark, frequently used in bequests, was thirteen shillings and fourpence - or two thirds of a pound.

The Roper and Brocket Connections

Leonard was succeeded (as we might expect) by his son George. George was married first to Alice Roper of Kent, who was the sister of William Roper, the son-in-law and biographer of Sir Thomas More. Although the Roper estates were in Kent, in and around Canterbury, they seem to have many links with the Hertfordshire families.

George and Alice had several daughters who all married into well-known local families - Fyshe, Boteler, Perient, Pratt and Kympton - and two sons, Leonard and William. After the death of Alice Roper, George married another Alice, a widow, the daughter of John Brocket of Wheathampstead.

George died in 1553 and asks to be buried "in the chaunsell of the parishe churche of Throkkyng by the litle dore on the north side of the said chaunsell as nyghe the place where the course or bodye of Leonard Hyde my father lyeth buried as may be conveniently". As we saw earlier, he left bequests to the poor of many surrounding parishes, and there are bequests to his children and grandchildren.

The Death of the young Heir

Sadly George's eldest son Leonard had predeceased him. There emerges here a very sad story. Leonard was only 28 years old when he died, leaving a young widow Anne, the daughter of Sir Philip Boteler of Watton Woodhall, and three little daughters, Ellen, Mary and Grissel. The middle daughter, Mary, was later to marry Sir John Cary, Lord Hunsdon, who was almost certainly a grandson of Henry VIII (see footnote).

Leonard made his will in May 1549 and died five months later. The will seems to indicate that he knew he had not long to live. It may have been an illness, but more likely the result of a hunting accident, which was the most common cause of death of a young man at this time. A broken limb or an infected wound could cause a lingering and painful death.

He made small bequests to friends and neighbours and to the poor of Ashwell, Baldock and Watton, and he leaves £30 each to "Ellyn, Grysell and Marie" on attaining the age of 18. His sword he leaves to his brother-in-law Thomas Fyshe, and to all his cousins the choice of his bows "lying at Plummers of Baldock and my arrowes to be devyded betweene them". He leaves rings to his father, mother, Lady Elizabeth Butler (Boteler), his brother William, Thomas Fyshe, Edmund Kympton, John Pratte, Thomas Bowles, William Butler and their wives. The remainder to his wife Anne. He must have had an amazing collection of rings! Gold rings of course were a valuable part of a gentleman's wealth, and were sometimes used as currency. We have an example of another member of the family, William Kympton, paying a fine of 40s. with a gold ring.

The New Heir

A few weeks after Leonard's death Anne gave birth to their first and only son. He was named William, probably after Leonard's younger brother of whom he was very fond. The little son was now the heir to his grandfather's estate which he inherited when George died four years later. George's younger son, William, inherited Daniels. This William was of course the uncle of little William, so to avoid confusion we shall now refer to him as Uncle William.

In 1561, for some reason which we shall never know, all the estates of young William were conveyed to his uncle.

Uncle William, now a very wealthy man, decided to build a grand new house to replace the old manor house at Sandon, which was now to be called Hyde Hall.

The historian Chauncy gives an artist's impression of the house which appears to be very grand indeed. It was built for William's son Leonard who was about to be married. Chauncy accuses Leonard of having used the tombstones from Throcking Church to pave his new kitchen! The story could be true, because outside the present-day Hyde Hall there are certainly some large engraved paving stones, situated

Throcking Church

on what could be the site of the old kitchen. Significantly the historian Cussons, writing around 1870, adds "It is a curious fact that no memorials to the Hydes now remain, although they were all buried in Throcking Church".

All the estates would now descend through Uncle William's son Leonard, while the deceased Leonard's son William, with his widowed mother Anne, and his three sisters, would be left with nothing.

Later young William married Mary Bristow of Ayot St Lawrence and they had several children including a son Nicholas. William died while the children were still young, and it seems that the widow and her family were in dire poverty.

Mary's father, Nicholas Bristow, in his will, desires his wife "to consider the great necessitie that our daughter Hide and hir children are in".

Uncle William accused of Forgery

Soon after this began a long and bitter law suit, and we can assume that for many years there had been a tremendous family row going on over young William's lost inheritance. It seems that Uncle William was actually accused of forgery, for in his will he writes, "for the discharge of my conscience I do here before God … purge and discharge myselfe of the forgerye untrulye laid to my charge and do protest yt my said nephew did deale and delyver ye same writing of release unto me as his deed in forme of law".

Poor Uncle William - perhaps he did buy the estate, and perhaps little William's mother wished to sell it so that she could live on the money. From another document we discover that for many years Uncle William had also been paying an annuity of £60 a year for life to young William's widow Mary, and £20 a year to her son Nicholas. He makes it clear that this is an act of charity because of the affection and respect he has for Mary, and not because he considers it to be a duty.

Connections with The Royal Family

But we can also understand how young Nicholas was feeling. His cousin Leonard inherited all the estates which, had it not been for his grandfather's tragic death, would have been his. However, it seems that there was no ill feeling between the younger generations. Leonard was now a very wealthy man, and was knighted by James I in 1603 just before his Coronation. It is possible that his cousin Mary, William's sister, put in a good word for him at Court, because her husband, John Cary Lord Hunsdon, was a close friend (and cousin) of Queen Elizabeth. When the Queen died John Cary had the privilege of going to Scotland to escort King James VI to London to take up his place as James I of England.

In 1625 Leonard's son Robert inherited the Hyde estates, but soon afterwards he sold Hyde Hall to the Earl of Exeter, from whom it went to Sir Julius Adelmere, sometimes known as Julius Caesar, who had been physician to Queen Elizabeth and Treasurer of the Exchequer to James I.

Throcking Hall followed a different descent. It was sold to Thomas Soame, the son of Sir Stephen Soame who was Lord Mayor of London in 1598. There is a large memorial slab to Sir Thomas on the floor of Throcking Church. Later the manor descended through their kinsmen to the Elwes family. Both the Soames and the Elwes were part of the same vast family network. In an earlier chapter we read that the Elwes are mentioned in "Timpson's English Eccentrics" under the heading "Oddness can run in the family". Certainly the Hydes had their share of eccentrics. Who else would want to pave their kitchen with tombstones from the church, presumably with the names of their ancestors engraved upon them! Those of us who can claim descent from the Hydes of Throcking should watch out for the warning signs!

* * * * * * *

Footnote: Mary Boleyn, Henry VIII and their descendants.

Historians have always agreed that Henry VIII had an affair with Mary Boleyn, the wife of William Cary of Hunsdon, but the relationship was thought to be childless. However, in 1997 new research by Anthony Hoskins, Librarian of the Newbury Library in Chicago, has shown that the two children, Henry and Catherine, were not the children of William Cary, but of Henry VIII. Catherine later married Sir Francis Knollys, and Henry's son John married Mary, the daughter of Leonard Hyde of Throcking.

Queen Elizabeth the Queen Mother was descended from the Knollys family, which means that our present Queen is the first Sovereign since Elizabeth I to have descended from Henry VIII and the House of Tudor.

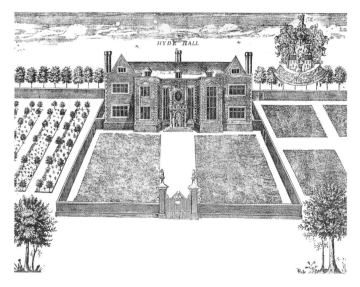

Hyde Hall, Sandon

Drawing by John Drapentier, reproduced in Chauncy's
Historical Antiquities of Hertfordshire c.1700

Chapter 10

The Knightons, the Herveys
and the Wicked Lady of Markyate Cell

The network of related families in Hertfordshire and Bedfordshire was closely bound up with a group of families in Suffolk and Essex, and it was here, in the quiet Suffolk village of Little Bradley, that we find vital clues about the rather elusive Knighton family of Hertfordshire.

Arthur Mee, writing in 1941, gives this description of his visit to the little church of All Saints:

> The cluster of cottages and a farmhouse share the quiet of a country lane, and amid finely wooded fields stands the little church, its walls and chancel arch Norman, the top of its tower mediaeval.

> On the chancel wall is a figure of Richard le Hunt, kneeling here in his armour since 1540, with his headless family. There are many brasses to folk who were baptised long ago at the big 14th century font. An early 16th century Underhill kneels with his wife; and Thomas Knighton, who must have known them both, is near, armoured but headless, with two sons and a daughter.

All these people were part of a large family group which included the Kymptons, Hydes, Bulls, Herveys, Harmers and Alingtons, the link being Thomas Knighton of Bayford near Hertford. Thomas Knighton of Bayford was the father of the headless Thomas in Little Bradley Church, and he was married to Ann Underhill, daughter and co-heiress of Thomas Underhill of Little Bradley Manor which is also known as 'Harveys'. The name 'Harveys' is interesting, for not far away is Ickworth Hall, the home of the Suffolk branch of the Harvey (or Hervey) family.

John Knighton of Bayfordbury and Brickendon

Clutterbuck tells us that 'the vill of Beyford', together with Essingdon, Hertingfordbury and the Castle of Hertford, belonged in the 14th century to the Duchy of Lancaster, and descended from John Duke of Lancaster to his son King Henry IV. In the early 1500's the manor of Bayford was bought by John Knighton from Henry VIII for £317 13s 8d. It was John's son Thomas who married Ann Underhill of Little Bradley.

When his father died Thomas Knighton inherited Bayford, but seems to have chosen to go and live on his wife's estate in Suffolk. All his children were born there, but his eldest son, Thomas, married a Hertfordshire lady, Alice Bull of Hertford. This Thomas is described in the Hertfordshire Visitations as Thomas Knighton of Brickendon (a manor near Bayford which was later held by the Kympton family). But in the Suffolk Visitations he is described as Thomas Knighton of Harveys in Little Bradley and, as we know, his memorial is in Little Bradley Church.

Bayfordbury
The Hertfordshire home of the Knightons from the 16th century

Links with the Bull Family of Hertford

There were still, however, strong links with Hertfordshire, and particularly with the Bull family. Thomas Knighton's sister Jane married Alice Bull's brother Charles, and while Thomas and Alice stayed in Suffolk, Jane and Charles lived in Hertford, where Charles was soon to inherit considerable estates from his father Richard Bull.

Thomas and Alice also continued their links with Hertfordshire in later generations. Their daughter, Ann Knighton, was married first to Richard Hunt of Ashen, and secondly to Thomas Soame. One of their 14 children was Sir Stephen Soame, who lived at Brickendon Manor and was a patron of St Andrew's Church in Hertford. In 1598 he became Lord Mayor of London. Later his son bought the manor of Throcking, previously the home of the Hyde family.

Returning once again to Suffolk, we know that the Herveys of Ickworth Hall were related to the Knightons because the Hervey arms appear on the Knighton memorial brass, but the exact relationship is not clear. We do know, however, that the Herveys have been closely connected with many other branches of the family - the Faircloughs, St Johns, and Lyttons - for many generations. There is also an interesting connection with the Harmer family going right back to the 13th century. In the year 1286 we find that John Harmer held the manor of Wroxhill in Marston Moreteyne. He acquired it from Richard de Argentein for one quarter of a Knight's fee, together with the "advowson of the church of Wroxhill". This was probably a chapel of ease to Marston Parish Church. There still remains in Marston Moreteyne a farm known as Roxhill Manor, but the chapel, dedicated to St Lawrence the Martyr, has disappeared.

The Herveys of Bedfordshire and Suffolk

When John Harmer died, around 1296, his son John inherited Wroxhill, while his daughter Joan inherited his other manor at Thurleigh, sometimes known as Whitwick Manor. Joan Harmer married John Hervey of Riseley who took over the Thurleigh estate, and the Herveys remained there until the 17th century.

Both the Suffolk and the Bedfordshire branches of the Hervey family were descended from the Harmers of Marston. The grandson of John Hervey and Joan Harmer was Sir John Hervey (or Harvey) who was Justice of the Peace for Bedford from 1382 - 1394. Elizabeth Hervey, Abbess of Elstow, whose memorial remains in Elstow Abbey, was Sir John's great-granddaughter.

It was during this generation that the family split into two distinct branches. Abbess Elizabeth's brother Thomas had two sons, John, who was the Member of Parliament for Bedford in 1472, and Thomas, who was admitted to Lincoln's Inn in 1475.

John Hervey remained in Bedfordshire, his descendants marrying into various well-known families such as Luke, St John, Piggot, Fairclough and Wingate, while Thomas Hervey married a Suffolk heiress, Jane Drury of Ickworth, thus founding the family which has given its name to a well-known brand of sherry!

The Suffolk branch still retained its connection with Bedfordshire. Around 1480 William Hervey, son of Thomas, married Joan Cokett of Ampthill, and their son, Sir Nicholas Hervey of Bakenloo Manor, who was Ambassador to Emperor Charles V, was buried at Ampthill in 1532.

The Bedfordshire branch continued to be closely linked with the Faircloughs of Weston in Hertfordshire, thus retaining their links with the Harmer family which began back in 1297.

Thurleigh remained in the Hervey family until 1715 when on the death of John Hervey it was sold. But the Bedfordshire links still went on. In 1680 John had bought Ickwell Bury from his kinsman Robert Barnardiston, and the Herveys lived there for nearly 200 years. They sold it in 1860 and bought The Old House from the Fish-Palmers, who were also part of the family network.

The Fish (or Fyshe) family and also the Barnardistons were related to the Knightons, but there is very little in the history books to tell us more about the direct links, and at this stage the Knightons almost disappear from the scene, with one notable exception. Her name was Katherine Ferrers, and she was the daughter of Sir Knighton Ferrers of Markyate Cell.

Sir Knighton Ferrers of Markyate Cell

At this time the Knightons continued to hold land in various parts of Hertfordshire, including part of the manor of Kimpton, and also Bayfordbury, which was the Knighton family home.

When Thomas Knighton left Bayford to live on his wife's estate in Suffolk, his younger brother John took over the Hertfordshire estates, and his grandson Sir George inherited in 1585. Sir George's eldest son predeceased him and the estates went to his daughter Ann, who married Sir John Ferrers of Markyate. Their eldest son, Sir Knighton Ferrers, inherited from his father, but died soon afterwards, just before the birth of his daughter Katherine in 1628.

Katherine's mother later married Viscount Thomas Fanshawe of Ware Park, and when she was only 12 years old Katherine was forced, much against her will, to marry Sir Thomas's son from his first marriage. The registers record, "Simon de Fanshawe married Katherine Ferrers on 29th September 1640". But Katherine never seems to have taken her husband's name.

Markyate Cell
The home of 'The Wicked Lady'

This was the time of the Civil War, and Sir Thomas Fanshawe was an ardent Royalist. When the Parliamentarians took control of Ware, the family were forced to flee from their comfortable home at Ware Park, and stay with friends in Huntingdonshire. Later they were able to return to Hertfordshire and they lived at the Ferrers family home at Markyate (previously part of Caddington in Bedfordshire). Their house, Markyate Cell, had originally been a Benedictine nunnery founded by Abbot Geoffrey of St Albans in 1145. The first prioress was the famous Christina of Markyate.

Poor Katherine, like so many children throughout history, was the victim of war and of the disruption which this had caused to her privileged and peaceful life. By the time she returned from her exile she was an angry and rebellious young lady, married to a man she did not love, and with no young siblings or cousins of her own age to keep her company.

Katherine Ferrers, 'The Wicked Lady'

Katherine soon became infatuated with a wild and handsome young farmer called Ralph Chaplin and, dressed in man's clothing, she joined him in holding up and robbing wealthy travellers on Watling Street which passed near her home.

There are many versions of this story, which has been the subject of two films, and Katherine Ferrers is now widely known as The Wicked Lady. One account suggests that Katherine's first victim was her own sister-in-law, whom she disliked almost as much as she disliked her husband. After a dinner party at Markyate Cell, Fanshawe said goodbye to his guests and went to bed. Katherine also retired to her room, but instead of going to bed she put on her highwayman's attire and crept down a secret staircase into the grounds, where her horse was waiting for her. She then set off for Watling Street, intercepted the Fanshawe coach, and relieved her sister-in-law of all her jewellery - a very satisfying gesture towards the family who had helped to ruin her life!

After Chaplin was killed during a robbery on Finchley Common, Katherine continued her life as a highwaywoman. Then one night, on Nomansland Common, she herself was shot and fatally wounded. She managed to ride back to her home at Markyate Cell, where she died alone in a secret room, which is still said to be haunted by her ghost.

Markyate Cell, now known as Cell Park, has been much altered and rebuilt since the 17th century, but part of the old building still remains - presumably enough to enable Katherine's ghost to find its way around!

And so it happens that the most well-known descendant of the Knightons is the notorious Katherine Ferrers, the granddaughter of Ann Knighton of Bayford-bury, immortalised because of her evil deeds. But in their day the Knightons were noble and influential members of the community, and many of their descendants were well-known families who did much to shape the history of Hertfordshire.

The ancient manor house of Howells in Weston

Chapter 11

The Kymptons of Howells and Clothallbury
Country Squires and City Merchants

On the 25th July 1568 a wedding was taking place at the little church of St Leonard in Bengeo. The bridegroom was a certain George Kympton, and his bride was a lady called Catherine Brooke, whose identity still remains something of a mystery. It is likely, however, that she was the daughter of George Brooke, 9th Lord Cobham, and an aunt of Elizabeth Brooke who married Robert Cecil, 1st Earl of Salisbury.

As for the bridegroom, George Kympton, we know a great deal about him! He was the only son of Edmund Kympton and Lucy Hyde who owned manors in Clothall, Weston and Astwick, and also held lands in Mundon, and the manors of Kingswoodbury and Brickendon.

After their wedding, George and Catherine settled down to begin their married life in the beautful manor house of Howells in Weston.

By this time the Kymptons (or Kimptons) had already been established in the area for several years. A manor called 'Kimptons' in Stanbridge near Dunstable was held by members of the Kympton family as early as 1400, but we hear no more of them until 1539, when Edmund Kympton bought Astwick and Kingswoodbury from John Poley and his brother-in-law Richard Sheldon. The Poleys and the Sheldons were already related to the Harmer ancestors through the Suffolk line and it is possible that they were also related to the Kymptons.

Strangely we have found no Kympton connections with Kimpton Hoo, although there probably is a link somewhere, because the families who lived there during this period, Hoo, de Vere, Keate, Mordaunt, Knighton, Trevor, and Brand, are all part of the network.

Clothallbury, 'A Mansion of Considerable Importance'

Edmund Kympton and Lucy Hyde started their married life either at Astwick or Clothallbury - the latter being a beautiful manor house situated between Kingswoodbury and Quickswood (home of the Earl of Salisbury). Clothallbury is described by Cussons as 'a mansion of considerable importance, judging from the fishponds and extensive terraces and avenues which surrounded it'. Parts of the old 15th century house still survive, though it has been much altered and extended.

Sadly Edmund and Lucy had very few years to enjoy their beautiful home together. Edmund died just five years after the marriage, leaving Lucy to bring up their 4-year-old son George and to manage the vast estates. Lucy, however, seems to have been well able to rise to the occasion. Sixteenth century ladies were often very well educated and strong minded - not as fragile and helpless as

Clothall Church

we are sometimes led to believe. One of the Hertfordshire historians makes a point of telling us that "Lucy Hyde, the widow of Edmund Kympton, held court at Astwick at the age of 24", and she presumably managed the whole estate until George came of age in 1565.

The Wool Trade

In 16th century England many changes were taking place. Until this time most of the land was held by small country squires, who might have two or three manors which were occupied by various members of the family. But gradually, in the 16th and 17th centuries, the more enterprising gentlemen were buying out the small landlords and building up large estates.

These men were often merchants, who had made their wealth from wool or some other trade, and were now investing it in land. Both Richard Hale of King's Walden and William Hyde of Throcking were London grocers, or grossers (general merchants), and many long-established families were becoming wool merchants.

The wool trade had been flourishing since mediaeval times, but was mainly in the hands of a few wealthy merchants who traded with France and belonged to an association known as the Staple. But now the number of wool merchants was increasing, and the cloth trade was beginning to emerge. The landowners were not only breeding sheep and producing wool, but were also employing local people as weavers and dyers to produce the finished cloth.

The rich merchants in the city were also commissioning their own ships. Until now the trading ships had been mainly Venetian, the exotic goods from the East being brought overland to Venice and then shipped to England. Now English ships would carry the wool or woollen cloth to the continent, and bring back spices, wine and silken goods which were more and more in demand by the English gentry and nobility.

The City Guilds

The old Trade Guilds took on an even greater importance and gradually changed their character, so that each guild or Livery Company was made up of a group of powerful merchants who were not necessarily connected with the trade from which the Company took its name. They were often general merchants trading in a variety of commodities, and their wealth and influence became such that they were virtually in control of the country. The Sovereign and government relied on the merchants to create the wealth to run the country, to expand its industries, to finance grand new buildings and endow universities, schools and colleges.

Hertfordshire was very well placed for the London trade, not only for export, but also for the needs of the city itself. Large herds of cattle, fattened on the Hertfordshire pastures, would be driven up to London to supply the inhabitants with meat. Geese were also reared and driven to London in large flocks, often passing through the county from areas further north, their feet having been dipped in tar to prevent them from becoming sore on the long journey. There was also grain and flour, produced on the local farms, and taken by ox cart to the capital. It is thought that Wheathampstead took its name from the wheat which was grown and milled there to supply the Abbots of Westminster.

The Rise and Fall of the Hertfordshire Gentry

While some local landowners began to accumulate wealth, others went into decline, and found it difficult to live on their incomes. There were a number of reasons for this, including the Civil War, which in the 17th century caused great hardship and loss of property. Land and possessions would be confiscated as a punishment for supporting the wrong side, and high taxes were demanded from both sides to pay the extra costs incurred by the war. Many of the wealthy families were also 'recusants' (faithful to the 'old religion', Roman Catholicism), and lost thousands of pounds and much of their land as a penalty.

Back in 1588 we find a list of gentlemen who contributed to the defence of the country at the time of the Spanish Invasion. Most, including Thomas Harmer and George Kympton, were required to pay £25 each (probably equivalent to about £2,500 in today's money), but a few, like Robert Hyde of Throcking, had to pay twice that amount. There were many such demands for extra taxes during the 16th and 17th century.

The Harmers and the Faircloughs, for various reasons, were among the families who lost most of their land in the 17th century, but the Kymptons were more fortunate because they were not relying solely on their rents, but were also city merchants. In the Victoria County History of Hertfordshire we find:

> More significant are the Londoners who took farms in Hertford-shire. In 1551 a clothworker of London held chantry lands in Bishop's Hatfield. At the same time one Edward Kimpton of Westminster held a lease of the meadows, feedings and pastures of Clothall, Yardley and Rushden. In 1552 he sold them to William Kimpton, a London Merchant Tailor.

This William Kimpton (more frequently spelt Kympton) would have been the brother of Edmund Kympton who married Lucy Hyde, and Edward would have been their father. The family had probably been living in London for several generations for they do not appear in Hertfordshire until 1539, though there were earlier links with the area and the Kymptons were probably already part of the network. In the 16th century the family still had their house in Westminster as well as land and property in Hertfordshire and Bedfordshire. The records show that William was married to Jone Maryman at St. Margaret's Westminster in 1539, and there are several other family baptisms and marriages recorded in the St. Margaret's parish registers.

The Merchant Taylors Company

William Kympton was Master of the Merchant Taylors Company for the year 1570, and there are many references to him in the Company's records. In 1576 he was elected Sheriff, only one step away from the very top position of Lord Mayor of London. Several other local gentlemen are listed as members of the Merchant Taylors at this time, including Henry Palmer, Walter Fyshe, Andrew Osborne and Jeffery Elwes.

One very well-known Merchant Taylor from Bedfordshire was William Harpur. He was Master of the company in 1553 and Lord Mayor of London in 1561, after which, as was the custom, he was awarded a knighthood. He put his wealth to good use in the county, and is best remembered for the founding of the four Harpur Trust schools in Bedford. Every year on Founder's Day the pupils still give thanks for their founder Sir William Harpur and his wife Dame Alice.

William Kympton's two sons, Edward and William, were also members of the Merchant Taylors company, and Edward was Master in 1596. Details concerning the life and character of William Kympton (the elder) which appear in Clode's 'Early History of the Guild of Merchant Taylors' are quite fascinating. Especially exciting is a record of the actual words spoken by our kinsman more than 400 years ago, (even if they did get him into trouble!). Clode reports this incident which took place in 1562:

> Some freeman complained of William Kympton's conduct towards him. The offender ought to have known better manners, for he was Warden two years later and became (as we read in these pages) a well-known citizen. This is his case ... 29th August 1562 - William Kympton fined 40s for calling Stephen Myliney a 'craftie boye', whereupon the said William lefte in pawne with the Master a ring of gold in payment of the said 40s. Nevertheless the Master and Wardens upon gentle submysion of the said Kimpton [sic] have remytted the moytee of the said fyne.

But that was not the end of the matter. William had to apologise in the presence of the assembled company in the following words:

> I know I have offended you and not used myself well in speaking such evil words against you. I am sorry for them from the bottom of my heart, and do ask your hearty forgiveness, for they were uttered in coller, but rudely rashly and immoderately. I pray you that we may be friends and so continue.

Later, William is described as 'A man of reputation, who was Sheriff in 1570, but was brought before the Star Chamber in 1576'. When he was Senior Sheriff, William had to search the Charter House for Roman recusants, and there is a graphic description of the search:

> On Sunday last, at six of the clock in the afternoon Mr Sheriff Kympton and Mr Sheriff Barnes and I (the Recorder) did repair to the Charter House and knocking at the gates no man answered ... Mr Sheriff Barnes, by agreement, went upon the backsyde to see that no Mass hearers should escape, and after divers knockings at the gate the porter comes ... The Porter answered us very stubbornly and at length he opened the gate, and being half in and half out ... he thrust the gate so sore upon my leg that I shall carry the grief thereof to my grave. Sittens that time my pain has been so great that I can take no rest, and if Mr Sheriff Kympton had not thrust the gate from me, my legge had been utterlie bruised into skyvers, and besides the porter began to bussel himself to his dagger, and tooke me by the throat, and then I thrust him from me, for indeed he was but a testy little wretche. And so I willed Mr Sheriff and his officers to stay the fellow from doing any hurte to any other in his furye.

Whether or not Sheriff Kympton and his companions found any Roman recusants, or whether they even managed to search the Charter House, we are not told.

The Manor of Howells in Weston

While William and his sons were enjoying the excitement and pageantry of life amongst the London merchants, Edmund's son George was looking after the Hertfordshire estates, probably rearing sheep and producing wool for the London and overseas markets. He was living in the manor house of Howells in Weston, and this is where all his children were born.

George and his wife Catherine Brooke had seven children, whose baptisms are all recorded in the Weston parish registers. Jane, the eldest, was born in 1573, followed by Anne, Leonard, George, another George, another Anne, and finally a third George. This last George survived and became his father's heir. Leonard, named after his Hyde ancestors, evidently died, as we hear no more of him. The second Anne may have lived, but again there is no further record of her, so it seems likely that Jane and George, the oldest and the youngest, were the only surviving children.

Young George was later to marry Dorothy Becher, the daughter of William Becher of Howbury Hall in Renhold, Bedfordshire. George and Dorothy lived in the beautiful mansion house of Clothallbury, previously the home of George's grandparents, Edmund and Lucy Kympton. They sold the manor of Astwick in 1620 to John Hudson of London, for the sum of £2,100.

The Marriage of Jane Kympton and Thomas Harmer

Jane Kympton, the only surviving daughter of George and Catherine, was married in 1592 to Thomas Harmer, the eldest son and heir of Thomas Harmer and Elizabeth Fairclough. It was a very suitable marriage, probably planned from the moment Jane was born, for Thomas Harmer held the neighbouring manor of Newberry (known as Dane End), and now most of the land in Weston would belong to the family.

Jane fulfilled her role very well, and just a year after the marriage she produced a healthy baby boy - the son and heir. He was named George, after his Kympton grandfather.

We can imagine the joy in both families at the arrival of their first grandchild. There would have been a wonderful Christening Party at Howells, with a large gathering of friends and relations, and a feast with special delicacies brought from London by the merchant uncles and cousins.

Guests at the Christening would have included members of the Becher family of Renhold, including perhaps three-year-old Dorothy. The Bechers (or Beechers) were a well-known Bedfordshire family. Dorothy's brother William (later Sir William, a Member of Parliament for Bedford) was married to Elizabeth St John of Bletsoe.

Most of the guests would have arrived on foot or on horseback, but the Bechers - trend-setters in 16th century Hertfordshire and Bedfordshire - would probably have arrived in the family coach.

The family coach at this time would have been a heavy wooden structure on four wheels, with no springs, and leather curtains to draw over the windows when it rained. But it was mainly used by the very young or the very old, for it was considered quite inappropriate for able-bodied people to 'coddle' themselves in this way!

The Death of Jane Kympton

Jane went on to have three more children - a daughter Susan in 1595, Ann in 1596 and Joseph in 1597. Then in November 1598 came the tragic day when Jane gave birth to their third son Thomas. The baby survived, but Jane, like so many young mothers, died in childbirth. She was only 25 years old, and had produced five babies in the six years of her marriage. On November 2nd baby Thomas was baptised in Weston church and on the same day his mother was laid to rest in the churchyard.

It must have been particularly hard for the Kymptons to lose their only daughter, and young George, now 16 years old, would also sadly miss his sister who had been his devoted companion from the time he was born. But life in the manor house went on as usual.

It seems that the young family had been living at the old home at Weston with Thomas's parents and some of his younger brothers and sisters. We know from the Marriage Settlement that Thomas Harmer had recently built a "mansion house" at Dane End to replace the old manor house, so there would have been plenty of room for several generations to live comfortably together.

Thomas Harmer and Elizabeth Clarke

In 1601 Thomas Harmer married again. His new wife was Elizabeth Clarke, the daughter of George Clarke of Benington and Elizabeth Bristow. Elizabeth's father was Nicholas Bristow of Ayot-St-Lawrence, who, as we read in another chapter, was 'Clarke of the Jewells' to the Queen. Mary Bristow, the young widow of William Hyde, was Elizabeth's sister.

George Clarke had property in Benington but was also Lord of the Manor of Therfield and Ashwell. He also held the manor of Chesfield, which was later absorbed into Graveley. There still remain the ruins of the old church at Chesfield, and also a farmhouse and another house called Rook's Nest. This was once the home of the writer E M Forster and was the setting for his well-known novel 'Howard's End'. For many years Newberry Manor descended with the manor of Chesfield, so it is possible that Chesfield and the house which inspired 'Howard's End' once belonged to the Harmer ancestors.

Rook's Nest, originally part of Chesfield Manor

Inscribed on the wall plaque "E M Forster ... lived here and loved this place"

The Clarkes and the Bristows were already related to the Kympton family, and the Clarkes also had Bedfordshire connections. Sir Francis Clarke of Houghton and John Clarke of Henlowbury were part of the same family. They also had links with the Kents of Astonbury and the Josselyns of Hyde Hall in Sawbridgeworth.

George Kympton died in 1608, but we have no record of Catherine's death. George would have lived to see his son married to Dorothy Becher, and would no doubt have visited his grandchildren at Clothallbury. Hopefully there would have been sons to carry on the Kympton name.

The lovely manor house of Howells, the home of the Kympton ancestors, still stands in Weston today. The barns and out-buildings have been converted to living accommodation, but the house remains, surrounded by the ancient moat and weeping willow trees, and probably looking very much the same as it did when George and Catherine with their young family lived there 400 years ago.

Chapter 12

Lady Cathcart of Tewin and the Famous Five

Lady Cathcart of Tewin must have been one of the most notable Hertfordshire ladies of the 18th century. She even had a write-up in the Gentleman's Magazine for 1789! After the death of her fourth husband she had a 'poesie' inscribed inside her wedding ring:

> If I survive I will have five.

The 'Famous Five' might also refer to the five grand mansion houses of Tewin, surrounded by their beautiful parks and gardens, all of them connected with the family network, and four of them still standing today.

Lady Cathcart was born Elizabeth Malyn, a family name about which we know nothing. Her fame derived entirely from her various husbands, particularly the fourth and last.

Tewin Church and its Memorials

The little church of Tewin is full of history. Around its walls are memorials of men and women long since dead and forgotten. But perhaps not quite forgotten! Most of the families were related to each other, and the names recur generation after generation down the various family lines. Many of them have also made their way into the history books.

They include Boteler, North, Beckingham, Dewhurst, Sabine, Colett and Fleet, (who was the first husband of Lady Cathcart). On the floor of the south aisle is a small but rather beautiful brass showing our ancestor Thomas Piggot, whose wife Elizabeth was the sister of the poet George Chapman, and who lived in one of the Tewin mansions.

The Manor of Tewin Bury

The manor of Tewin, before the Dissolution, belonged to the monastery of St Bartholomew in Smithfield. About 1540 it was bought by the Wroth family from whom it went to the Botelers or Butlers. The manor, known as Tewin Bury, descended to Beckingham Butler who married Elizabeth, the younger daughter of Thomas Piggot and Elizabeth Chapman. In the 17th century it was sold to Richard Hale, from whom it went to William Cecil, 2nd Earl of Salisbury. After this it seems to have come back into the family when it was bought by James Fleet, son of Sir John Fleet who was Lord Mayor of London in 1692. It then descended to his great-nephews, John and Edmund Bull. In the 18th century Tewin Bury, like several other properties in Tewin, was bought by George the 3rd Earl Cowper.

Tewin Bury Farm

The present house, known as Tewin Bury Farm, has been partly rebuilt over the years, but many of the old features remain, including two original fireplaces. It stands beside the river Mimram, and part of the old water mill has survived, and is now used for parties and weddings. The old stables and farm buildings have been converted into a restaurant and conference centre - so life at Tewin Bury is probably just as busy and purposeful as it was when our ancestors lived there 400 years ago.

Waterside or Tewin Water

Not far away, just up the river from Tewin Bury, was the mansion now known as Tewin Water, but at the time when Thomas Piggot was writing his will in 1610 it was referred to as Waterside. Thomas Piggot and his wife Elizabeth Chapman lived here for many years, although according to various documents they lived for a while at Wymondley Bury.

Their two daughters Rebecka and Elizabeth were probably born at Tewin Water and the younger daughter, Elizabeth, when she married Beckingham Butler, would simply have moved next door to become mistress of Tewin Bury. The elder daughter, Rebecka, was married to Henry Bull of Hertford.

It is possible that Tewin Water was handed over to Beckingham Butler as part of Elizabeth's marriage settlement, because it seems to have followed the same descent as Tewin Bury. It was certainly in the possession of James Fleet in the 18th century, and he is said to have 'repaired and beautyfied' it before bequeathing it to his great-nephews John and Edmund Bull of Battersea. Finally, like Tewin Bury, it passed to the Cowper family. We know that Lady Cathcart died at Tewin Water, but why she was still there in 1789 is not clear. Presumably she retained the property after the death of James Fleet, and either continued to live there, or moved back in her old age, after the disaster of her fourth marriage.

Tewin Water still remains as a beautiful mansion, with grounds running down to the river, and has been used in recent years as a school.

Queenhoo Hall

The third of the five grand houses of Tewin was known as Queenhoo Hall. It stood on high ground just over a mile to the north-east of the church, and was built by Edward Skeggs in 1550. The Skeggs (or Skegg) family were ancestors of Ann Warren who married John Harmer in 1698. The Victoria County History describes Queenhoo as 'a small house of red brick, very little altered, and there are no indications that it has ever been larger.' There follows a very detailed description of the house, together with plans of the ground and upper floors, but we are given no indication of its history. However, we find from other sources that Queenhoo was once the home of Aphabelle Partriche, a London goldsmith. Later, as we know from the

Queenhoo Hall, Tewin

memorials in Tewin church, it went to the Boteler family, and then to the Abel Smiths of Watton Woodhall. There is a theory that Queen Elizabeth sometimes stayed here, using it as a hunting lodge, hence the name Queenhoo Hall.

Tewin House

The fourth house, once known as Tewin House, no longer remains, but we know it occupied a site just to the east of the church, and adjacent to the churchyard. As one might expect from its proximity, it had close links with the church, though there is no indication that it was ever used as the rectory. It was built by John Mountford, Doctor of Laws and Residentiary of St Paul's London. John Mountford was the son of Dr Thomas Mountford, Rector of

Tewin in 1633, and brother of James Mountford who followed his father as rector, but was turned out of the living in 1643 (see page 150). James Mountford was presumably a friend of Thomas Piggot as he is named as one of the executors of his will. The house built by John Mountford was later pulled down and replaced in 1715 by a 'handsome modern house', which was demolished in 1807.

Marden Hill

Marden, or Marden Hill, was perhaps the grandest of the five mansion houses of Tewin. It stood on high ground about half a mile to the east of the church, and the park and gardens ran down to the river. The estate belonged to Edward North, Master of the Harriers to King Edward VI. It descended to his son Edward, then to his grandson Edward, who was Serjeant-at-Arms to Charles I. It then went to his great-grandson Hugh, who sold it to Richard Hale. Thomas Piggot in his will left a bequest to 'my welbeloved brother in Christ, Edward North the elder of Marden.'

In 1672 Marden was bought by Edmund Field, who was Member of Parliament for Hertford from 1671 until his death in 1676. From Edmund Field, the estate went to his kinsmen the Warrens and the Collets of Hertford Castle. One of the Collet (or Colet) family was Dean of St Paul's and founder of the famous Colet's school.

The Dewhursts of Cheshunt

In describing the memorials in Tewin Church, Clutterbuck gives details of many of the families who lived in these stately homes. The name of Affabel Battel of Tewin Berry (sic) turns up yet again. We also learn that Julyan Dewhurst, the daughter of Beckingham Butler of Tewin Bury, died at Cheshunt Nunnerie in 1637.

This information was at first rather puzzling, as there were no nuns or nunneries in 1637 - they had all been swept away by Henry VIII a hundred years earlier. Then we discover that Cheshunt Nunnerie was now the private home of the Dewhurst family, but had retained its original name. Robert Dewhurst, Julyan's husband, had bought it from the descendants of Sir Anthony Denny, to whom it was granted in 1537. Robert Dewhurst is still remembered in Cheshunt as the founder of the Dewhurst School, which bears his arms and initials on the east wall.

Among the many Botelers buried in Tewin church are: Sir George (a Gentleman of the Privie Chamber to Charles I), Edward (of the Honourable Order of the Bath), and Ralph of Queenhoo Hall (who is buried with his wife Susannah, and their infant grandson George). In the churchyard lies the body of Lady Ann Grimston, wife of Sir Samuel Grimston of Gorhambury. She is remembered because of the tree which grew up through her gravestone as a direct result, it is said, of her challenging the doctrine of the resurrection!

The Right Honourable Dowager Lady Cathcart,

Finally we come to the memorial of the "Right Honorable Dowager Lady Cathcart who died at Tewin Water in 1789". Amongst all the distinguished and noble ladies and gentlemen whose bones are interred within these walls, Lady Cathcart could probably be described as the most remarkable.

She was married first to our kinsman James Fleet of Tewin Bury, then to Captain William Sabine of Queenhoo Hall, then to Lord Cathcart, and finally to Hugh Macguire, for whom she bought a Lieutenant Colonel's commission in the British Service. She was soon to discover, however, that he only wanted her money! She plaited some of her jewels into her hair and quilted some into her

St Peter's Church, Tewin

petticoats. She also hid her will, but Macguire's mistress managed to find it, and Macguire proceeded to alter it in his own favour, threatening to shoot her if she tried to stop him. Then things got even worse. Clutterbuck quotes the following account from her obituary in the Gentleman's Magazine for 1789:

> One morning when she and her caro sposo were out to take an airing from Tewin in the coach, she proposed to return but he desired to go a little further. She remonstrated that 'they should not be back by dinner-time'. At length the Colonel told her ... they should not dine at Tewin, for they were on the high road to Chester.

When her friends found out what had happened they sent an attorney chasing after her with a writ of Habeas Corpus. The attorney caught up with them at the inn at Chester.

The attorney found him and demanded a sight of my lady but he did not know her person. The Colonel told him that he should see her immediately and he would find that she was going with him to Ireland with her own free consent. The Colonel persuaded a women, whom he had properly tutored, to impersonate her. The attorney asked the supposed captive if she were going to Ireland....of her own free will? 'Perfectly so.' Astonished at such an answer, he begged her pardon, made her a low bow, and set out again for London.

Lady Cathcart remained a prisoner in Ireland, but after a time her husband died and she returned in triumph to her house in Tewin. She is said to have danced at Welwyn Assembly with the spirit of a young woman when she was over 80 years old! She died at Tewin at the great age of 97.

What her Ladyship had to leave she left among her domesticks. Her body was dressed in linen and laid in a leaden coffin; the outside coffin was covered with velvet trimmed with gold, on which was a gold plate, whereon were engraven the names of her husbands, her age etc. She was carried in a hearse and six, followed by two coaches and six...to the church of Tewin, where she was buried in a vault near her first husband. Hatbands and gloves were given in general to all those who chose to attend and a sumptuous entertainment was provided ...

This very spectacular funeral is just what might have been expected from such a flamboyant character as Lady Cathcart! Strangely enough, Tewin may be best remembered in folk-lore, not by its politicians, lawyers and theologians, but rather by such eccentric personalities as Lady Grimston, whose tombstone was cleft by a tree, and Lady Cathcart, who never quite achieved her ambition of having five husbands.

Tewin Water

Chapter 13

The Mordaunts of Turvey, the Petres of Ingatestone Hall
and links with The Gunpowder Plot

The lovely Jacobean house now known as Turvey Abbey, which is home to a small community of Benedictine monks and nuns, only took on its role as a religious house in 1981. It was originally built by the Mordaunts as a family home, probably on the site of an earlier manor house. The Abbey is well known today as a tranquil place of prayer and meditation where people can go for study or retreat, and can if they wish join with the religious community in some of their daily services.

The Mordaunts were in Turvey as far back as the 13th century and owned estates known as Mordaunt's Manor. The remainder of the manorial lands belonged to the Abbots of St James at Northampton. However, there is no evidence that they ever built an Abbey here, so why the Mordaunt home later acquired the name of Turvey Abbey remains a mystery. At the time of the Dissolution the monastic lands went to the Dudley family, later Earls of Leicester, and took on the name of Turvey Manor. This probably included the other house, Turvey Old Hall, which was on the site where Turvey Hall Farm now stands. In 1660 the two manors were united and descended in the Mordaunt family until the whole estate was sold to Claude Higgins towards the end of the 18th century.

A Staunch Roman Catholic Family

The Mordaunts were a staunch Roman Catholic family, who suffered greatly at various times because of their unswerving loyalty to their religion. There was a time around 1608 when the Government took away the Mordaunt's eldest son so that he would be brought up as a Protestant, but the determination of his mother, Lady Mordaunt (then a widow), never flinched. We are told that she had resident in her home at Turvey the Vicar Apostolic, who travelled round the county in a coach with four horses, accompanied by 9 or 10 priests!

Although the Mordaunts seem to have had no doubts about their religious views, they were more divided when it came to political issues. In the Wars of the Roses, back in the 15th century, Robert Mordaunt, we are told, was a supporter of the House of York. He died in 1448, having "considerably impoverished the estate to support the Yorkist army".

Changing Loyalties

In the next generation his son William and his wife "were frugal and provident, and the family became prosperous again". Then we read that Sir John Mordaunt, the son of William, was wounded when fighting on the Lancastrian side in the battle of Barnet. What would his poor grandfather have felt about that!

But to go back to the beginning - Eustace Mordaunt was named lord of the manor of Turvey at an assize of Morte d'ancestor in 1225. He was succeeded by his son and grandson - both called William, and then by Robert who held the manor in 1346.

Domestic Problems

Robert's son Edmund seems to have had domestic problems. We are told that "the Sunday before the feast of St Simon and St Jude he was seized with homicidal mania, killed his wife Ellen, and drowned himself in a pool at Turvey". We do not know where this pool was, but it may even have been in the peaceful grounds of Turvey Abbey. No doubt the house, like all family homes, has witnessed many scenes of human joy and sadness over the long years of its history.

The family had certainly been going through difficult times. It was Edmund's son Robert who impoverished the family by supporting the Yorkist army, and Robert's grandson John (son of William) who fought for the House of Lancaster. But though exasperated by their family's costly involvement in war and politics, John's parents (William and his frugal wife whose name we do not know) would finally have been very proud of their son. He was knighted by the king and became Speaker of the House of Commons in 1487. He is said to have been instrumental in arranging the marriage between Mary Tudor and James IV of Scotland.

The parents would also have been happy about the marriage of their daughter Maud to Sir Weston Browne of Abbess Roding. The Brownes were friends and kinsmen of the Petres of Ingatestone Hall and they also played a prominent part in the historical events of the time.

The Field of the Cloth of Gold

In every generation the Mordaunts seem to have had one or more interesting and influential characters. The son of Sir John was John Lord Mordaunt, created baron in 1533. He accompanied Henry VIII to the Field of the Cloth of Gold. He also received Anne Boleyn at the Tower when she came to be crowned, and took part in her trial three years later. He lived at one of the other family homes, Drayton Park in Northamptonshire, and used Turvey Park as a Dower House.

While many members of the family still lived at Turvey, the eldest son and heir now seems to have lived mainly at Thorndon in Essex. John, the 2nd Lord Mordaunt, lived here at West Horndon, quite close to Ingatestone Hall, the home of their friends the Petre family.

Sir William Petre, Chief Deputy to Thomas Cromwell

At the time of the dissolution of the monasteries under Henry VIII, Sir William Petre was one of the King's Visitors and Chief Deputy to Thomas Cromwell. He travelled all over the country obtaining the surrender of a large number of Abbeys and Priories. We are told that "Unlike many of the royal agents Petre emerged with no stain, and even earned a few encomiums on his leniency and honesty in this arduous task".

Ingatestone Hall, Essex

The nuns of Barking Abbey were very happy with the terms he offered them. Petre paid the full market price for the property. The Abbess of Barking and thirty nuns assembled on 14th November 1539 to hand the Deed of Surrender to Dr Petre. Among them were ladies of many leading families in Suffolk and Essex, including the Mordaunts, Tyrrells, Wentworths, Drurys, Sulyards and Kemps. All were very happy with their annuities, Abbess Barley's being £133-13s.-4d.

Many of the ladies were probably very pleased to be released from their vows, having entered the nunnery, not from any religious conviction, but because they were sent there by their parents. Unmarried daughters of noble families were not allowed to sit around at home doing nothing, but were packed off to the nearest nunnery, the religious houses being only too pleased to accept the young ladies in return for the substantial sums of money paid by their wealthy fathers.

The Mordaunts were not only neighbours but also friends and kinsmen of the Petres. John, Lord Mordaunt made a gift of an ox at the wedding of Sir William Petre's step-daughter Catherine Tyrrell in 1552, and for the christening of Master John Petre we hear that Lady Mordaunt (previously Elizabeth de Vere) sent a gift of "a guinea fowl, a mallard, a woodcock, two teals, a basket of wafers and other cakes".

William Byrd, Court Musician and Composer

John, Lord Mordaunt often came to play backgammon with Sir William Petre at Ingatestone Hall, and together with other friends, would gather to hear musical performances by William Byrd, the Court musician and composer, who spent as much of his time as possible with the Petres who were his friends and patrons.

This John Mordaunt was a supporter of Queen Mary, who made him a Privy Counsellor. He had inherited part of the manor of Kimpton in Hertfordshire by his marriage to Elizabeth de Vere, who was the daughter of Henry de Vere, and sister to Audrey and Ann, who both married into the Browne family of Abbess Roding.

The Barnardiston Connection

In the next generation Lewis, 3rd Lord Mordaunt, lived at Northill in Bedfordshire. His uncle, George Mordaunt, already had links with Northill, as his daughter Katherine was married to Robert Barnardiston of Ickwell Bury. There were also links with the Brand family at Kimpton who later acquired the house now known as Turvey Abbey.

Lewis was a Judge who took part (un-willingly) in the trial of Mary Queen of Scots and also of Thomas Duke of Norfolk. Later he sold his share of the manor of Kimpton to Thomas Hoo of St Paul's Walden, from whom the manor took its name of

Turvey Abbey, Bedfordshire

Kimpton Hoo. He was married to Jane Nedham of Wymondley Priory - the great-aunt of Mary Nedham who later married Thomas Harmer of Weston.

The son of Lewis Mordaunt and Jane Nedham was Henry, 4th Lord Mordaunt, a very staunch Roman Catholic, who seems to have lived once again at Turvey. He was sent to the Tower under suspicion of being involved in the Gunpowder Plot, and remained imprisoned there until just before his death in 1608. In his will he states that his conscience is clear, and that he had no knowledge of the Gunpowder Treason.

His widow lived on at Turvey, and it was her eldest son John who was taken away by the government so that he would not be influenced by the "old religion". This was the lady who hid and cared for many Jesuit priests and who sometimes as an act of defiance drove them round the countryside in a coach and four!

This is also the lady whose house furnishings are described by Joyce Godber in her 'History of Bedfordshire':

> Lady Mordaunt's house at Turvey .... had three parlours (one of them wainscotted), drawing room (where were chairs of turkey-work), red room and gallery, and 14 bed-chambers - her own contained a white wrought bed; among miscellaneous items were 5 bellows and 6 chamber pots.

John, the son who was taken away and brought up as a Protestant, was made Earl of Peterborough in 1628. He took the Parliamentarian side in the Civil War, and died in 1642.

Henry, 2nd Earl of Peterborough, unlike his father, took the Royalist side (reminding us of an earlier father and son who had taken opposite sides in the Wars of the Roses). Henry was wounded at Newbury, and several times imprisoned. His estates were sequestered in 1648, but were recovered in 1655 at a cost of £5,106-15s.-0d!!

Henry Mordaunt, Member of the Privy Council

Like most of his predecessors Henry played an important part in the history of the country. At the Restoration he was made a member of the Privy Council, and conducted negotiations for the marriage of the Duke of York (later James II) and Mary of Modena. The Duke of York's previous marriage of course was to Anne Hyde, a relative of the Hydes of Throcking.

Obviously the fact that John had been taken away and brought up as a Protestant had had no permanent effect on his family's allegiance to Roman Catholicism. His grandson Henry was impeached for High Treason, but later released, probably on payment of a large fine. He was created Earl of Monmouth in 1689 and died at an advanced age in 1697 without male issue. His only daughter Mary died unmarried in 1705.

The Mordaunt dynasty at Turvey was coming to an end. Henry was succeeded by his nephew Charles, 3rd Earl of Peterborough, the 4th Earl being his grandson. In 1786 the 5th and last Earl sold all the property at Turvey to Claude Higgins, Sheriff of London, and the estates remained in the Higgins family until the 19th century.

The Gunpowder Plot

But before we leave the Mordaunts of Turvey we look back once more at a particularly turbulent period in their history. We have already come across several links with the Gunpowder Plot of 1605, and we know that Henry, 4th Lord Mordaunt, was imprisoned in the Tower, but he stated that his conscience was clear and that he had no knowledge of the Treason. We can, however, quite understand how he might come under suspicion.

One of the conspirators, Robert Keyes, was closely connected with the family. Robert's wife, Christina, was governness to the Mordaunt children, and Lord Mordaunt was Robert's patron and friend. Because of this involvement we are told that he was not only imprisoned in the Tower, but tried in front of the Star Chamber and fined £10,000.

Another of the conspirators, Robert Wintour, was married to Gertrude Talbot, a member of a well-known recusant family at Grafton Manor near Bromsgrove. Her mother was Katherine Petre, daughter of Sir William Petre of Ingatestone Hall. Another friend of the Mordaunts, Eliza Vaux, a highly educated woman, devoted her life to her children and also to the rebuilding of Harrowden Hall, to include ingenious hiding places for the many priests who found refuge there. She was known with respect and affection, even by non-Catholics, as the Dowager of Harrowden.

Other equally strong and determined women did much to support the cause of Catholicism, among them Elizabeth Tresham of Rushton Hall in Northampton-shire and Elizabeth Throckmorton, wife of Sir Walter Raleigh and cousin of the conspirator Robert Catesby. Then there was the "Monteagle Letter", a letter received by Lord Monteagle warning him not to attend parliament on November 5th. Because of this letter the Plot was discovered and disaster averted. Lord Monteagle's daughter Catherine was married to John Petre, the "Master John" to whom Lady Mordaunt sent a christening present!

And so we leave these colourful characters - the Mordaunts of Turvey. Perhaps the strongest image which remains is that of Lady Mordaunt driving round the Bedfordshire countryside in her coach and four, accompanied by the distinguished Vicar Apostolic and nine assorted priests, determined to assert her right to worship according to her own convictions.

Chapter 14

The Nedhams of Wymondley Priory and the Warrens of Bygrave

In the church at Little Wymondley is a brass plaque in memory of James Nedham and his son John. It tells us that James was advanced by King Henry VIII for his service in England and France, and lies buried in the church of Our Lady at Boulogne, where he was killed in 1545. The memorial was erected in 1605 by James's grandson George Nedham, and it was George's grand-daughter Mary who later married into the Harmer family of Weston.

James Nedham was 'accountant, surveyor general, and clerk' to King Henry VIII, and in 1536, in return for services to the King, he was granted the Augustinian Priory at Little Wymondley with all its extensive lands and properties. The Priory was founded by Richard de Argentein in the reign of Henry III, and owned land and property in many parts of Hertfordshire, including the manor of Marden at Tewin, and the water-mill at Ickleford. In addition to acquiring all these properties, James was also able to buy the entire contents of the Priory, which were valued at a sum total of only £13-12s-9d. Cussons quotes the original inventory, which was drawn up by the king's commissioners, one of whom was Thomas Perient Esquire, a familiar name in the family network.

It seems that the commissioners may have tried to keep the cost as low as possible, for they were very dismissive about some of the items. For example:

> **In the Kitchen** 3 kettles (very old) 4 pence. 2 spits (little worth) 4 pence. 3 platters, 3 dishes, 6 porringers, 2 sauces - 2 shillings.

> **In the Buttery or Pantry** 3 salts of pewter 3 pence. A chaffing dish 2 pence. 2 candlesticks 2 pence.

The sale of the contents of the Priory chapel seems even more ludicrous. In the Quire we find the alabaster altar valued at 2 shillings, 2 old linen altar cloths at 2d, a Mass Book 4d, sanctuary bell 1d, a vestment of blue silk (very old) 20d, one pair of 'orgaynes' (very old) 5 shillings, 2 crosses with a cross cloth 6d, one old senser 2d, 2 vestments, one of Bawdekyn and one of red silk 3d, one old Cope 8d.

At Our Lady's Altar was a 'table of alabaster of the resurrection' valued at 8d, and a Holywater Stoppe at 2d. At St Laurence's Altar a 'table of alabaster of the Trinity' was valued at 6d. But a pair of silver chalices at 24 shillings and 4 pence seems nearer the present-day value. In the farmyard things were in general rather more expensive, probably because they were more useful. A cart-horse and harness was 25 shillings, and the cart 3 shillings and 4 pence, though the plough was only valued at 8d.

Chauncy, writing about the Priory 150 years later, after it had been converted into a 'mansion' by James Nedham or his son John, gives the following description (spelling modernised):

> A fair old building with cloisters; there was a Chapel consecrated since the Dissolution. Almost surrounded with a moat, situated upon the side of a small hill, encompassed with near 400 acres of rich meadow, pasture and arable land enclosed to it, with a very fair orchard and garden, yielding the best sort of fruit. The house is supplied from a conduit with sufficient water to turn the spit in the kitchen upon all occasions.

Cussons, writing in the late 19th century says, "Nothing of the old religious house now remains". But this is not quite true. Although James Nedham pulled down most of the original building, he did leave the 13th century chapel, and incorporated it into his new house, where he used it for family baptisms and marriages. According to Chauncy, it seems that the cloisters also remained at least until the 18th century.

Extensive alterations in the 1970's uncovered considerable 13th century remains including the original high-pitched seven-sided rafter roof of the chapel nave, two south lancets, and the original north doorway. The conduit which supplied water to the mediaeval priory, and which turned the spit in the kitchen where our ancestors roasted their Sunday joint, has been carefully preserved, and is listed by the Department of the Environment as an Ancient Monument.

The Ancient Tithe Barn and Dovecote

The ancient tithe barn, built around 1400, has been restored, and the architectural detail of the nine-bay structure, with its magnificent raftered roof, is probably more appreciated now than at any time in its long history. The dovecote, again a listed building, has now been converted into a house known as Dove Cottage.

One other very interesting feature is the grove of box trees about thirty feet high, claimed to be the oldest in England. They are almost certainly the descendants of those which are known to have been here in ancient times. Some box leaves were found with a Roman burial urn nearby, and it could well be that the original trees were introduced by the Romans nearly two thousand years ago.

Family Baptisms in the Priory Chapel

The pedigree of the Nedham family has been documented by various historians, but there are slight discrepancies, probably due to the fact that most of the baptisms, and at least one of the marriages, took place in the private chapel of the Priory and the records were later incorrectly copied into the parish registers.

Wymondley Priory

We cannot be sure whether the baby daughter, who later married John Harmer around 1657, was Mary or Margaret because there are two possible entries in the registers. The first one states that 'Mistress Margaret Needham [sic], daughter to the right worshippfull Mr Eustace Nedham was baptised 21st May 1629'. The second simply records, 'Mary Nedham baptised 23 February 1636/7.' The second entry seems the more likely, as the Weston parish registers later refer to John's wife as Mary, although there is still some doubt because one of John's daughters is baptised Margaret. We do know, however, that she was the daughter of Eustace Nedham and his second wife, Frances Wingate, whose father was Lord of the Manor of Lockleys at Digswell.

The Wingate family came originally from Harlington in Bedfordshire, and included Edmund Wingate, a renowned mathematician, who went to France to teach English to Princess Henrietta Maria, the future wife of King Charles I.

Eustace was the son of George Nedham, the grandson of James who acquired the Priory in 1536 and built the house which we see today. George's brother James, and his two sisters Juliana and Bridget, all had connections with the family. James was married to Elizabeth, sister of Beckingham Butler of Tewin Bury, whose wife Elizabeth was sister of Rebecka Piggot. Bridget Nedham married Benjamin Piggot of Gravenhurst in Bedfordshire - a member of the same Piggot family, and Juliana married William Warren, alias Bygrave, of whom we shall hear more later.

Camfield Place, Essendon

When Eustace Nedham died the Priory descended through his eldest son George, the son of his first wife, Ann Norton. George died in 1669, and was succeeded in turn by his son and grandson, both named George. But there were to be no more Georges or any other male heirs. The third George had only daughters - Susan, Barbara and Martha, who jointly inherited the property. Martha married Thomas Browne, an eminent surveyor, who later became Garter King of Arms. They lived for a time at Wymondley Priory, and then moved to Camfield Place in Essendon. Martha died in 1773 and Thomas died seven years later at the age of 79. They were buried in Essendon church where there are monuments to their memory.

In more recent times Camfield Place was the home of the novelist Barbara Cartland, who died there in August 2000, and is buried within the grounds.

Robie Sherwin, Rector of Ashwell

Barbara Nedham married John Sherwin of Nottingham and their son Robie Sherwin became Rector of Ashwell. The third sister, Susan, seems to have remained unmarried, and later went to live at Graveley, possibly with her aunt Elizabeth Nedham, whose husband, Simon Degge, was Lord of the Manor.

Around 1733 the Priory, which had been the home of the Nedhams for nearly 200 years, was finally sold. It was bought by Samuel Vanderplank, and descended to his son-in-

Little Wymondley Church

law, Gilbert Joddrell, and then to the Clitherow family of Essendon. In 1806 they sold it to Samuel Heathcote of Shephallbury (of whom we read in another chapter) who had recently bought Wymondley Bury and was now Lord of the Manor of Wymondley.

The Warren Family of Bygrave

The Warren family were related to the Nedhams through Juliana, an aunt of Eustace, and sister of Bridget who married Benjamin Piggot. Juliana Nedham married William Warren alias Bygrave, who had taken the name Bygrave in order to inherit estates belonging to that manor.

The manor of Bygrave lay below the northern slopes of the Hertfordshire chalk hills, in the angle formed by the Icknield Way and the Great North Road, which met at the adjacent town of Baldock. The church stood in the highest part of the village, and adjoining the churchyard on the south side was the old fortified manor house surrounded by moats, which at one time also enclosed the church.

The Thornbury and de Somery Connections

In the 13th century the manor was held by the de Somery family, and in the 14th century it was sold to Sir John Thornbury, who obtained a licence to crenellate his two houses within the manor of Bygrave. From the Thornbury family it passed to Laurence Warren of Poynton in Cheshire and his wife Joan.

Laurence bought the manor of Bygrave in 1550, but he died in 1556, leaving the manor to his son William, who apparently took the name of Bygrave for the Visitations of 1586. They had several children, but in 1589 William died leaving a young family, with his eldest son still only five years old. He had left an annuity for Juliana to help her bring up the children, but the manor was held in trust for his heir, also named William, to inherit when he came of age at eighteen.

During his long minority there was evidently some bad management, for the debts accumulated, and when he took over the manor in 1602, things were in a very bad way. Not only was William burdened with debts, but he also had to support his young brothers and sisters. In 1613, in order to make fitting provision for them, he sold the Bygrave estate to William Whettall of Thetford and Sir John Heveningham of Norfolk, 'endeavouring to raise the price by hinting that the estate was desired in high quarters'.

The Sale of Bygrave Manor

After all these years the details have been lost, but it seems that somewhere here is a rather sad story. William, having sold the estate, now moved to London, where he possibly became a merchant. But he really did not want to part with the family home. He offered to retain the mansion house, dove-house, buildings, gardens and orchards on a ten-year lease. But Whettall refused, even though he complained that he did not want to live there himself because it was too far from his home, and tried to get William to reduce the price on this account.

So Juliana and the children would have had to move out of their home and find somewhere else to live. It seems likely that William may have managed to buy a small estate at Ashwell, not far from Bygrave, where he settled his mother and family while he himself returned to London, desperately trying to earn money to pay off the debts and revive the family fortunes.

At this stage the descent of William's family becomes rather uncertain, probably because the name 'William' occurs in several different branches. We know that they were all connected because of the distinctive arms described as "Checky Or and Azure, a quarter Gules with a lion Argent therein". There are three Warren pedigrees in the Heralds' Visitations - Warren of Harpenden, Warren of Colney, and Warren alias Waller of Ashwell, all descended from Sir John Warren of Poynton in Cheshire.

The Warrens and the Manor of Marden

In the 17th century the Warrens of Ashwell were holding the manor of Marden in Tewin, and there is evidence that the Harpenden Warrens also had connections with Tewin through the Field and Thornton families. We find the name 'Field' (married to Bridgett Warren) and also Jeremy Thornton whose daughter married Bridgett's brother Gregory. Both these names occur later in the history of Marden. The Harpenden pedigree includes marriages with the Booth family who were connected with the Newports of Pelham, the Snagges of Letchworth and Marston Moreteyne, and the Skipwiths of St Albans (ancestors of the Bull family). The Booth family lived at Shrublands Hall in Suffolk - a mansion which in the 20th century had connections with the de Someries, the family who held Bygrave back in the 13th century.

Marden Hill, Tewin

But where does William alias Bygrave fit in? If, as seems likely, the family had acquired an estate at Ashwell, it would be one of their descendants, Richard (or Edward), who inherited the manor of Marden from his cousin Edmund Field in 1692. From Richard it went to his son Richard who died in 1768 and was succeeded by his son Arthur.

This fits in with Clutterbuck's account of the descent of the manor of Marden. He writes:

> In the year 1692 this estate was possessed by Richard Warren, Rector of South Warnborough in the County of Southampton, Clerk, LL.D. He devised it by will, dated in that year, to his son Richard Warren, who in 1728, upon his marriage with Mary, one of the four daughters and co-heiresses of Joseph Collet, then late of Hertford Castle, Esq. settled this estate on the issue of that marriage, under which settlement it passed to his only son Arthur Warren Esq.

He goes on to say that on Christmas Day 1785 Arthur Warren sold Marden to Robert Mackey of Tewin House who pulled down the house in 1790 and built a handsome modern mansion on the site, (the house which we see today). In 1809 it was sold to Richard Flower of Hertford. He sold it in 1817 to Claude-George Thornton Esq., Governor of the Bank of England.

Memorials in Tewin Church

The memorials in Tewin church give us more information about the Warren family. First we have on the north wall of the Nave, the arms of Warren quartered with Collet and underneath the following inscription:

> In a vault in this church lies ye body of Mary Warren, wife of Richard Warren of Marden, Esq. daughter of Joseph Collet of Hertford Castle, Esq. a woman of extraordinary sweetness of temper, great probity, and extensive knowledge; she died December 28th 1733 in the 31st year of her age leaving two sons, Arthur and Collet.

Underneath is a verse in praise of Mary Warren who was wise, humble, fair and 'chaste as a Roman dame'.Below this is the Latin inscription 'Ricardus Warren ortus comitibus de Warren et Surrey, natus A.D. 1686, obiit 1768', confirming that the family was descended from the Earls of Surrey.

It will be remembered that Clutterbuck states that Marden passed from Richard Warren to his 'only son' Arthur Warren, so it appears that the other son, Collet, died in infancy. We have one more reference to Arthur Warren and to his wife Mary, whose children are buried in the churchyard at Hertingfordbury. The inscription reads:

> Here are interred Arthur Warren, son of Arthur Warren Esq. and Mary his wife, late of Marden in this County, who died January 28 1762 aged 9 years. Likewise Louisa Warren, their daughter, who died August 25 1762 aged two years. Also, Frances-Maria Warren

their daughter, who died Sept. 14 1762 aged three years. Mary Warren, wife of the above mentioned Arthur Warren, died the 11th of November 1787 aged 57.

It must have been a very sad time for Mary and Arthur, losing three of their children in one year. The two little girls probably died of smallpox, which was the most frequent cause of death until the introduction of vaccination in the 19th century.

There are very few further references to the Warren family of Hertfordshire - the only significant entries being in the Hitchin Parish Registers:

20th August 1688 - baptism of Jacob son of William Warren als. Wood de Gosmore.

5th March 1688/9 - marriage of Edward Warren de Clothall and Elizabeth Wood of Bigrave.

This shows the Warren family once again taking an alias (we already have Waller and Bygrave). There is almost certainly a family connection here.

But perhaps, having established links between the ancient families of Nedham and Warren, and having followed them in their relationships with numerous well-known Hertfordshire and Bedfordshire families, we should be satisfied that we have finally brought them back to the old familiar manor of Marden Hill in Tewin.

Marden Hill, Tewin
Home of the Warren family 1692-1785

Chapter 15

The Piggots of Hertfordshire and Bedfordshire

Anyone searching for Piggot ancestors in Hertfordshire and Bedfordshire will find it is not an easy task. What we do know is that the Piggots have been here since the 13th century, and they are still here today!

There were Piggots or Picots on the Bedfordshire borders as early as 1224 when young Hugh Piggot brought a case before the court stating that he had been wrongfully deprived of 20 shillings of rent which his father William, recently deceased, had been in the habit of receiving from tenants in Luton. It is thought that the family held land in Stopsley before the Conquest, and their descendants have remained in the area up to the present day.

The Early Piggots of North Mymms and Wheathampstead

One of the earliest Piggots to be mentioned in Hertfordshire was Peter Piggot (or Picot) who held the manor of North Mymms from 1239. A manor known as Piggots remained in the area until the 15th century when it was part of the estate of Thomas Knollys. Throughout the 13th century we find references to Piggot in Wheathampstead where there was also a manor known as Piggots. It is in connection with this manor of Piggots in Wheathampstead that we first come across the name of Baldwin Piggot who owned the manor in 1307.

Fifteenth Century Connections at Wallington

In the 15th century there were strong Piggot connections in the parish of Wallington. In the church is a 15th century altar tomb bearing the arms of Piggot and Prysot, and in the north window of the Lady Chapel are fragments of 16th century glass, also bearing the Piggot arms. These were probably memorials of the family of Richard Piggot who owned the nearby manor of Kingswoodbury in 1481, and also the manor of Astwick, both of which later passed to the Kympton family.

Although by the 15th century there were two distinct branches of the Piggot family, there was certainly not a Hertfordshire branch and a Bedfordshire branch. Both families flitted backwards and forwards between the two counties, and both seem to be descended from a certain Baldwin de Clare, who owned vast areas of the country during the 12th century. Baldwin de Clare was a kinsman of Gilbert de Clare, Earl of Pembroke, who died in 1148.

Hugh de Beauchamp of Bedford Castle

Another common ancestor was Hugh de Beauchamp of Bedford Castle who owned large estates in Bedfordshire, Hertfordshire and Buckinghamshire from the time of the Norman Conquest. He was also an ancestor of the Greys of Wrest Park and of Margaret Beauchamp of Bletsoe.

The senior branch of the Piggot family is probably the one which descended from Baldwin Lord Wake (a grandson of Baldwin de Clare). He married Ela de Beauchamp around the year 1250. Ela and her two sisters, Beatrice and Maud, jointly inherited the Beauchamp estates when their brother John, the last male heir, was killed at the battle of Evesham in 1265. Beatrice (ancestor of the Latimers and Nevills) inherited the largest of the three manors of Renhold, also Astwick and Cardington. Maud (ancestor of the Mowbray family) inherited the smallest of the manors of Renhold, while Ela finally inherited all three! She then married Baldwin Lord Wake, thus bringing into the family the manors of Stapleford, Gobions and Blakemoor.

The Manor of Cardington

Baldwin Lord Wake and Ela had only one child, a daughter called Joan, who inherited all the estates, and married John (or Michael) Piggot of Wheathampstead and Houghton. The family probably made their home at Howbury Hall in Renhold, the house which was later the home of the Becher family. The Piggot arms can be seen on the tower of Renhold church. But two generations later their grandson, John, handed over Renhold to their Nevill relations in exchange for the manor of Cardington.

Cardington now seems to have been the principal manor, and was almost certainly the Piggot family home. Two of John's children found their way into the history books - Sir Baldwin Piggot, a Member of Parliament for Bedford, and his sister Margaret, who was Abbess of Elstow in 1409. Sir Baldwin served in three parliaments from 1381 to 1401. He also left a very interesting will, from which we learn quite a lot about his character. Joyce Godber in her 'History of Bedfordshire' tells us:

> From his will we get some idea of the kind of man he was - attached to his family, his servants and his tenants. He mentions his sister Margaret, a nun of Elstow Abbey, and two sisters 'in religion at Sempringham'. He refers to six servants by name, one of whom was to have a cow; and to all servants unnamed he left 40d each; to the poor 40s; and to the fabric of Cardington Church 40s; while his tenants were to be excused rent for one term.

The Piggot links with Houghton are also interesting. At the time of John Piggot's marriage to Baldwin Lord Wake's daughter, one of the manors of

Houghton was already part of the Piggot estates. The other manor came through the Wake family, from the Beauchamp ancestors.

Houghton House, John Bunyan's 'House Beautiful'

In the 15th century Baldwin Piggot sold one of these manors to the Conquest family, who held it for the next 200 years, during which time it took its present name of Houghton Conquest. When Lewis Conquest died around 1640 the whole manor (including Houghton House, John Bunyan's 'House Beautiful') came once again to the Piggot family. Later they sold it to Robert Bruce of Aylesbury, from whom it went to the Duke of Bedford.

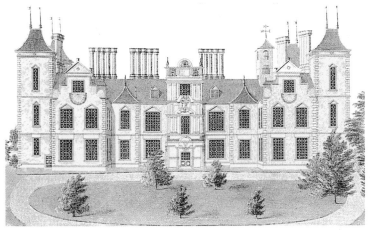

Houghton House

The second distinct branch of the ancient Piggot family begins (in our records) with Sir Randolf Piggot, who would probably be either a brother or a cousin of the John Piggot who married Joan Wake. It was Randolf's great grandson, Richard Piggot, who lived in Wallington and owned Kingswoodbury and Astwick, and Richard's grandson was Thomas Piggot of Totternhoe, Sergeant-at-Law to Henry VIII. The manor of Totternhoe descended through his younger son William for at least three more generations.

The Rabbit Warren at Rowney Grange

At this stage it is difficult to identify the various members of the family because the same names are used in each generation. In 1570 a Thomas Piggot and George Fyshe were responsible for supplying armour and weapons in the Hundred of Wixamtree. George Fyshe, who was the King's Surveyor for Bedfordshire, held the manor of Holme Hill Grange from Warden Abbey. Long before this, however, there had been Piggots at Stratton and Holme, who served as Sheriffs as early as 1408. Meanwhile a Francis Piggot was holding the manor of Southill with Rowney, land later held by the Whitbread family. The rabbit warren at Rowney Grange was sold by Sir Michael Fisher to Francis Piggot in 1544 for £698 6s.

Going forward a few generations we find that in 1609 the Rectory of Studham descended to a Thomas Piggot and his father-in-law Thomas Sankey and their heirs for ever. They sold it to William Halsey who was related to the Hare and Roberts families of Thrales End.

Eleanor Piggot, Prioress of Harrold

We hear less of the female members of the Piggot family, but several seem to have been drawn (or pushed) towards the nunneries. In addition to Margaret, who was Abbess of Elstow from 1392 to 1409, there was also Eleanor, who was Prioress of Harrold in 1501 until her death in 1509.

One of the most valuable sources of information about the Piggot family is a memorial plaque in the church at Lower Gravenhurst, which firmly links these ancient families with our 17th century ancestors, and also with two ancient and historic houses in Hertfordshire.

The memorial is to Benjamin Piggot who died in 1606 at the age of 55. It gives a long and detailed account of the descent of the Piggot family over nine generations. Benjamin's grandfather was Thomas, Sergeant-at-Law to Henry VIII, the same Thomas who acquired Totternhoe Manor in 1518. His father was Francis and his mother was Margery St John, daughter of Sir John St John of Bletsoe. It also lists Benjamin's three wives. The first was Mary Astry of Harlington, the second was Anne Wiseman of Essex and the third was Bridget Nedham of Little Wymondley in Hertfordshire.

Links between the Piggot and Nedham Families

Bridget was the daughter of John Nedham of Little Wymondley Priory. Her sister was married to Lewis Mordaunt of Northill, and another sister, Juliana, was married to William Warren of Bygrave, another ancestor of the Harmer family. Their brother Thomas was married to Elizabeth, the sister of Beckingham Butler of Tewin Bury. Now comes a link with another historic house in Little Wymondley. We discover that in 1544 a certain Thomas Piggot bought the manor of Wymondley Bury for his son John who was about to be married. Thomas turns out to be the half-brother of Benjamin Piggot of Gravenhurst.

Benjamin would no doubt have visited his brother Thomas at Wymondley, and would have met the three lovely Nedham daughters and fallen in love! Unless of course it was an arranged marriage which most marraiges would have been in the 17th century, especially when money and property were involved.

We learn from the plaque at Gravenhurst that the father of Thomas and Benjamin was Francis Piggot, High Sheriff of Bedfordshire in 1527 and 1558, and Francis was the son of another Thomas whom we have already met - the Sergeant-at-Law to Henry VIII and Lord of the manor of Totternhoe.

Wymondley Bury, a Fourteenth Century Manor House

Wymondley Bury, the home of the Piggot family for at least two generations, still stands at Little Wymondley. It is a Grade I listed building dating back to the late 14th century. It was originally the Manor House for Great and Little Wymondley, and was built by William de Argentein around the year 1380.

Wymondley Bury

Much of the original house remains, but there were once two more bays which have now disappeared. The 13-foot-wide fireplace with its massive carved beam above, would have been put in by a member of the Piggot family soon after they bought the property in 1544. They would also have built the fine solar on the upper floor, which would have been used for various forms of recreation - perhaps as a shovelboard room. There is a cellar under the dining room (the old hall) which has brick niches round the walls, probably once used for storing wine flasks.

The Victoria County History (written about 100 years ago) gives not only a detailed account of the house but also of the surrounding gardens and grounds:

> Close to the house on the north is an old brick dovecote which still contains some 300 nests, and a little to the south-east of the house stands a fine Spanish chestnut of great age but still flourishing. Gilpin refers to it in his 'Forest Scenery' about the year 1798.

This tree is also described by Cussons who says that the trunk is 44 feet in circumference. Chauncy also remarks on it, so it must already have been renowned for its size and antiquity as early as 1700.

At the present time, although the tree has split into several parts, it is still sending out new growth from its gnarled and twisted trunks, and the ancient dovecote still stands in the garden beside the moat, where a bridge marks the site of the original drawbridge.

The Argenteins, Cup Bearers to the King

Although the Piggots bought Wymondley Bury and lived there for several generations, they were never Lords of the Manor. The Lordship of Wymondley was granted soon after the Conquest to the Argentein family and was passed down through their descendants, the Alingtons and the Grosvenors, in an unbroken line until the 18th century.

Thomas Piggot obviously bought a lease or a tenancy which would have been almost identical to a freehold of today, but did not include all the manorial rights and privileges. One of these privileges was the office of Cup-bearer to the King, which was granted to the Lords of Wymondley in the 13th century. The duty of presenting the first cup of wine at the Coronation feast was carried out by members of the Argentein family and their successors for seven centuries, the last occasion being the coronation of George IV in 1820.

John Piggot, as we have seen, carried out extensive alterations to the house, adding the chimney and fireplace, and building the upper floor. But he did not have many years to enjoy his new home. He died in 1558, and the property reverted to his father, although the widow, Margaret, and later her second husband, John Palmer, continued to live in the manor house with their young family.

Thomas Piggot, John's father, died in 1581 and his grandson Maurice inherited the property. Maurice died in 1609, presumably without a direct heir, and Wymondley Bury went to Thomas Piggot of Tewin.

Thomas Piggot of Tewin Water

We know a great deal about Thomas Piggot of Tewin because we have a copy of his will. He lived at 'Waterside', now known as Tewin Water, and he was married to Elizabeth, the sister of George Chapman the poet. We hear about his two daughters - Rebecka, later the wife of Henry Bull of Hertford, and Elizabeth, who married Beckingham Butler of Tewin Bury.

Thomas died in 1610 and is buried under the south aisle of Tewin Church. But here is a mystery which we still cannot solve.. The inscription on the brass memorial plate begins "Here lyeth the body of Thomas Piggot whose ancestors have remayned dwelling in this town this 300 years and upwards". Strangely we have no record of any Piggots living in Tewin, except for Thomas himself, and his family appear to have lived in Gravenhurst.

We do know from manorial records that the Piggots had held land in Tewin for many years, so perhaps Tewin Water, or an earlier house on the same site, was the birthplace of some of the Piggot ancestors. One historian suggests that the Piggots may have lived at Queenhoo Hall, but we have found no evidence of this.

The Thomas Piggot Memorial in Tewin Church

The mystery remains, and will probably never be solved. So here we must leave the Piggots of Hertfordshire and Bedfordshire, with their long line of Sheriffs, Members of Parliament, Sergeants-at-Law, and at least one poet, a line which takes us back to the days of the Beauchamps of Bedford who inhabited this part of the country nearly 1000 years ago.

Pedigrees of inter-related families in Hertfordshire Bedfordshire, Suffolk and Essex

---

Abbreviations

osp - obit sine prole (died without offspring); **MI** - Memorial Inscription;
m - married; **d** - daughter or died (according to context)

The arms and blazons are reproduced from the Victoria County Histories
by permission of the General Editor

The Barnardiston Family
of Suffolk and Ickwell Bury in Bedfordshire

THOMAS de BARNARDISTON, of Barnardiston in Suffolk, lived in the reign of Edward II (1307-27). m. Margery, d. of William Willoughby of Suffolk

SIR THOMAS BARNARDISTON lived in the reign of Edward III (1327-77). m. Lucie, d. of Robert Havering of Norfolk

WALTER BARNARDISTON lived in the reign of Richard II (1377-99) m. Frances, d. of Thomas Kingsman

ROGER BARNARDISTON of Grimsby, d. about 1440 m. Elizabeth, d. of Sir Edmund Perpoint

THOMAS BARNARDISTON of Suffolk. m. Joan Vavasour

BARNARDISTON. *azure a fesse dancetry ermine between six crosslets argent.*

SIR THOMAS BARNARDISTON of Keddington at the time of Edward IV, Edward V and Richard III. m. Elizabeth, d. of John Newport of Pelham in Hertfordshire (connected with Bulls and Casons)

SIR THOMAS BARNARDISTON of Ketton (Keddington). m. Ann, d. of Thomas Fitz Lucas of Saxham.

A daughter, m. Thomas, Lord Audley, Chancellor of England

GEORGE BARNARDISTON, m. Elizabeth, d. of Thomas Burley of Lynn in Norfolk. In 1543 he acquired Ickwell Bury in Northill, Bedfordshire

SIR THOMAS BARNARDISTON, m. c1520, Mary, d. of Sir Edward Walsingham, Lieutenant of the Tower. (Mary later m. Francis Clopton of Kentwell)

JOHN BARNARDISTON of Ickwell Bury, m. Joan, d. of Thomas Mellor (or Miller) of Lynn in Norfolk. Joan d. 1568. John d. 1587 (buried in the aisle of Northill Church)

ELIZABETH BARNARDISTON m① ... Brookesbye. m② Francis Clopton of Kentwell Hall in Suffolk

SIR THOMAS BARNARDISTON m① Elizabeth Hanchett | m② Ann Bygrave (alias Warren) of Hertfordshire

MARGARET BARNARDISTON, m. 1573, William Fyshe of Stanford Manor in Southill. The Old House at Ickwell Green came to the Fyshe family from the Barnardiston estate.

GEORGE BARNARDISTON of Ickwell Bury. d.1577. m. Mary, d. of Sir George Perient of Digswell.

SIR THOMAS BARNARDISTON m. Mary, d. of Sir Richard Knightly of Fawsley.

GYLES BARNARDISTON of Clare in Suffolk m. Philippa, d. of Sir William Waldegrave of Smallbridge in Bures, Suffolk

SIR WILLIAM FYSHE of The Old House, Ickwell Green. m. Elizabeth, d. of Sir Thomas Barnardiston of Suffolk (his 3rd cousin once removed) (See Fyshe Tree)

ROBERT BARNARDISTON of Ickwell Bury. m. Katherine, d. of George, son of John, the first Lord Mordaunt of Turvey. (see Mordaunt Tree)

HANNA BARNARDISTON m. John Brograve of Hammels in Hertfordshire, (Related to the Leventhorpes of Shingle Hall and to the Brownes of Abbess Roding)

SIR NATHANIAL BARNARDISTON m. Jane, d. of Sir Stephen Soame (Lord Mayor of London in 1598) and grand-daughter of Ann Knighton and Richard Hunt.

ELIZABETH BARNARDISTON m. Sir William Fyshe (her 3rd cousin once removed)

HENRY BARNARDISTON of Ickwell Bury, d. 1640. m. Margaret, d. of Robert Hares of the town of Bedford

RICHARD BARNARDISTON of Ickwell. bapt 19th August 1604

ROBERT BARNARDISTON, d. 1652. In 1680 his son George conveyed Ickwell Bury to John Harvey

The Barre Family
of Knebworth, Ayot St Lawrence and Panshanger

A DAUGHTER of Lawrence de Ayot m. ... Pembrugge of Ayot St Lawrence

SIR RICHARD de PEMBRUGGE	HAWISE PEMBRUGGE	ALICIA PEMBRUGGE
d. 4th August 1375	m. Thomas Barre	m. ... de Beurlee

HENRY de PEMBRUGGE b. 1360. Inherited Ayot but died two months later, age 15.	SIR THOMAS BARRE m. Elizabeth ... Died 30th December 1421. Member of Parliament for Hertford in 1420. Inherited Ayot on the death of his cousin Henry in 1375. Also held the manor of Aldenham in 1391. Monument (mutilated) in Ayot St Lawrence Church to Sir Thomas and his wife Elizabeth.	RICHARD de BEURLEE Jointly inherited Ayot but the whole estate later went to his cousin Sir Thomas Barre

THOMAS BARRE - predeceased his father

A SON - probably the ancestor of Milliscent Barre who m. Thomas Fairclough and was the grandmother of Thomas Harmer of Weston	SIR JOHN BARRE, d. 1482. Inherited Ayot from his grandfather. m. Indonea, d. of John Hotoft, from whom he inherited the manors of Knebworth and Panshanger.	JOAN BARRE m. ... Delabere	ANCRET BARRE m. ... Hanmer (or Harmer)

ISABEL BARRE (Isabel Countess of Devon) 1443-88		RICHARD DELABERE	EDWARD HANMER
m① Humphrey Stafford, Earl of Devon who was beheaded for treason in 1469	m② Sir Thomas Bourchier, younger son of the Earl of Essex		

ISABEL BOURCHIER died before her parents and the manors descended to her mother's cousins Richard Delabere and Edward Hanmer

DESCENT OF THE MANORS OF AYOT, KNEBWORTH AND PANSHANGER.

Thomas Bourchier survived his wife and daughter, and from him the estates went first to his wife's (Isabel Barre's) three cousins, Richard Delabere, Thomas Cornwall and Edward Hanmer (or Harmer). They sold them to Thomas Bourchier's nephew, Henry Bourchier, 2nd Earl of Essex, who married Mary, eldest daughter of Sir William Say. Their only child, Anne Bourchier, married Sir William Parr, who inherited the property, then divorced his wife and retained most of her estates. Soon afterwards his sister, Catherine Parr, became Queen Consort. Sir William was created Earl of Essex, and later Marquis of Northampton. He tried to advance Lady Jane Grey to the throne but failed and was committed to the Tower, and all his honours forfeited, though his life was spared. His lands were later returned to him by Queen Elizabeth who, in 1559, re-created him Marquis of Northampton, made him Privy Councillor and Knight of the Garter.

The manor of Ayot was the portion of the estate which was retained by the divorced wife and went to her niece Gertrude, daughter of Elizabeth Say and William, Baron Blount. Gertrude was the wife of Henry Courtenay, 2nd Earl of Devon and 1st Marquis of Exeter, who lived at Powderham Castle in Devon. In 1538, because of disputes about succession (Henry Courtenay was a relative of the king and had some claim to the throne) he was arrested and imprisoned in the Tower and was executed for High Treason in 1540. The manor was forfeited to the crown, and soon afterwards was granted to Nicholas Bristow. It remained in the Bristow family for 4 generations and was sold by the widow of William Bristow in 1714.

The manor of Knebworth went to Sir Robert Lytton, of Litton in Derbyshire, by his marriage to Agnes, another daughter of John Hotoft. The manor of Panshanger was granted in 1546 to Nicholas Throckmorton. In 1567 it went to Edward Skeggs (an ancestor of Ann Warren who married John Harmer in 1698) In 1693 it was acquired by Sir Gervase Elwes, whose family also acquired the manor of Throcking and the manor of Stoke College at Clare in Suffolk. In 1719 Panshanger went to Earl Cowper, Lord Chancellor, who lived at Cole Green, and later built the mansion house known as Panshanger.

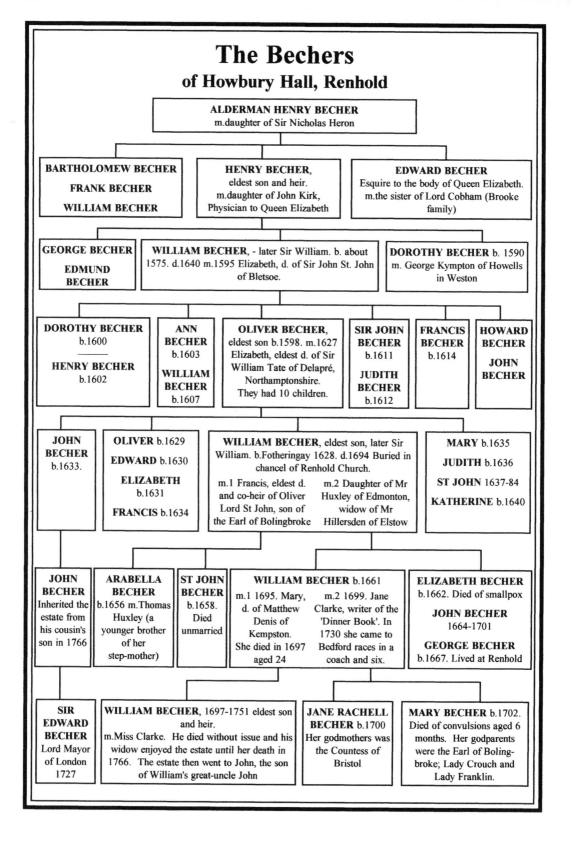

The Bechers
of Howbury Hall, Renhold

ALDERMAN HENRY BECHER
m.daughter of Sir Nicholas Heron

BARTHOLOMEW BECHER

FRANK BECHER

WILLIAM BECHER

HENRY BECHER,
eldest son and heir.
m.daughter of John Kirk,
Physician to Queen Elizabeth

EDWARD BECHER
Esquire to the body of Queen Elizabeth.
m.the sister of Lord Cobham (Brooke family)

GEORGE BECHER

EDMUND BECHER

WILLIAM BECHER, - later Sir William. b. about 1575. d.1640 m.1595 Elizabeth, d. of Sir John St. John of Bletsoe.

DOROTHY BECHER b. 1590 m. George Kympton of Howells in Weston

DOROTHY BECHER
b.1600

HENRY BECHER
b.1602

ANN BECHER
b.1603

WILLIAM BECHER
b.1607

OLIVER BECHER,
eldest son b.1598. m.1627
Elizabeth, eldest d. of Sir
William Tate of Delapré,
Northamptonshire.
They had 10 children.

SIR JOHN BECHER
b.1611

JUDITH BECHER
b.1612

FRANCIS BECHER
b.1614

HOWARD BECHER

JOHN BECHER

JOHN BECHER
b.1633.

OLIVER b.1629

EDWARD b.1630

ELIZABETH
b.1631

FRANCIS b.1634

WILLIAM BECHER, eldest son, later Sir William. b.Fotheringay 1628. d.1694 Buried in chancel of Renhold Church.

m.1 Francis, eldest d. and co-heir of Oliver Lord St John, son of the Earl of Bolingbroke

m.2 Daughter of Mr Huxley of Edmonton, widow of Mr Hillersden of Elstow

MARY b.1635

JUDITH b.1636

ST JOHN 1637-84

KATHERINE b.1640

JOHN BECHER
Inherited the estate from his cousin's son in 1766

ARABELLA BECHER
b.1656 m.Thomas Huxley (a younger brother of her step-mother)

ST JOHN BECHER
b.1658. Died unmarried

WILLIAM BECHER b.1661

m.1 1695. Mary, d. of Matthew Denis of Kempston. She died in 1697 aged 24

m.2 1699. Jane Clarke, writer of the 'Dinner Book'. In 1730 she came to Bedford races in a coach and six.

ELIZABETH BECHER
b.1662. Died of smallpox

JOHN BECHER
1664-1701

GEORGE BECHER
b.1667. Lived at Renhold

SIR EDWARD BECHER
Lord Mayor of London 1727

WILLIAM BECHER, 1697-1751 eldest son and heir.
m.Miss Clarke. He died without issue and his widow enjoyed the estate until her death in 1766. The estate then went to John, the son of William's great-uncle John

JANE RACHELL BECHER b.1700
Her godmothers was the Countess of Bristol

MARY BECHER b.1702.
Died of convulsions aged 6 months. Her godparents were the Earl of Bolingbroke; Lady Crouch and Lady Franklin.

The Boteler Family
of Hatfield and Watton Woodhall.

SIR RALPH BOTELER, Lord of Woodhall, m. Hawise, d. and heir of Richard, son of Hugh Gobion. Died before 1300 (Inquisition 35 Edward I)

SIR JOHN BOTELER, m. Joan, d. of John de Argentein of Throcking, who d. in 1318 leaving his two daughters as heirs.

WILLIAM BOTELER, m. Elizabeth Argentein, sister of Joan

RALPH BOTELER, m. Katherine, d. of Sir Philip Peletoot who died in 1361. (Brass in Watton Church)

EDWARD BOTELER, b.1339, sold Throcking to William Hyde about 1395

SIR PHILIP BOTELER of Woodhall, d. 1421. m. Isabel ...

BOTELER. *Gules a fesse checky argent and sable between six crosslets or.*

PHILIP BOTELER of Woodhall, d. 1425, m. Elizabeth Cockain (first wife)

JOHN BOTELER, m. Constance Downhall of Goddington, in the North.

JOHN BOTELER, d.1514, m. Dorothy, d. of William Tyrrell of Gipping, Suffolk.

SIR PHILIP BOTELER, m. Elizabeth, d. of Robert Drury of Halstead. They had 19 children.

SIR JOHN BOTELER of Woodhall, m. Grizel, d. and heir of Sir William Roche of Lamer in Hertfordshire, Lord Mayor of London in 1540.

ANN BOTELER m. Leonard Hyde of Throcking.

ELIZABETH BOTELER d. 1590, m. Sir Henry Coningsby of North Mymms

SIR PHILIP BOTELER of Woodhall m. Anne, d. of John Coningsby of North Mymms

SIR HENRY BOTELER of Hatfield Woodhall and Brantfield. High Sheriff 1603-4
m① Katherine Wallace | m② Alice Pulter

SUSAN BOTELER m. Julius Ferrers of Markyate. Their son John m. Ann Knighton whose son was Knighton Ferrers, the father of Kathleen Ferrers ('The Wicked Lady')

SIR PHILIP BOTELER of Watton Woodhall m. Catherine, d. of Sir Francis Knollys

SIR JOHN BOTELER, of Hatfield Woodhall. m. Elizabeth Villiers, sister to George Villiers, Duke of Buckingham.

PHILIP BOTELER of Stapleford m. Alice, Shotbolt

SIR ROBERT BOTELER m. Frances, d. of Sir Drew Drury

WILLIAM BOTELER osp. m. Joan Wingate of Lockleys

AUDREY BOTELER m. Sir Francis Anderson of Eyworth

ELEANOR BOTELER m. Sir John Drake

JANE BOTELER Duchess of Marlborough

ANN BOTELER Countess of Newport

SIR JOHN BOTELER, Knight of the Bath, m. Ann (or Elizabeth) Spencer, granddaughter of Sir John Spencer of Althorpe.

JOAN BOTELER sole daughter and heir. m. John, Lord Bellysis

SIR PHILIP BOTELER, Knight of the Bath. m. d. of Sir John Langham, Alderman of London

JOHN BOTELER, m. d. of Sir Edward Atkins, Lord Chief Baron

CATHERINE BOTELER m. Sir John Gore

ELIZABETH BOTELER m. Ralph Gore

SIR JOHN BOTELER, m. Elizabeth, d. of Sir Nicholas Gold of London

MARY BOTELER, m. Sir William Gostwick, Baronet, of Willington, Beds.

The Bull Family
of Hertford, Stapleford and Tewin

RICHARD BULL of London, m. Helen, d. of William Skipwith of St Albans, High Sheriff of Herts and Essex in 1504 and 1505. Richard Bull held the manor of Halfhide or Westmill in 1483.

CHARLES BULL of Hertford. Held Benwick Hall (on the site of the present Bullsmill) in 1532. m. Jane, d. of Thomas Knighton of Bayford and Ann Underhill of Harveys in Little Bradley, Suffolk

ALICE BULL m. Thomas Knighton (The brother of Jane Knighton who married Charles Bull.) (See Knighton tree)

RICHARD BULL, Bailiff (Mayor) of Hertford in 1578. Died 1585. He owned at least 11 messuages in Hertford, as well as Benwick Hall and various properties in Tewin and Welwyn. m. Alice Hunt of Stanford, Bedfordshire. (Alice was the sister of Richard Hunt who m. Ann Knighton)

CHRISTOPHER BULL d.1588

ANN KNIGHTON m. Richard Hunt (The brother of Alice Hunt who m. Richard Bull)

ELIZABETH BULL b.1563

ALICE BULL b.1575

HENRY BULL 1565-1637. Justice of the Peace, Mayor of Hertford in 1600, held land in Hertford, Stapleford, Tewin and Burnt Pelham.

m① Cecily Graves d. in childbirth 1593

m② 1596, Rebecka, d. of Thomas Piggot of Tewin Water

RICHARD BULL b.1571 Probably Major Richard Bull of Marwell, Southampton.

CECILY BULL b.1590 m. John Dayle

RICHARD BULL b.1593 and died a few days after birth.

ALICE BULL, b.1598 died in infancy

RICHARD BULL, b.1599, eldest son and heir, inherited property in Hertford, Sacombe, Great and Little Munden, and Stapleford

REBECKA BULL 1603-85 m.1623 George Harmer of Weston (See Harmer tree)

EDWARD BULL b.1609

ELIZABETH BULL mentioned in father's will

ELIZABETH BULL m. Thomas, s. of Sir Robert Dacres of Cheshunt and Elizabeth Mannock of Gifford's Hall, Stoke-by-Nayland

RICHARD BULL, m. .... d. of Sir John Fleet (Lord Mayor of London 1692)

There were two sons, **EDMUND BULL** and **JOHN BULL** of Battersea who inherited property from the Bull family and also from their great-uncle James Fleet (1687-1733) including Wymondley Bury which was once the home of their Piggot ancestors.

NOTES: Henry Bull held the manor of Burnt Pelham (or Brent Pelham) jointly with Edward Cason (a descendant of Ann Hyde and Thomas Bowles). The Casons held the manor of Astonbury and Furneaux Pelham. Edward Cason's mother was Susan Oxenbridge of Hurstbourne Priors (Chauncy wrote about her - see Chapter 2). The Casons had connections with Sir Francis Mannock of Gifford's Hall, Stoke-by-Nayland, who also had connections with the Bull family.

William Bull Clk, MA., Rector of St Andrew's Hertford from 1643 to 1660, was almost certainly a member of the family. Rebecka Harmer (née Bull) was baptised, married and buried in St Andrew's Church and the family home was in St Andrew's Street.

The Capell Family
of Little Hadham, Hertfordshire, and Abbess Roding, Essex

SIR WILLIAM CAPELL
b. at Stoke by Nayland in Suffolk, Lord Mayor of London in 1504 and 1509,
Knighted by Henry VII. Bought the manor of Walkern about 1510.
m. Margaret, d. of Sir Thomas Arundell (ancestor of the Earls of Essex).

SIR GILES CAPELL of Hadham
d. 1556 (buried beside his father at St Bartholomew's),
m. ..., d. of Sir John Newton (alias Craddock)

ELIZABETH CAPELL
m. Sir William Pawlett, Knight of the Garter, Marquis of Winchester, Treasurer of the Household to Henry VIII.
He died in 1571.

SIR EDWARD CAPELL of Hadham,
m. Ann, d. of Sir William Pelham of Burnt (Brent) Pelham.

MARGARET CAPELL
m. Robert Warde of Brooke (alias Kirkby), in Norfolk

SIR HENRY CAPELL of Raynes and Little Hadham Hall. High Sheriff 1585, Muster Captain for Herts.

m① Mary, d. of Sir Anthony Browne of Sussex and widow of Lord John Grey of Pirgo.	m② Lady Catherine, d. of Thomas Manners Earl of Rutland KG

MARY CAPELL, m. Weston Browne of Rookwood (or Clovills). She died childless. Weston Browne then m. Elizabeth, d. of Giles Pawlett (a kinsman of Sir William Pawlett who m. Elizabeth Capell) and they had a daughter, Jayne, who m. Sir Gamaliel Capell. (see below)

SIR ARTHUR CAPELL of Little Hadham, 1558-1632, High Sheriff of Herts 1592, m. Mary, d. of Lord Grey of Pirgo

JOHN CAPELL b. 1561, High Sheriff 1587, m. Helen, d. of Thomas Leventhorpe.

FRANCIS CAPELL and **ANN CAPELL** (twins) b. 1565. Ann m. Sir Robert Chester of Cockenhatch near Royston.

SIR GAMALIEL CAPELL of Raynes, 1566-1613, acquired Abbess Roding in 1692, knighted 1603, m. Jayne, d. of Weston Browne by his 2nd wife, Elizabeth Pawlett, (Jayne was marrying her father's first wife's nephew)

SIR HENRY CAPELL son and heir, m. Ann Wentworth

DAUGHTER m. Sir John Corbett of Sproston in Norfolk. Their d. Bridget m. Brian Darcy of Tiptree, s. of Thomas Darcy of Tolshunt Darcy

SIR GAMALIEL CAPELL inherited Abbess Roding from his mother. His son and grandson (both Gamaliel) inherited. Finally sold to the Duke of Bedford about 1700.

MARY CAPELL
———
PENELOPE CAPELL m. Litton, s. of Edmund Pulter.

ARTHUR CAPELL
MP for Hertford 1641. Executed 1649. At the Restoration his son Sir Arthur was created Earl of Essex

The Chapman Family
of Mardocks Manor (Ware) and Hitchin, Herts

HUGH CHAPMAN of Cambridge
m. 1420, Ann, d. and heir of John Mardock of Mardocks Manor at Ware

---

ROBERT CHAPMAN
eldest son and heir
m. Elizabeth ... , inherited Mardocks

JOHN CHAPMAN

JOHN CHAPMAN eldest son and heir, sold the manor of Mardocks in 1580, m. Ann, d. of Henry Mannock (related to the Mannocks of Gifford's Hall, Stoke by Nayland)

THOMAS CHAPMAN of Hitchin, d. 1589 (Will dated 1581) m. Joan, who died 1566, d. of George Nodes of Shephallbury. They lived at Western House, Hitchin (35 Tilehouse Street) where their famous son George was born. (see Nodes tree)

THOMAS CHAPMAN (*1)	**JOHN CHAPMAN**	**GEORGE CHAPMAN (*2)**	**ELIZABETH CHAPMAN**	**JOAN CHAPMAN**	**MARGARET CHAPMAN**
A wealthy gentleman who had probably inherited property from his grandfather, George Nodes of Shephallbury.	d. 1624 m. Anne ... He was Rector of Willian in 1606 (memorial in Willian Church). His widow gave communion silver to Hitchin church	1559-1634 osp Poet and translator of Homer. Buried at St Giles, London, where a monument designed by his friend Inigo Jones marked the grave.	m. 1571 Thomas Piggot of Tewin Water. (Memorial brass in Tewin Church)	m ... Monk (mentioned in her father's will, and also Elizabeth Piggot's will.)	m. ... Chambers (mentioned in her father's will)

REBECCA CHAPMAN	**REBECCA PIGGOT**	**ELIZABETH PIGGOT**	**JOHN and THOMAS MONK.**	**JOAN CHAMBERS.**
m. Sir Rowland Lytton of Knebworth. Their d. Rebecca m. Lord Falkland. (See Lytton tree)	b. 1577. m. 1596 Henry Bull (See Bull and Harmer tree)	b. 1563 m. Beckingham Butler, Lord of the Manor of Tewin (See Butler tree)	Mentioned in their grandfather's will.	Mentioned in her grandfather's will

(*1) In 1669 a Thomas Chapman, son or grandson of this Thomas, left a cottage and yard in Stevenage, the rent to provide bread to be given to the poor each year on St Andrew's day. He was probably the Thomas Chapman described elsewhere as Clerk of Little Wymondley. There were several Clerks (Clergy) in the Chapman family. George's brother was Rector of Willian, and William Chapman of Therfield was one of the four clergy of Hertfordshire who had to contribute £40 each towards the defence of the Kingdom in 1593. In Walkern Church there is a brass to Edward Chapman who died in 1636 and may also have been a priest.

(*2) GEORGE CHAPMAN the poet died in poverty, but his brother Thomas was an extremely wealthy man, being assessed to pay £25 for the defence of the Kingdom at the time of the Spanish invasion in 1588, and similar amounts in 1590 and 1593. In 1595 Thomas set aside £10 to be laid out in barley and converted into malt, the yearly income thereof to redound to the use of the poor of Hitchin.. He was presumably able to afford a good dowry for his daughter Rebecca, who married into the Lytton family of Knebworth.

The Clarke Family
of Walkern, Benington, Chesfield and Ashwell

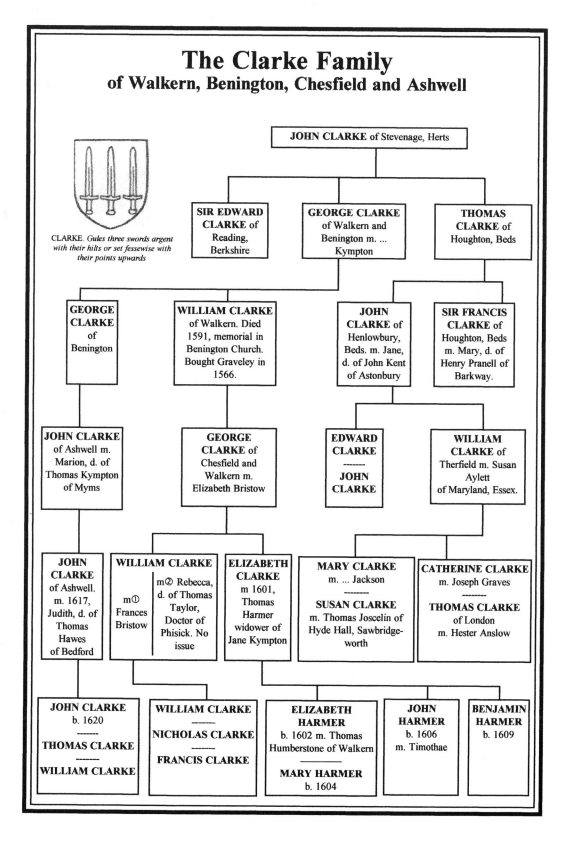

JOHN CLARKE of Stevenage, Herts

SIR EDWARD CLARKE of Reading, Berkshire

GEORGE CLARKE of Walkern and Benington m. ... Kympton

THOMAS CLARKE of Houghton, Beds

CLARKE. *Gules three swords argent with their hilts or set fessewise with their points upwards*

GEORGE CLARKE of Benington

WILLIAM CLARKE of Walkern. Died 1591, memorial in Benington Church. Bought Graveley in 1566.

JOHN CLARKE of Henlowbury, Beds. m. Jane, d. of John Kent of Astonbury

SIR FRANCIS CLARKE of Houghton, Beds m. Mary, d. of Henry Pranell of Barkway.

JOHN CLARKE of Ashwell m. Marion, d. of Thomas Kympton of Myms

GEORGE CLARKE of Chesfield and Walkern m. Elizabeth Bristow

EDWARD CLARKE

JOHN CLARKE

WILLIAM CLARKE of Therfield m. Susan Aylett of Maryland, Essex.

JOHN CLARKE of Ashwell. m. 1617, Judith, d. of Thomas Hawes of Bedford

WILLIAM CLARKE

m① Frances Bristow

m② Rebecca, d. of Thomas Taylor, Doctor of Phisick. No issue

ELIZABETH CLARKE m 1601, Thomas Harmer widower of Jane Kympton

MARY CLARKE m. ... Jackson

SUSAN CLARKE m. Thomas Joscelin of Hyde Hall, Sawbridgeworth

CATHERINE CLARKE m. Joseph Graves

THOMAS CLARKE of London m. Hester Anslow

JOHN CLARKE b. 1620

THOMAS CLARKE

WILLIAM CLARKE

WILLIAM CLARKE

NICHOLAS CLARKE

FRANCIS CLARKE

ELIZABETH HARMER b. 1602 m. Thomas Humberstone of Walkern

MARY HARMER b. 1604

JOHN HARMER b. 1606 m. Timothae

BENJAMIN HARMER b. 1609

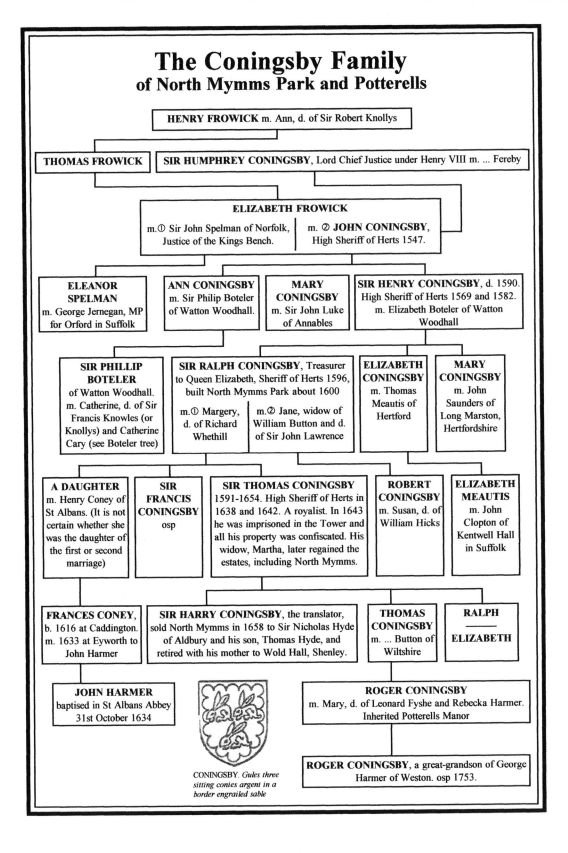

The Coningsby Family
of North Mymms Park and Potterells

HENRY FROWICK m. Ann, d. of Sir Robert Knollys

THOMAS FROWICK

SIR HUMPHREY CONINGSBY, Lord Chief Justice under Henry VIII m. ... Fereby

ELIZABETH FROWICK
m.① Sir John Spelman of Norfolk, Justice of the Kings Bench.
m. ② **JOHN CONINGSBY**, High Sheriff of Herts 1547.

ELEANOR SPELMAN
m. George Jernegan, MP for Orford in Suffolk

ANN CONINGSBY
m. Sir Philip Boteler of Watton Woodhall.

MARY CONINGSBY
m. Sir John Luke of Annables

SIR HENRY CONINGSBY, d. 1590. High Sheriff of Herts 1569 and 1582.
m. Elizabeth Boteler of Watton Woodhall

SIR PHILLIP BOTELER
of Watton Woodhall.
m. Catherine, d. of Sir Francis Knowles (or Knollys) and Catherine Cary (see Boteler tree)

SIR RALPH CONINGSBY, Treasurer to Queen Elizabeth, Sheriff of Herts 1596, built North Mymms Park about 1600
m.① Margery, d. of Richard Whethill
m.② Jane, widow of William Button and d. of Sir John Lawrence

ELIZABETH CONINGSBY
m. Thomas Meautis of Hertford

MARY CONINGSBY
m. John Saunders of Long Marston, Hertfordshire

A DAUGHTER
m. Henry Coney of St Albans. (It is not certain whether she was the daughter of the first or second marriage)

SIR FRANCIS CONINGSBY
osp

SIR THOMAS CONINGSBY 1591-1654. High Sheriff of Herts in 1638 and 1642. A royalist. In 1643 he was imprisoned in the Tower and all his property was confiscated. His widow, Martha, later regained the estates, including North Mymms.

ROBERT CONINGSBY
m. Susan, d. of William Hicks

ELIZABETH MEAUTIS
m. John Clopton of Kentwell Hall in Suffolk

FRANCES CONEY, b. 1616 at Caddington. m. 1633 at Eyworth to John Harmer

SIR HARRY CONINGSBY, the translator, sold North Mymms in 1658 to Sir Nicholas Hyde of Aldbury and his son, Thomas Hyde, and retired with his mother to Wold Hall, Shenley.

THOMAS CONINGSBY
m. ... Button of Wiltshire

RALPH
———
ELIZABETH

JOHN HARMER
baptised in St Albans Abbey 31st October 1634

ROGER CONINGSBY
m. Mary, d. of Leonard Fyshe and Rebecka Harmer. Inherited Potterells Manor

CONINGSBY. *Gules three sitting conies argent in a border engrailed sable*

ROGER CONINGSBY, a great-grandson of George Harmer of Weston. osp 1753.

The Docwra Family
of Putteridge and Pirton, Hertfordshire

PETER DOCWRA of Kendal in Westmorland

ROBERT DOCWRA m. Sibil, d. of Sir Thomas Leybourne

ROGER DOCWRA m. Elizabeth, d. of Edward Brocket of Brocket Hall in Yorkshire

REGINALD DOCWRA

THOMAS DOCWRA, Last Prior of the Knights of St John of Jerusalem at Hitchin. Lived at Brotherhood House, Hitchin

JAMES DOCWRA m. Katherine, d. of John Haspedine of Murden and Chesterfield in Cambridgeshire

RICHARD DOCWRA m. Alice, d. of Thomas Green of Gresingham

DOCWRA. Sable a cheveron engrailed argent between three roundels argent each having a pale gules upon it

JOHN DOCWRA bought the manor of Putteridge from Sir Edward Darrell - it was held by a yearly rent of one pound of pepper and one pound of cummin. He married Ann, d. of Thomas St George of George Hatley and his wife Alice Rotherham, who was sister of Sir Thomas Rotherham of Someries Manor, Luton

THOMAS DOCWRA of Putteridgebury, 1518-1602, m. 1548 Mildred Hales (d. age 70 in 1596). Thomas was educated at Gray's Inn (1540). JP for Herts in 1559, Sheriff 1580-81, Clerk to the Receiver General of the Duchy of Lancaster 1578-83 and 1586-7 and Receiver General in 1588. Bought the manor of Lilley and also inherited the property of his great-uncle Thomas - the Prior of the Knights of St John at Hitchin. Died in his house at Putteridge in 1602, buried with his wife in the church at Lilley, where there is a monument on the north side of the chancel. (*1)

THOMAS DOCWRA (*2)
d.1620 at the age of 92, about 1611 bought the manor of Pirton.

m① Ellen, d. of George Horsey and Ann Sadlier. They had one d. Jane, who m. Sir Henry Pakenham.

m② Jane, d. of Sir William Periam Chief Baron of the Exchequer 1593-1603. She was the widow of Thomas, s. of Sir Gabrielle Pointy. Jane d. at Pirton in 1645. (monument in church)

FRANCES DOCWRA
m. Peter Taverner of Hexton (monument in Hexton church). Their son John Taverner is mentioned in the will of his grandfather, Thomas. (See Taverner tree)

HELEN DOCWRA
m. Jasper Horsey (brother of Sir Ralph Horsey and of Ellen Horsey who m. Thomas Docwra)

RALPH DOCWRA of Fulbourne, Cambridgeshire

EDWARD DOCWRA
1553-1610 of Brotherhood House, Hitchin.
m. Elizabeth Carpenter

PERIAM DOCWRA
m. Martha, sister of Oliver St John of Bletsoe, Earl of Bolingbroke.
(see Harvey & Piggot trees)

HENRY DOCWRA
of North Mymms

ANN DOCWRA
m. Humphrey Walcott of Salop,

ELIZABETH DOCWRA
m. James Beverley, JP for Bedford

JANE DOCWRA
m. John Powell, Merchant Adventurer. She d. in Hamburg

HELEN DOCRWA
m. George Nodes of Shephallbury (See Nodes tree)

THOMAS DOCWRA
Son and heir
m. Dorothy Stone of Ridgmont, Beds.

HENRY DOCWRA
———
LANCELOTT DOCWRA

MARGARET DOCWRA
———
ELIZABETH DOCWRA

MARTHA DOCWRA
———
DOROTHY DOCWRA

SAMUEL POWELL
b. in Hamburg

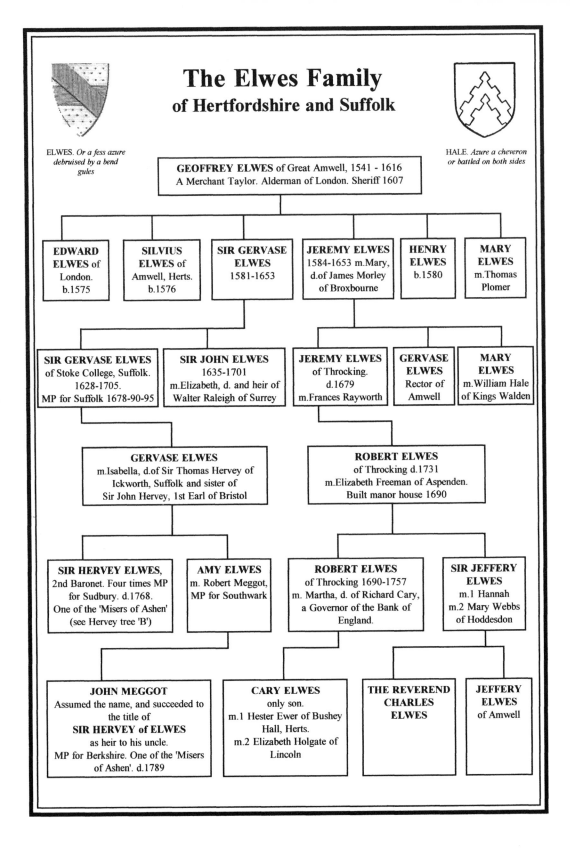

The Elwes Family
of Hertfordshire and Suffolk

ELWES. *Or a fess azure debruised by a bend gules*

HALE. *Azure a cheveron or battled on both sides*

GEOFFREY ELWES of Great Amwell, 1541 - 1616
A Merchant Taylor. Alderman of London. Sheriff 1607

EDWARD ELWES of London. b.1575

SILVIUS ELWES of Amwell, Herts. b.1576

SIR GERVASE ELWES 1581-1653

JEREMY ELWES 1584-1653 m.Mary, d.of James Morley of Broxbourne

HENRY ELWES b.1580

MARY ELWES m.Thomas Plomer

SIR GERVASE ELWES of Stoke College, Suffolk. 1628-1705. MP for Suffolk 1678-90-95

SIR JOHN ELWES 1635-1701 m.Elizabeth, d. and heir of Walter Raleigh of Surrey

JEREMY ELWES of Throcking. d.1679 m.Frances Rayworth

GERVASE ELWES Rector of Amwell

MARY ELWES m.William Hale of Kings Walden

GERVASE ELWES m.Isabella, d.of Sir Thomas Hervey of Ickworth, Suffolk and sister of Sir John Hervey, 1st Earl of Bristol

ROBERT ELWES of Throcking d.1731 m.Elizabeth Freeman of Aspenden. Built manor house 1690

SIR HERVEY ELWES, 2nd Baronet. Four times MP for Sudbury. d.1768. One of the 'Misers of Ashen' (see Hervey tree 'B')

AMY ELWES m. Robert Meggot, MP for Southwark

ROBERT ELWES of Throcking 1690-1757 m. Martha, d. of Richard Cary, a Governor of the Bank of England.

SIR JEFFERY ELWES m.1 Hannah m.2 Mary Webbs of Hoddesdon

JOHN MEGGOT Assumed the name, and succeeded to the title of **SIR HERVEY of ELWES** as heir to his uncle. MP for Berkshire. One of the 'Misers of Ashen'. d.1789

CARY ELWES only son. m.1 Hester Ewer of Bushey Hall, Herts. m.2 Elizabeth Holgate of Lincoln

THE REVEREND CHARLES ELWES

JEFFERY ELWES of Amwell

The Fairclough Family
of Weston

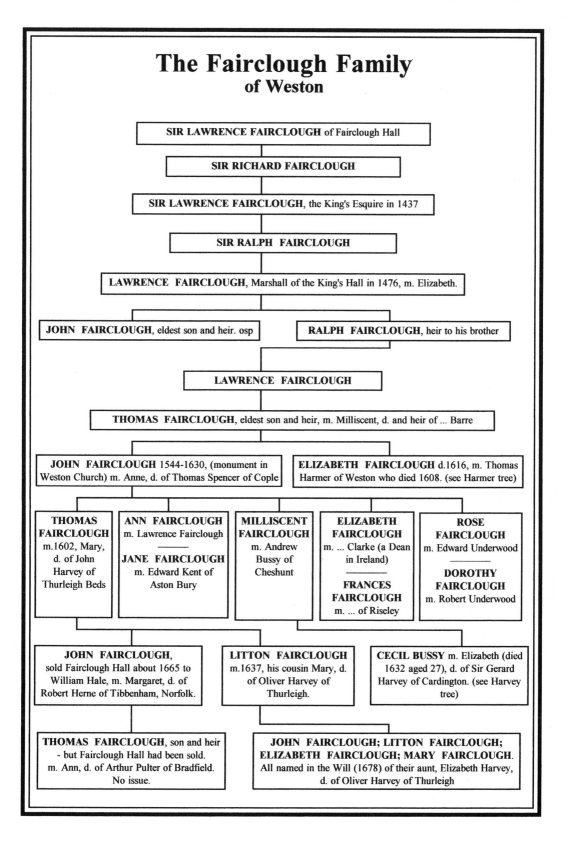

SIR LAWRENCE FAIRCLOUGH of Fairclough Hall

SIR RICHARD FAIRCLOUGH

SIR LAWRENCE FAIRCLOUGH, the King's Esquire in 1437

SIR RALPH FAIRCLOUGH

LAWRENCE FAIRCLOUGH, Marshall of the King's Hall in 1476, m. Elizabeth.

JOHN FAIRCLOUGH, eldest son and heir. osp

RALPH FAIRCLOUGH, heir to his brother

LAWRENCE FAIRCLOUGH

THOMAS FAIRCLOUGH, eldest son and heir, m. Milliscent, d. and heir of ... Barre

JOHN FAIRCLOUGH 1544-1630, (monument in Weston Church) m. Anne, d. of Thomas Spencer of Cople

ELIZABETH FAIRCLOUGH d.1616, m. Thomas Harmer of Weston who died 1608. (see Harmer tree)

THOMAS FAIRCLOUGH m.1602, Mary, d. of John Harvey of Thurleigh Beds

ANN FAIRCLOUGH m. Lawrence Fairclough
———
JANE FAIRCLOUGH m. Edward Kent of Aston Bury

MILLISCENT FAIRCLOUGH m. Andrew Bussy of Cheshunt

ELIZABETH FAIRCLOUGH m. ... Clarke (a Dean in Ireland)
———
FRANCES FAIRCLOUGH m. ... of Riseley

ROSE FAIRCLOUGH m. Edward Underwood
DOROTHY FAIRCLOUGH m. Robert Underwood

JOHN FAIRCLOUGH, sold Fairclough Hall about 1665 to William Hale, m. Margaret, d. of Robert Herne of Tibbenham, Norfolk.

LITTON FAIRCLOUGH m.1637, his cousin Mary, d. of Oliver Harvey of Thurleigh.

CECIL BUSSY m. Elizabeth (died 1632 aged 27), d. of Sir Gerard Harvey of Cardington. (see Harvey tree)

THOMAS FAIRCLOUGH, son and heir - but Fairclough Hall had been sold. m. Ann, d. of Arthur Pulter of Bradfield. No issue.

JOHN FAIRCLOUGH; LITTON FAIRCLOUGH; ELIZABETH FAIRCLOUGH; MARY FAIRCLOUGH. All named in the Will (1678) of their aunt, Elizabeth Harvey, d. of Oliver Harvey of Thurleigh

The Fyshe Family
of Ayot Mountfitchet, Southill, Northill and Biggleswade

JOHN FYSHE, of Ayot Mountfitchet, d. 5th June 1494

THOMAS FYSHE, b. 1483, d. before 1527, osp.

WILLIAM FYSHE, heir to his brother, d. 1531

THOMAS FYSHE, 1508-1553., m. 1544 Elizabeth (1523-83), d. of George Hyde of Throcking. Elizabeth later m. William Perient and had a son, Sir George Perient, who inherited Ayot Mountfitchet

GEORGE HYDE FYSHE of Southill, Beds, 1545-1614 m① Elizabeth Thompson m② Judith Hamley of London

WILLIAM FYSHE of Stanford Manor, m. Margaret, d. of George Barnardiston of Ickwell Bury. Lived at The Old House (part of the Barnardiston Estate) on Ickwell Green.

LEONARD FYSHE of Little Ayot, m. Emma Graves, (Sister of Cicely Graves - the first wife of Henry Bull)

SIR JOHN FYSHE of Southill, created Baronet of Ireland 1621, d. 1623, m. Mary, d. of Edward Pulter of Wymondley

EDWARD FYSHE, living in 1634, m. Mary Nodes (see Nodes tree)
———
DOROTHY FYSHE m. Dr Michael Boyle, Bishop of Waterford and nephew of Richard, Earl of Cork.

SIR WILLIAM FYSHE of Biggleswade and Gray's Inn, m. Elizabeth, a 3rd cousin of his mother and d. of Sir Thomas Barnardiston of Suffolk

JOHN FYSHE, Rector of Little Hallingbury Essex, m. Susan Price
HUMPHREY FYSHE of Ickwell (Northill) 1585-1647, JP for Bedford, m.1608, Margaret Scroggs
OLIVER FYSHE m.1620, Mercy, d. of Thomas Smythe of Biggleswade

ANNE FYSHE m. Dr John Partington, Rector of Maulden, Beds
THOMAS FYSHE of Southill 1588-1646 m. Dorothy Bonington (widow) of Stansted, Herts

THOMAS FYSHE of Hatfield, d. 1660, m. Alice, d. of John Geves

SIR EDWARD FYSHE, Baronet in Ireland, m. Elizabeth, d. of Martin Heton, Bishop of Ely.

MARY FYSHE, m. John Blundell (Brother to Sir Francis Blundell)

ANN FYSHE, m. Sir George Sexton, in Ireland

BARNARDISTON FYSHE eldest daughter and co-heir
———
MERCY FYSHE m. Mark Mott of Keddington in Suffolk, MA Cambridge

WILLIAM FYSHE
———
MARY FYSHE m. Richard Palmer

HUMPHREY FYSHE 1629-1720, m. Katherine Constable (died 1709), inherited The Old House

LEONARD FYSHE of Hatfield, m. Rebecka, d. of George Harmer of Weston. (see Harmer tree)

CHARLES PALMER His cousin Henry inherited

HUMPHREY FYSHE d.1728, lived at The Old House at Ickwell

HENRY FISH PALMER d.1785, added the Palmer surname and inherited from his cousin Charles.

MARY FYSHE, b. 1661 m. Roger Coningsby of North Mymms Park. Inherited Potterells. (see Coningsby tree)

CAPTAIN LEONARD FYSHE, 1652 - 1713 (memorial in Hatfield churchyard).

The Harmer Family of Weston

John Harmer of Rushden bought a messuage and land in Weston in 1541. He died in 1552 leaving lands in Clothall, Wallington and Rushden to his son John. Thomas was probably a younger son, and inherited the Weston property.

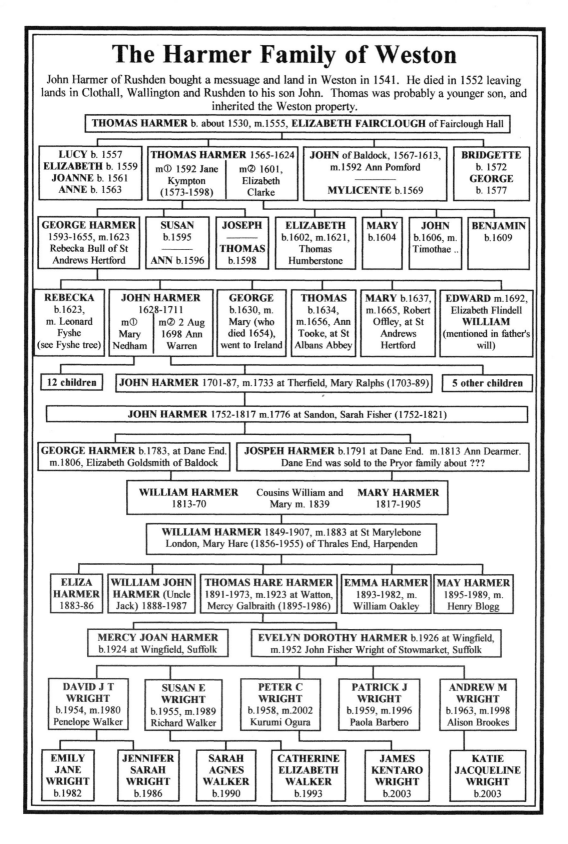

THOMAS HARMER b. about 1530, m.1555, **ELIZABETH FAIRCLOUGH** of Fairclough Hall

| LUCY b. 1557
ELIZABETH b. 1559
JOANNE b. 1561
ANNE b. 1563 | THOMAS HARMER 1565-1624
m① 1592 Jane Kympton (1573-1598) / m② 1601, Elizabeth Clarke | JOHN of Baldock, 1567-1613, m.1592 Ann Pomford
MYLICENTE b.1569 | BRIDGETTE b. 1572
GEORGE b. 1577 |

| GEORGE HARMER 1593-1655, m.1623 Rebecka Bull of St Andrews Hertford | SUSAN b.1595
——
ANN b.1596 | JOSEPH ——
THOMAS b.1598 | ELIZABETH b.1602, m.1621, Thomas Humberstone | MARY b.1604 | JOHN b.1606, m. Timothae .. | BENJAMIN b.1609 |

| REBECKA b.1623, m. Leonard Fyshe (see Fyshe tree) | JOHN HARMER 1628-1711
m① Mary Nedham / m② 2 Aug 1698 Ann Warren | GEORGE b.1630, m. Mary (who died 1654), went to Ireland | THOMAS b.1634, m.1656, Ann Tooke, at St Albans Abbey | MARY b.1637, m.1665, Robert Offley, at St Andrews Hertford | EDWARD m.1692, Elizabeth Flindell
WILLIAM (mentioned in father's will) |

| 12 children | JOHN HARMER 1701-87, m.1733 at Therfield, Mary Ralphs (1703-89) | 5 other children |

JOHN HARMER 1752-1817 m.1776 at Sandon, Sarah Fisher (1752-1821)

| GEORGE HARMER b.1783, at Dane End. m.1806, Elizabeth Goldsmith of Baldock | JOSPEH HARMER b.1791 at Dane End. m.1813 Ann Dearmer. Dane End was sold to the Pryor family about ??? |

| WILLIAM HARMER 1813-70 | Cousins William and Mary m. 1839 | MARY HARMER 1817-1905 |

WILLIAM HARMER 1849-1907, m.1883 at St Marylebone London, Mary Hare (1856-1955) of Thrales End, Harpenden

| ELIZA HARMER 1883-86 | WILLIAM JOHN HARMER (Uncle Jack) 1888-1987 | THOMAS HARE HARMER 1891-1973, m.1923 at Watton, Mercy Galbraith (1895-1986) | EMMA HARMER 1893-1982, m. William Oakley | MAY HARMER 1895-1989, m. Henry Blogg |

| MERCY JOAN HARMER b.1924 at Wingfield, Suffolk | EVELYN DOROTHY HARMER b.1926 at Wingfield, m.1952 John Fisher Wright of Stowmarket, Suffolk |

| DAVID J T WRIGHT b.1954, m.1980 Penelope Walker | SUSAN E WRIGHT b.1955, m.1989 Richard Walker | PETER C WRIGHT b.1958, m.2002 Kurumi Ogura | PATRICK J WRIGHT b.1959, m.1996 Paola Barbero | ANDREW M WRIGHT b.1963, m.1998 Alison Brookes |

| EMILY JANE WRIGHT b.1982 | JENNIFER SARAH WRIGHT b.1986 | SARAH AGNES WALKER b.1990 | CATHERINE ELIZABETH WALKER b.1993 | JAMES KENTARO WRIGHT b.2003 | KATIE JACQUELINE WRIGHT b.2003 |

The Harvey (or Hervey) Family - Tree A
of Thurleigh and Northill in Bedfordshire

All the Harveys (or Herveys) of Thurleigh and Ickworth are said to be descended from **DE HARVEY, DUKE OF ORLEANS** who came to England with William the Conqueror. **HENRY HARVEY** was settled in Bedfordshire in the reign of Richard I (1189-99). He had a son **HENRY**, and a grandson **OSBERT DE HERVEY** who died 1206. Osbert's son **ADAM** m. Julien, d. and heir of John Fitzhugh.

JOHN HARVEY (Hervic de Risely), died 1297, m. **JOAN**, d. and co-heir of **JOHN HARMER** of Thurleigh

WILLIAM HARVEY of Thurleigh, died 1376, m. Mary, d. and heir of Richard Folliot

SIR JOHN HARVEY of Thurleigh, JP for Bedford 1382-94, m. Margaret d. of Sir John Neyrnute of Fleetmarston.

JOHN HARVEY died 1426, m. Margery, d. of Sir William Calthorpe of Norfolk.

THOMAS HARVEY died 1475, Master of the King's Ordnance 1461, m. Jane, d. of William Paston of Norfolk.

ELIZABETH HARVEY, Abbess of Elstow, d.1524	**THOMAS HARVEY** m. Christian, d. of John Chicheley, Chamberlain of London

THOMAS HARVEY, admitted to Lincoln's Inn 1475, m. Jane, d. and heir of Henry Drury of Ickworth in Suffolk. Inherited the Suffolk estate. (see tree B)	**JOHN HARVEY**, MP for Bedford 1472, died 1474, m. Alice, d. of Nicholas Morley. Alice later m. one of the Pastons of Norfolk

SIR GEORGE HARVEY 1474-1522, m. Margaret (or Elizabeth) Stanford

GERARD SMART d 1569, natural son of Sir George Harvey, changed his name to Harvey, MP for Bedford 1554. m① Elizabeth (widow), sister of John Lord Williams of Thame. m② Ann (widow), d. of Nicholas Luke

JOHN HARVEY m. Mary, d. of Sir John St John, sister of Margery St John who m. Francis Piggot of Gravenhurst

MARY HARVEY b.1580, m.1602 Thomas Fairclough of Weston	**OLIVER HARVEY** 1568-1627, eldest son and heir, m. Ann Browne of London. In 1605 King James I stayed with him for two nights at Thurleigh	**JOHN HARVEY**, 3rd son 1572-1619, "died at Knebworth at Sir William Litton's house there in the County of Hertford"	**SIR GERARD HARVEY** of Cardington, 2nd son b.1569, knighted at Caddez, being the first to enter the town, m. Dorothy, d. of John Gascoigne of Cardington	**SAMUEL HARVEY** of Shenfield, 5th son b.1576, m. Dorothy, d. of George Wingate.
LITTON FAIRCLOUGH m.1637 his cousin Mary Harvey	**MARY HARVEY** m.1637 her cousin Litton Fairclough	**ELIZABETH HARVEY** 1606-78, left a bequest to her sister Mary Fairclough and her children.	**JOHN HARVEY** heir, m. his cousin Elizabeth, d. of Stephen Harvey of London.	**ELIZABETH HARVEY** m. Cecil, s. of Andrew Bussy and Milliscent Fairclough (sister of Thomas who m. Mary Harvey)

JOHN HARVEY 1632-1715, left a cottage & land at Thurleigh for the poor. Sold Thurleigh to the Holts. In 1790 Rowland Holt sold it to the Duke of Bedford for £1,796. The next Duke sold it in 1880 to William Thompson.

The Harvey (or Hervey) Family - Tree B
of Ickworth in Suffolk

THOMAS HARVEY of Thurleigh, admitted to Lincoln's Inn 1475, m. Jane, d. and heir of Henry Drury of Ickworth.

WILLIAM HERVEY of Ickworth Hall, admitted to Lincoln's Inn 1479/80, died 1538, buried in St Mary's Church, Bury St Edmunds (M.I.), m. Joan Cokett of Ampthill.

SIR NICHOLAS HERVEY of Bakenloo Manor, Bedfordshire, member of the royal household (Henry VIII), ambassador to Emperor Charles V in 1530, died 1532, buried at Ampthill, Beds. m① Elizabeth Fitzwilliam; m② Bridget Wiltshire (*1)

JOHN HERVEY d.1556 m.1511, Elizabeth, d. of Henry Pope of Mildenhall.

EDMUND HERVEY d. before 1560, member of the royal household (Henry VIII) granted part of the abbey of Elstow, Beds in 1541

1998

WILLIAM HERVEY, eldest son and heir, d.1592, m.1554 Elizabeth, d. of John Poley of Boxted

14 OTHER CHILDREN including two named John - known as John the Elder and John the Younger

JOHN HERVEY, eldest son and heir, born about 1550, buried at Ickworth 1620, m.1582 Frances Bocking of Ashbocking

SIR WILLIAM HERVEY b.1555
m① Susan Jermyn of Rushbrooke
m② Penelope, d. of Thomas Lord Darcy (Earl Rivers) of Hengrave Hall. (no issue)

8 OTHER CHILDREN The older children were baptised at Boxted, the later ones at Ickworth.

SIR THOMAS HERVEY m. Isabella, d. of Sir Humphrey May and Judith Poley

ISABELLA HARVEY 1659-97 m. Gervase Elwes of Stoke by Clare (*2)

JOHN HARVEY 1st Earl of Bristol

(*1) Bridget was the d. of Sir John Wiltshire of Stone Castle in Kent. She was the widow of Sir Richard Wingfield of Kimbolton Castle, a descendant of Sir John Wingfield of Wingfield Castle.

(*2) Isabella and Gervase had a son, Sir Harvey Elwes who, with his nephew, John Elwes, were known as 'The Misers of Ashen' and are mentioned in 'Timpson's English Eccentrics' (see Chapter 5).

Ickworth Hall, home of the Suffolk branch of the Harvey family from about 1475 until John Hervey 7th Marquis of Bristol vacated in 1996.

The Hyde Family
of Throcking and Sandon

WILLIAM HYDE, a citizen and grocer of London, bought Throcking from the Botelers and de Argenteins in 1398. He died about 1460. m.1414, Joyce ....

LAWRENCE HYDE b.1415

WILLIAM HYDE osp

HYDE. *Azure a cheveron between three lozenges or.*

ROBERT HYDE Lord of the Manor in 1486

GEORGE HYDE b.1443, m.1468, Agnes ...

HYDE OF THROCKING. *Azure a saltire engrailed or and a chief ermine.*

LEONARD HYDE 1469-1509, m. Elizabeth Lyster of Norfolk. In 1492 acquired the manor of Sandon, sometimes known as Olivers, which was later known as Hyde Hall. Asked to be buried 'by the little dore on the north side of the chaunsell of Throcking Church'. One of his executors was John Knighton.

GEORGE HYDE 1495-1553, built mansion at Throcking. Asked to be buried near his father in Throcking Church.

m① Alice Roper of Eltham, Kent (*1) — m② Alice Brocket of Wheathampstead

LEONARD HYDE	LUCY HYDE,	ELIZABETH HYDE	WILLIAM HYDE
1521-49, m.1546, Ann Boteler of Watton Woodhall, died just before the birth of his only son.	b.1527, m.1546 at Weston, Edmund Kympton. 'Held court' at Astwick at the age of 24 after the death of her husband. (See Kympton tree)	1528-83, m.① Thomas Fyshe, (See Fyshe tree). m.② William Perient	1533-90, m. Elizabeth Shipman, acquired Hyde Hall in 1561 from nephew William.

MARY HYDE	WILLIAM HYDE	SIR LEONARD HYDE (*2)	LUCY HYDE	DUDLEY HYDE	ANN HYDE
m. Sir John Cary Lord Hunsdon (memorial in Hunsdon Church) ——— ELLEN HYDE ——— GRISSEL HYDE	b.1549, m.1572, Mary Bristow, inherited Hyde Hall from his grandfather, but it was handed over to his uncle William in 1561	1555-1624, High Sheriff of Herts 1606, m. Ann Tryce	Lady of the Bedchamber to Queen Elizabeth, m. Sir Robert Osborne	(a daughter) b.1559, mentioned in her father's will. (Probably named after Robert Dudley, Earl of Leicester who was a friend of the family and executor of her father's will.) (*3)	m. Thomas Bowles of Wallington (brother of Richard Bowles who m. Alice Perient) (*4)

NICHOLAS HYDE, named after his Bristow ancestors.	ROBERT HYDE inherited Hyde Hall but sold it in 1609	WILLIAM HYDE m. Grissell, d. of Thomas Stutville of Dalham, Suffolk (a relative of the Knightons)	MARGARET HYDE m. Captain Henry Lane, Esquire of the Body to King James I	ELIZABETH BOWLES m. Edward Cason

(*1) Alice Roper was the sister of William Roper who married Margaret, the daughter of Sir Thomas More..

(*2) Leonard inherited all his father's estates. Around 1608 he granted Hyde Hall to his son Robert, who sold it in 1609 to the Earl of Exeter. It then went to the Caesars and the Franklyns, and then to Sir Nicholas Miller and his descendants.

(*3) Robert Dudley, 1532-88, was the son of the Duke of Northumberland, and was created Earl of Leicester in 1564. He was a favourite of the Queen, who would have liked to marry him, but he was already married. When his wife died he married again (secretly), and when the Queen found out she was furious and sent him to the Tower.

(*4) Mary, the grand-daughter of Ann Hyde and Thomas Bowles, m. Sir John Spencer of Althorpe.

The Knighton Family
of Bayford in Hertfordshire and Little Bradley in Suffolk

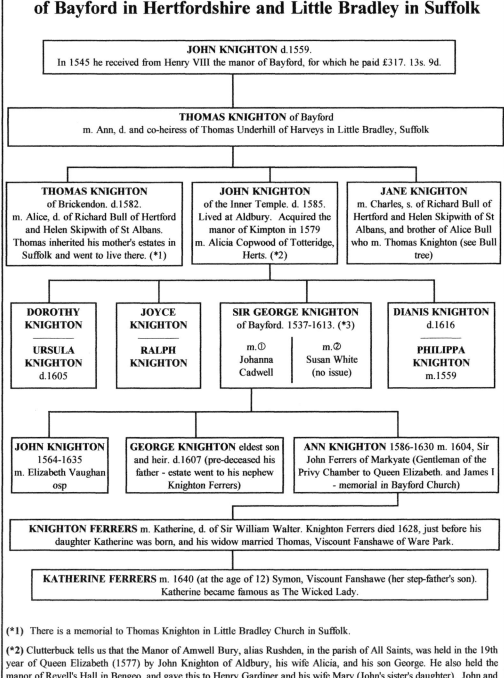

JOHN KNIGHTON d.1559.
In 1545 he received from Henry VIII the manor of Bayford, for which he paid £317. 13s. 9d.

THOMAS KNIGHTON of Bayford
m. Ann, d. and co-heiress of Thomas Underhill of Harveys in Little Bradley, Suffolk

THOMAS KNIGHTON
of Brickendon. d.1582.
m. Alice, d. of Richard Bull of Hertford
and Helen Skipwith of St Albans.
Thomas inherited his mother's estates in
Suffolk and went to live there. (*1)

JOHN KNIGHTON
of the Inner Temple. d. 1585.
Lived at Aldbury. Acquired the
manor of Kimpton in 1579
m. Alicia Copwood of Totteridge,
Herts. (*2)

JANE KNIGHTON
m. Charles, s. of Richard Bull of
Hertford and Helen Skipwith of St
Albans, and brother of Alice Bull
who m. Thomas Knighton (see Bull
tree)

DOROTHY KNIGHTON
———
URSULA KNIGHTON
d.1605

JOYCE KNIGHTON
———
RALPH KNIGHTON

SIR GEORGE KNIGHTON
of Bayford. 1537-1613. (*3)

m.① Johanna Cadwell | m.② Susan White (no issue)

DIANIS KNIGHTON
d.1616
———
PHILIPPA KNIGHTON
m.1559

JOHN KNIGHTON
1564-1635
m. Elizabeth Vaughan
osp

GEORGE KNIGHTON eldest son
and heir. d.1607 (pre-deceased his
father - estate went to his nephew
Knighton Ferrers)

ANN KNIGHTON 1586-1630 m. 1604, Sir
John Ferrers of Markyate (Gentleman of the
Privy Chamber to Queen Elizabeth. and James I
- memorial in Bayford Church)

KNIGHTON FERRERS m. Katherine, d. of Sir William Walter. Knighton Ferrers died 1628, just before his
daughter Katherine was born, and his widow married Thomas, Viscount Fanshawe of Ware Park.

KATHERINE FERRERS m. 1640 (at the age of 12) Symon, Viscount Fanshawe (her step-father's son).
Katherine became famous as The Wicked Lady.

(*1) There is a memorial to Thomas Knighton in Little Bradley Church in Suffolk.

(*2) Clutterbuck tells us that the Manor of Amwell Bury, alias Rushden, in the parish of All Saints, was held in the 19th
year of Queen Elizabeth (1577) by John Knighton of Aldbury, his wife Alicia, and his son George. He also held the
manor of Revell's Hall in Bengeo, and gave this to Henry Gardiner and his wife Mary (John's sister's daughter). John and
George Knighton at this time also held Kimpton, Bayford and Brickendon.

(*3) There is a memorial to George Knighton in Bayford Church showing a knight in armour on an altar tomb.

The Kympton (or Kimpton) Family
of Westminster, Clothall and Weston

The family held land in Herts and Beds, including the manor of Kimptons in Stanbridge, from the 14th century. By the 16th century they were also city merchants, but still held their estates in Hertfordshire. There is no apparent link with the manor of Kimpton Hoo in Hertfordshire.

EDMUND KYMPTON of Westminster, held land in Clothall, Yardley, Rushden and Astwick. He was probably related to the Poley and Sheldon families of Suffolk, from whom he acquired Astwick in 1539.

WILLIAM KYMPTON, Merchant Taylor. b. about 1515, m. 1539 Joan Maryman at St Margaret's Westminster, became Freeman of the Merchant Taylors Company in 1544 and Master of the Company in 1570. (*)

EDMUND KYMPTON of Clothall, 1527-51, m. 1546 (at Weston) Lucy, d. of George Hyde of Throcking and Alice Roper of Well Hall, Eltham in Kent. (see Hyde tree) When Edmund died his wife held court until her son George came of age. Lucy was afterwards married to John Shipman.

WILLIAM KYMPTON, Merchant Taylor, Freeman of the Company 1575, m. 1577 Cecily Burse at St Margarets Westminster. Held the manor of Brickendon in Hertfordshire jointly with his cousin George.

EDWARD KYMPTON, bapt. 1556. Merchant Taylor, Master of the Company 1596.

GEORGE KYMPTON c.1546-1608, of Clothall and Weston (Howells). m.1568 at Bengeo, Catherine Brooke of High Cross. George and his cousin William also held the manor of Brickendon near Hertford

---

EDMUND KYMPTON m. 1619 Joanna Chaukell at St Margarets Westminster

JANE KYMPTON 1573-98 m. Thomas Harmer of Weston (see Harmer Tree)

ANNE b.1574; **LEONARD** b.1576; **GEORGE** b.1577; **GEORGE** b.1580; and **ANNE** b.1581. All died young

GEORGE KYMPTON b. 1583, only surviving son and heir, m. Dorothy, d. of Henry Becher of Howbury Hall, Renhold, and lived at Clothallbury. George sold Astwick in 1420 for £2,100 to John Hudson (or Hodgeson) of London.

WILLIAM KYMPTON baptised 1621 at St Margarets Westminster.

(*) One of the most well-known local members of the Merchant Taylors Company was Sir William Harpur of Bedford, who was Master in 1553 and Lord Mayor of London in 1561.

1586

MERCHANT TAYLORS COMPANY

KYMPTON. *Azure a pelican between three fleurs de lis or.*

The Lytton (or Litton) Family
of Knebworth

LYTTON of Knebworth.
*Ermine a chief indented azure
with three crowns or therein*

SIR ROBERT LYTTON of Litton in Derbyshire, Under-Treasurer of the Exchequer and Keeper of the Great Wardrobe to Henry VII and member of the Privy Council, knighted by Henry VIII when he became Duke of York, died 1504. Bought Knebworth from the Barre family about 1488. m. Agnes, daughter of John Hotoft (*1).

WILLIAM LYTTON, Governor of the castle at Boulogne and Sheriff of Hertfordshire in 1510, d.1517, m. Audrey, d. and heir of Sir Philip Booth of Shrublands in Suffolk.

SIR ROBERT LYTTON created Knight of the Bath in 1547 at the Coronation of Edward VI, d. without male issue and his brother Rowland inherited.

ROWLAND LYTTON m. Ann, d. of George Carlton of Brightwell, Oxfordshire, d.1582

HELEN LYTTON m. Sir John Brocket of Brocket Hall . He was MP and High Sheriff for Hertfordshire in 1581

SIR ROWLAND LYTTON, d.1616, Lord Lieutenant of Hertfordshire, conducted the Forces of Hertfordshire at Tilbury 1588, High Sheriff 1594, MP for Hertford 1597, knighted 1603.

m① Anne, d. of Oliver Lord St John of Bletsoe (see St John tree).   m② Margaret Tate

JUDITH LYTTON, m① Sir George Smyth of Annables (*2), m② Sir Thomas Barrington

SIR WILLIAM LYTTON, MP for Hertford 1628 and 1641, d.1660 m. Ann, d. of Stephen Slaney of Norton, Salop.

MARY LYTTON, m. Edward Pulter.

SIR ROWLAND LYTTON 1614-74, MP for Hertford 1672

m① Judith d.1659, d. of Sir Humphrey Edwards.   m② Rebecca, d. of Thomas Chapman. She was cousin of Rebecca Piggot and niece of the poet George Chapman

MARGARET LYTTON m① Thomas Hillersden of Elstow, Beds, m② Thomas Hewitt of Ampthill, Beds

SIR WILLIAM LYTTON, died without issue 1705. He was the last male descendant

JUDITH LYTTON, d.1662, eldest daughter, m. Sir Nicholas Strode. When Sir William Lytton died in 1705 her grandson, Lytton Strode Lytton, inherited the estate (*3).

REBECCA LYTTON m. Lord Falkland

Knebworth House, Hertfordshire about 1824

(*1) There were family connections with the Barres through the Hotofts. Sir John Barre (d.1482) was married to Indonea Hotoft, the sister of Agnes, (see Barre tree).

(*2) Annables, sometimes known as Kinsbourne Hall, was later the home of the Luke family and then the Bissels and the Roberts, relations of Mary Hare who married William Harmer in 1883

(*3) He died without issue in 1710 and one of the other descendants took the name of Lytton and inherited the estate, which came down to the Bulwer Lyttons in the 19th century.

The Mordaunt Family of Turvey

The manor of Mordaunts in Turvey was held by the Mordaunt family from the early 13th century.

EUSTACE MORDAUNT named in 1225 in an assize of Morte d'ancestor

WILLIAM MORDAUNT succeeded and his son WILLIAM held the manor in 1278

ROBERT MORDAUNT inherited the manor before 1346

EDMUND MORDAUNT, d.1372. The Sunday before the feast of St Simon & St Jude he was seized with homicidal mania, killed his wife Ellen and drowned himself in a pool at Turvey.

MORDAUNT. *Argent a cheveron between three stars sable*

ROBERT MORDAUNT. United the two manors of Mordaunt and Ardres. Died before 1397

ROBERT MORDAUNT, a supporter of the house of York in the Wars of the Roses. Died 1448, having considerably impoverished the estate to support the Yorkist army.

WILLIAM MORDAUNT and his wife were 'frugal and provident' and the family became prosperous again.

MAUD (or Elizabeth) MORDAUNT m. Sir Weston Browne of Abbess Roding

SIR JOHN MORDAUNT succeeded about 1475. He was Speaker of the House of Commons 1487. Died 1504

JOHN LORD MORDAUNT, created baron in 1533. He accompanied Henry VIII to the Field of the Cloth of Gold. He received Anne Boleyn at the Tower when she came to be crowned and took part in her trial three years later. He lived at Drayton in Northamptonshire and used Turvey Park as a Dower House. Died 1561

JOHN 2ND LORD MORDAUNT. Lived at Thorndon, West Horndon, near Ingatestone Hall. Died 1571. John was a friend and kinsman of the Petres of Ingatestone Hall.

GEORGE MORDAUNT (3rd son) His daughter Katherine married Robert Barnardiston of Northill. (see Barnardiston tree)

LEWIS LORD MORDAUNT of Northill, Bedfordshire, d.1601. A judge who took part (unwillingly) in the trial of Mary Queen of Scots and also of Thomas Duke of Norfolk. Sold the manor of Kimpton to Thomas Hoo of St Paul's Walden. He m. Jane Nedham of Wymondley Priory (see Nedham tree)

HENRY 4TH LORD MORDAUNT. Was sent to the Tower under suspicion of being involved in the Gunpowder Plot (1605). Released after long imprisonment. Died 1608 and in his will he states that his conscience is clear, and that he had no knowledge of the Gunpowder Treason

JOHN MORDAUNT, made Earl of Peterborough in 1628. Took the Parliamentarian side in the Civil War. Died 1642

HENRY MORDAUNT 2nd Earl of Peterborough, was a Royalist (unlike his father). Wounded at Newbury and several times imprisoned. His estates sequestered in 1648 and recovered in 1655 at a cost of £5,106 - 15s. He died at an advanced age in 1697 without male issue. His only daughter Mary died unmarried in 1705.

CHARLES MORDAUNT 3rd Earl of Peterborough, d.1735, nephew of the 2nd Earl.

CHARLES MORDAUNT 4th Earl of Peterborough, grandson of the 3rd Earl. Died 1774

CHARLES MORDAUNT 5th (and last) Earl of Peterborough. Sold the property, including Turvey Abbey, in 1786 to Claude Higgins, Sheriff of London. The estates remained in the Higgins family until the 19th century.

The Nedham Family
of Wymondley Priory, Hertfordshire

JOHN NEDHAM of Nedham Grange in the High Peak of the County of Derby

CHRISTOPHER NEDHAM

JAMES NEDHAM, Surveyor to the King. Bought Marden in Tewin and the Priory at Little Wymondley about 1536. Fought for the King [Henry VIII] in France where he died in 1545 and was buried at Boulogne. (Memorial plaque in Little Wymondley church). He married Alice, d. of ... Merry (or Goodyer) of Hatfield.

m① Ann Coppin of Canterbury | **JOHN NEDHAM**, b. c.1523, d. 1591. | m② Jane Weldish of Cranbrooke, Kent.

| **GEORGE NEDHAM** 1557-1626 m. Margaret, (d. 1609), d. of Sir Henry Style of Kent | **SIR JOHN NEDHAM** 1565-1618 m. Elizabeth, d. of Sir Edward Watson. She later m. Sir Edward Tyrrell | **THOMAS (OR JAMES) NEDHAM** m. Elizabeth, sister of Beckingham Butler of Tewin Bury | **JANE NEDHAM** m. Lewis Mordaunt of Northill, Beds (see Mordaunt tree) | **JULIANA NEDHAM** m. William Warren (alias Bygrave) (see Warren tree) | **BRIDGET NEDHAM** m. Benjamin Piggot of Gravenhurst. (see Piggot tree) |

EUSTACE NEDHAM d.1658

m① Anne, d. of Luke Norton of Offley | m② 1626, Frances, d. of Edward Wingate of Lockleys and his wife Mary Taverner of Hexton. (see Wingate tree)

JOANNA NEDHAM d.1666
m. Francis Taverner of Hexton (brother of Eustace's mother-in-law) (see Taverner tree)

| **LETTICE NEDHAM** m① William Langhorne of Bedford m② Richard Shoard, Vicar of Shephall and Rector of Stevenage, d. 1679 M.I. at Shephall | **GEORGE NEDHAM** 1618-69 m. Barbara, d. of Sir William Fitch of Essex. Inherited Wymondley Priory. | **FRANCES NEDHAM** ——— **MARGARET NEDHAM** ——— **ANN NEDHAM** | **MARY NEDHAM** b. 1636, m. John Harmer of Weston (see Harmer tree) |

| **GEORGE NEDHAM** d. 1692 m. Lydia Banks d. 1728 | **FITCH NEDHAM** ——— **JAMES NEDHAM** | **MAURICE NEDHAM** b. 1653 ——— **CHARLES NEDHAM** b. 1655 | **BARBARA NEDHAM** ——— **ANN NEDHAM** ——— **ELIZABETH NEDHAM** |

| **GEORGE NEDHAM** 1672-1726 m. Barbara Gregory of Nottingham. Died with no male heir | **EUSTACE NEDHAM** 1675-1708 ——— **BANKS NEDHAM** b. 1676, d. in infancy | **BARBARA NEDHAM** b.1673 ——— **MARY NEDHAM** b. 1678 ——— **LETTICE NEDHAM** b. 1681 | **ELIZABETH NEDHAM** 1683-1753 m. Simon Degge (Memorial in Graveley Church) |

| **SUSAN NEDHAM** b. 1702 | **BARBARA NEDHAM** b. 1704, m. John Sherwin of Nottingham | **MARTHA NEDHAM** 1706-73, m. Thomas Browne, Garter King of Arms 1701-80, lived at Wymondley Priory and later Camfield Place, Essendon (Memorial in Essendon church) |

The Nodes Family
of Shephallbury

WILLIAM NODES of Barking in Essex

JOHN NODES served at the Court of Henry VIII

GEORGE NODES Serjeant at Arms and Serjeant of the Buckhounds to Henry VIII. m. Margaret, d. of Thomas Grimstone of Oxborough in Norfolk. Acquired the manor of Shephall in 1541. He left it in male tail to his nephew Charles

WILLIAM NODES of Stevenage

NODES. *Sable a pile argent with three trefoils sable therein.*

CHARLES NODES of Shephallbury, d. 1593 m. Elizabeth, d. of Thomas Mitchell of Codicote

JANE NODES m. William Kympton, who possibly m. afterwards Cecily Burse of Westminster (see Kympton tree).

JOAN NODES, d. 1566 m. Thomas Chapman of Hitchin. Their son, George Chapman, was the famous poet. (See Chapman tree)

EDMUND NODES of Graveley, m① Elizabeth Gwynne, m② Elizabeth Ashby

GEORGE NODES of Shephallbury m. Helen, d. of Edward Docwra of Brotherwood House, Hitchin. (see Docwra tree)

MARY NODES m. Edward Fyshe (grandson of Thomas Fyshe of Ayot and Elizabeth Hyde of Throcking). (see Fyshe tree)

CHARLES NODES m.. Jane, d. of Symeon Brograve of Hamells and Dorothy (née Leventhorpe) of Aldbury. (Jane's brother, John Brograve, was m. to Hannah Barnardiston of Suffolk)

JOHN NODES m. Margaret, d. of Thomas Crouch of Buntingford

GEORGE NODES a Freeman of the City of London

HELEN NODES m. William, s. and heir of Sir Thomas Boteler of Biddenham and Harrold Hall in Bedfordshire.

GEORGE NODES, s. and heir, b. 1630. Ancestor of the Heathcote family who were living at Shephallbury in the 19th century

THOMAS BOTELER
———
HELEN BOTELER

WILLIAM BOTELER
———
ANNE BOTELER

SHEPHALLBURY 1948

The Petre (Petter or Peter) Family
of Ingatestone Hall in Essex

SIR WILLIAM PETRE, 1505-72,
Deputy to Thomas Cromwell and later Chancellor and Principal Secretary to Queen Mary. He was a Doctor of Laws from Oxford, and tutor to George Boleyn (brother of Anne Boleyn). Built Ingatestone Hall in 1540-45.

m① Gertrude ... who died 1541. She was previously m. to John Tyrrell of Warley, a distant cousin of John Tyrrell of Heron Hall who was the first husband of Sir William Petre's second wife.

m②, in 1542, Anne Tyrrell, widow, b. 1509, d. of William Browne of Abbess Roding (who was Lord Mayor of London in 1507 and again in 1513/14). Anne had previously been married to John Tyrrell of Heron Hall, East Horndon. (*1)

DOROTHY PETRE
b.1535, m. 1555, Nicholas Wadham. They founded Wadham College, Oxford.

ELIZABETH PETRE
m. John, s. of William Gostwick, of Willington, Beds, and his wife Mary Boteler of Woodhall.

SIR JOHN PETRE
1549-1613, m. 1576, Mary, d. of Sir Edward Waldegrave (d. 1605). Sir John was created Lord Writtle by James I in 1603.

KATHERINE PETRE
m. John Talbot of Grafton Manor near Bromsgrove. Their daughter Gertrude was married to Robert Wintour, one of the conspirators in the Gunpowder Plot. (*2)

SIR WILLIAM PETRE, 2nd Lord Petre of Writtle, m. Katherine, d. of Edward Somersett Earl of Worcester.

JOHN PETRE, m. Catherine, d. of William Parker, Lord Monteagle and Morley. (*3)

THOMAS PETRE of Cranham in Essex, m. Elizabeth Baskerville of Wiltshire.

SIR ROBERT PETRE 3rd Lord Petre of Writtle, d. 1638, m. 1620, Mary (b.1603), d. of Anthony-Maria Browne 2nd Viscount Montague of Sussex. Mary died in 1684 and was buried at Ingatestone Hall. (*4)

FRANCES PETRE of Cranham, m. Elizabeth, d. of Sir John Gage, of Firle in Sussex, and his wife Penelope Darcy, of Hengrave Hall in Suffolk.

EDWARD PETRE

ELIZABETH PETRE

(*1) The wedding of Catherine Tyrrell, daughter of Anne and step-daughter of Sir William Petre, is described in Chapter 7.

(*2) Robert Wintour and his brother Thomas were two of the 8 main conspirators in the Gunpowder Plot. They were hung, drawn and quartered on 30th January 1606.

(*3) William Parker Lord Monteagle (later Lord Monteagle and Morley) was married to Elizabeth Tresham, a first cousin of the conspirator Robert Catesby. On 26th October 1605 Lord Monteagle received an anonymous letter (now known as the 'Monteagle Letter') warning him not to attend Parliament on 5th November. The letter led to the discovery of the Gunpowder Plot. Lord Monteagle was one of those who searched the cellars under the Houses of Parliament and discovered the barrels of gunpowder.

(*4) The Petres were closely connected with both the Brownes of Abbess Roding, who were close friends and neighbours, and the Brownes Lords Montague, of Sussex, who were connected with the family by this marriage and by other 'network' links.

The Piggot Family - Tree A
of Wheathampstead, Cardington, Houghton and Renhold

After the Norman Conquest the largest barony in the area was that of Hugh de Beauchamp of Bedford Castle. He held land in Beds, Herts and Bucks. There was a younger branch of the Beauchamp family at Eaton Socon who founded Bushmead Priory. They were the ancestors of the Greys of Wrest Park and of Margaret Beauchamp of Bletsoe. (see St John tree)

HUGH DE BEAUCHAMP, living 1066, was already married to Matilda Tallebosc at the time of the Conquest

MILES DE BEAUCHAMP, son or grandson of Hugh

BEATRICE DE BEAUCHAMP

PAYNE DE BEAUCHAMP, m.1144, Rose Mandeville who founded Chicksands Priory about 1150

SIMON DE BEAUCHAMP, founded Newnham Priory in 1166, Sheriff of Beds and Bucks 1198

WILLIAM DE BEAUCHAMP, grandson of Simon, held Astwick in 1261, and Renhold.

JOHN DE BEAUCHAMP, last male heir, killed 1265 in the Battle of Evesham. The family estate was divided among his 3 sisters

BEATRICE DE BEAUCHAMP, ancestor of the Latimers and the Nevills, inherited the largest of the 3 manors of Renhold, also inherited Astwick and Cardington.

MAUD DE BEAUCHAMP, ancestor of the Mowbray family (Earls of Nottingham and Dukes of Norfolk), inherited the smallest of the manors of Renhold.

ELA DE BEAUCHAMP, inherited (finally) all 3 manors of Renhold, m. Baldwin Lord Wake of Stapleford, Wheathampstead, Gobions and Blakemore.

ELIZABETH WAKE, inherited part of the manor of Renhold, m. John de Hoo and the manor became known as Hoobury (Howbury) Hall

JOAN WAKE, m. John (or Michael) Piggot of Wheathampstead (d.1318), inherited Houghton from the Piggot family and Howbury from Elizabeth Wake

BALDWIN PIGGOT named after his grandfather, predeceased his father.

JOHN PIGGOT, in 1318 inherited from his grandfather, Wheathampstead, Houghton and Howbury in Renhold, about 1360 exchanged Howbury for Cardington (which was previously owned by his kinsmen the Nevills and the Latimers.

MARGARET PIGGOT, Abbess of Elstow in 1409.

SIR BALDWIN PIGGOT of Cardington, Member of Parliament for Bedford 1389-1401, probably an ancestor or kinsman of Sir Randolf Piggot (who appears in Piggot tree B):

DOROTHY PIGGOT, m. c.1586, James Gascoigne. The Gascoigne family acquired Cardington through this marriage.

DOROTHY GASCOIGNE, m. Sir Gerard Harvey of Thurleigh (see Harvey tree).

ELIZABETH GASCOIGNE, m. Sir George Blundell

The Piggot Family - Tree B
of Wallington, Kingswoodbury, Edworth, Astwick, Stratton and Holme, and Gravenhurst

ALICE DE LANGTON, m. Edmund Peverell. Alice was sister and heir of Walter de Langton Bishop of Lincoln and Coventry and chief advisor to Edward I. Walter held Edworth from the Earls of Pembroke in 1307. He died in 1321

MARGARET PEVERELL
m. William de la Pole

JOHN PEVERELL,
osp, m. Isabella ...

SIR RANDOLPH PIGGOT, probably a kinsman of Sir Baldwin Piggot of Cardington, (see Piggot tree A)

KATHERINE DE LA POLE
m. John Bullok of Sharnbrook.
Inherited Edworth

SIR JOHN DE LA POLE, m. Joan, d. of John 3rd Lord Cobham

GEOFFREY PIGGOT

ROBERT BULLOK, m.1419

SIR RANDOLPH PIGGOT m. Anne Miniot

ELIZABETH BULLOK, m. William Furtho of Furtho

GEOFFREY PIGGOT, m. Margaret Plompton

JOHN ENDERBY of Astwick and Kingswoodbury, d.1457

m① ALICE FURTHO who inherited Edworth

m② Maud ... , who was probably related to the Piggots. When she died in 1471 her part of the Enderby estates went to Richard Piggot

RICHARD PIGGOT, m. Alice Finnet, acquired Kingswoodbury and Astwick in 1471 from Foljambes and **Enderbys**

RICHARD ENDERBY, inherited Edworth, d.1487

ROBERT PIGGOT m. Margaret Gifford

JOHN ENDERBY, inherited Edworth, d.1509

THOMAS PIGGOT, Sergeant-at-Law to Henry VIII, m. Agnes Forster, acquired Totternhoe Manor 1518, d.1521

FRANCIS PIGGOT of Gravenhurst, High Sheriff of Beds 1527 and 1548

m① ELEANOR ENDERBY. The marriage brought Edworth into the Piggot estates

m.② Margery St John, widow of Henry Grey Earl of Kent, d. of Sir John St John of Bletsoe

WILLIAM PIGGOT
of Totternhoe,
1497-1575

SIR THOMAS PIGGOT of Edworth and Stratton & Holme, High Sheriff of Beds 1552, 1557 and 1571, d.1581. Bought Wymondley Bury in 1544

m① Ann, d. of Richard Lord Rich who was Chancellor of England and a friend of the Petres of Ingatestone Hall

m② Elizabeth Thynne of Erith

BENJAMIN PIGGOT of Gravenhurst, 1551-1606, m③ Bridget Nedham of Wymondley Priory. Their d. Judith m.1617, Symon Hale of Clifton.

MICHAEL PIGGOT (Disinherited)

JOHN PIGGOT, b.1524, m.1544 Margaret Grainger, lived at Wymondley Bury

LEWIS PIGGOT inherited Edworth in 1581 and sold it in 1588

THOMAS PIGGOT of Tewin Water, 1540-1610, m.1571, Elizabeth, d. of Thomas Chapman of Hitchin, inherited Wymondley Bury in 1609 from his nephew Maurice.

MAURICE PIGGOT, d.1609, inherited Wymondley Bury in 1581.

REBECCA PIGGOT, 1577-1637, m.1596 Henry Bull of Hertford)

ELIZABETH PIGGOT, b.1583, m. Beckingham Butler of Tewin Bury

The St John Family
of Bletsoe

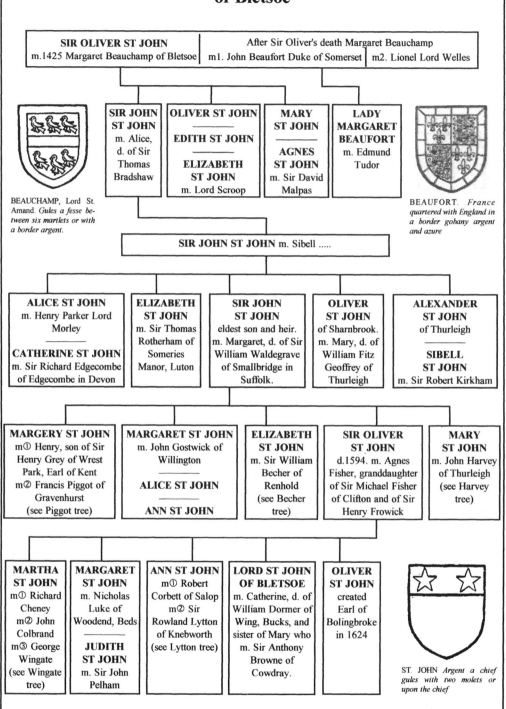

SIR OLIVER ST JOHN	After Sir Oliver's death Margaret Beauchamp
m.1425 Margaret Beauchamp of Bletsoe	m1. John Beaufort Duke of Somerset	m2. Lionel Lord Welles

SIR JOHN ST JOHN
m. Alice, d. of Sir Thomas Bradshaw

OLIVER ST JOHN
————
EDITH ST JOHN
————
ELIZABETH ST JOHN
m. Lord Scroop

MARY ST JOHN
————
AGNES ST JOHN
m. Sir David Malpas

LADY MARGARET BEAUFORT
m. Edmund Tudor

BEAUCHAMP, Lord St. Amand. *Gules a fesse between six martlets or with a border argent.*

BEAUFORT. *France quartered with England in a border gobany argent and azure*

SIR JOHN ST JOHN m. Sibell .....

ALICE ST JOHN
m. Henry Parker Lord Morley
————
CATHERINE ST JOHN
m. Sir Richard Edgecombe of Edgecombe in Devon

ELIZABETH ST JOHN
m. Sir Thomas Rotherham of Someries Manor, Luton

SIR JOHN ST JOHN
eldest son and heir. m. Margaret, d. of Sir William Waldegrave of Smallbridge in Suffolk.

OLIVER ST JOHN
of Sharnbrook. m. Mary, d. of William Fitz Geoffrey of Thurleigh

ALEXANDER ST JOHN
of Thurleigh
————
SIBELL ST JOHN
m. Sir Robert Kirkham

MARGERY ST JOHN
m① Henry, son of Sir Henry Grey of Wrest Park, Earl of Kent
m② Francis Piggot of Gravenhurst
(see Piggot tree)

MARGARET ST JOHN
m. John Gostwick of Willington
————
ALICE ST JOHN
————
ANN ST JOHN

ELIZABETH ST JOHN
m. Sir William Becher of Renhold
(see Becher tree)

SIR OLIVER ST JOHN
d.1594. m. Agnes Fisher, granddaughter of Sir Michael Fisher of Clifton and of Sir Henry Frowick

MARY ST JOHN
m. John Harvey of Thurleigh
(see Harvey tree)

MARTHA ST JOHN
m① Richard Cheney
m② John Colbrand
m③ George Wingate
(see Wingate tree)

MARGARET ST JOHN
m. Nicholas Luke of Woodend, Beds
————
JUDITH ST JOHN
m. Sir John Pelham

ANN ST JOHN
m① Robert Corbett of Salop
m② Sir Rowland Lytton of Knebworth
(see Lytton tree)

LORD ST JOHN OF BLETSOE
m. Catherine, d. of William Dormer of Wing, Bucks, and sister of Mary who m. Sir Anthony Browne of Cowdray.

OLIVER ST JOHN
created Earl of Bolingbroke in 1624

ST. JOHN *Argent a chief gules with two molets or upon the chief*

The Taverner Family
of Norfolk and Hexton in Hertfordshire

RALPH LE TAVERNER held land in North Elmham in Norfolk around 1272. His grandson, William, of Dunwich and Sibton Abbey, inherited in 1317. A grandson of William, Henry Taverner, was Councillor at Law to Henry VI, and another grandson, John Taverner, fought at Agincourt. Henry Taverner's son Nicholas inherited around 1460.

NICHOLAS TAVERNER d.1492
m. Margaret, d. of Thomas Dethick of Wrongey in Norfolk

JOHN TAVERNER d.1545, buried in Brisley Church
m① Alice, d. and heir of Robert Silvester of Brisley, Norfolk | m② Ann Crow (or Crane) of Bilney in Norfolk. (*1)

ROBERT TAVERNER
A Canon in the monastery of Walsingham

TAVERNER. *Argent a bend indented sable with a roundel gules in the cantle.*

RICHARD TAVERNER
of Oxford, d.1575. Clarke of the signet to Henry VIII, JP and High Sheriff of Oxfordshire.
m① Margaret, d. of Walter Lambert and Margaret Guildford | m② Mary, d. of Sir John Harecourt of Stanton Harecourt, Oxon (*2)

ROGER TAVERNER
of Upminster. Surveyor General of the King's Woods on this side of the Trent. His son John took over as Surveyor of the King's Woods.

ROBERT TAVERNER
of Lamborn, Essex. Surveyor of the King's Woods beyond the Trent. Had 2 sons: Robert and Thomas (a London merchant)

SILVESTER TAVERNER
of Marston in Bedfordshire. Father of Silvester, Thomas, John, and Richard, and grandfather of Henry Taverner, a sea captain.

JOHN TAVERNER
a Divine
___
MARTHA TAVERNER
m. George Calfield of Gray's Inn

PETER TAVERNER of Hexton, d.1601.
m. Frances, d. of Thomas Docwra of Putteridge, Herts. (There is a monument to Peter and Frances in Hexton Chucrh)
(see Docwra tree)

EDMOND TAVERNER, JP
of Soundess, Oxfordshire.
m. Lucy Hales

FRANCIS TAVERNER
of Hexton, JP. m. Joanna, d. of George Nedham of Wymondley Priory, Herts. (*3)

JOHN TAVERNER, one of the Professors of Gresham College, and Rector of Stoke Newington. d.1638. (*4)

MARY TAVERNER
m. Edward Wingate of Welwyn, JP for Hertford. (see Wingate tree)

RICHARD TAVERNER m. Martha, d. of Matthew Bedell, Alderman of London 1636

FRANCES WINGATE m.1626, Eustace Nedham. (*5)
(see Nedham tree)

(*1) John and Ann had 3 children: James, Thomas, and Margaret. James's daughter, Frances, m. Sir William Denny of Gray's Inn, Recorder of the City of Norwich..

(*2) Richard Taverner and his 2nd wife, Mary, had a son, Harecourt Taverner, and a daughter, Penelope.

(*3) The Taverners and Nedhams were closely related. Mary Taverner was the mother-in-law of Eustace Nedham, and Mary's brother Francis was married to Eustace's sister Joanna. There were also close links with the Docwra and Wingate families.

(*4) This is the John Taverner who was mentioned in Thomas Docwra's will (see Docwra tree). Thomas was John's grandfather and left John all his books, urging him to concentrate on his studies. John evidently fulfilled his grandfather's expectations and became a professor at Gresham College (see Docwra tree).

(*5) Eustace was brother of Joanna Nedham who m. Francis Taverner (uncle of Frances Wingate).

The Warren Family
of Hertfordshire

SIR JOHN WARREN of Poynton in Cheshire

LAURENCE WARREN
of Pointon, d. 1556, m. Joan ... .
Bought the manor of Bygrave in 1550

JOHN WARREN (5th son)
m. Margaret, d. of Sir William Booth of Shrublands in Suffolk
and Mary Newport of Brent Pelham.

LAURENCE WARREN
A younger son

WILLIAM WARREN, alias Bygrave, d. 1589
m. Juliana, d. of John Nedham of Wymondley Priory

HENRY WARREN m. Alice, d.
of Thomas Snagge of Letchworth

JOHN WARREN
of Harrow
m. .... Edlin

WILLIAM WARREN of Ashwell, b.1584,
m. Elizabeth Hammond, sold Bygrave in
1613 in order to pay his debts

GREGORY WARREN of St Peter's St
Albans, m. Alice, d. of William Pulter and
widow of George Skipworth of St Albans.

GILBERT WARREN of
Aldenham, m.
Martha, d. of
John Long,
Alderman of
London

WILLIAM WARREN
m. 1638,
Ann Skegg
of Baldock
(*1)

EDWARD WARREN,
alias Waller of Ashwell
and Simonds Inn

m① Margaret Gray	m② Margaret, d. of Richard Glascock

GREGORY WARREN
of Harpenden, m. Joan,
d. of Jeremy Thornton of
Greenford. (The
Thornton family later
owned Marden in the
19th century)

BRIDGET WARREN
m. .... Field of Ascot.
Probably the parents of
Edmund Field who sold
Marden to Richard
Warren in 1672.

GILBERT WARREN of Colney, m.
Margery, d. of Thomas Hickman Lord
of the Manor of Bushey and sister of
Alice Hickman who m. Nicholas
Tooke of Essendon Parsonage.

JOHN WARREN
b. 1639.
m.
Elizabeth ....

EDWARD WARREN
(alias Waller)

RICHARD WARREN
m. Elizabeth ... ,
acquired Marden from
his 4th cousin Edmund
Field in 1692

EDMUND FIELD
MP for Hertford
1671-76, related to
the Lamb family.

ANN WARREN b. 1676, m. 1698, John Harmer of
Weston who was previously m. to Mary Nedham.
(See Harmer Tree)

DR RICHARD WARREN MA LLD,
Rector of South Warnborough in Hampshire,
m. Catherine, d. of Sir Anthony Vincent of Stoke in Surrey

RICHARD WARREN 1686-1768
m. 1728, Mary Collet, 1703-33, d. of Joseph Collet of Hertford Castle (*2)

ARTHUR WARREN m. Mary ... ,
sold Marden in 1785. Mary d. 1787

COLLET WARREN,
died young

*WARREN. Checky or and azure
a quarter gules with a lion
argent therein.*

ARTHUR WARREN d. 1762 aged 9 years, buried at Hertingfordbury
FRANCES MARIA WARREN d. 1762 aged 3 years, buried at Hertingfordbury
LOUISA WARREN d. 1762 aged 2 years, buried at Hertingfordbury

(*1) The Skegg family, ancestors of Ann Warren, are frequently mentioned in the histories of Hertfordshire. Queenhoo Hall at Tewin was said to have been built by Edmund Skegg in 1550. He was Lord of the Manor of Brantfield (Bramfield) and in 1567 he acquired Panshanger, which later went to Gervase Elwes (who also acquired the manor of Throcking) and then to the Cowper family.

(*2) Joseph Collet (or Colet) of Hertford Castle, whose daughter Mary married Richard Warren, was a descendant of the Colet family of Barkway. Sir Henry Colet of Barkway was Lord Mayor of London in 1495 and his son John Colet was the famous Dean of St Pauls who, in 1505, re-founded St Paul's School.

The Wingate Family
of Sharpenhoe, Harlington and Lockleys Manor at Welwyn

EDMUND WINGATE of Sharpenhoe, Bedfordshire. Died 1559
m① Elizabeth, d. (or sister) of Ralph Astry of Wood End, Bedfordshire │ m② Mary, d. of William Belfield of Studham

GEORGE WINGATE of Harlington, Biscot and Lewsey; Justice of the Peace for Bedford.

| m① Ann Belfield of Studham | m② Ann, d. of William Wiseman of Canfield Hall in Essex | m③ Martha, d. of Oliver Lord St John of Bletsoe |

ROGER WINGATE
of Bourne End in Bedfordshire
m. Jane, d. of Henry Birch of Sundon

THOMAS WINGATE
m. the daughter of William Lockley of Welwyn

EDWARD WINGATE
of Lockleys Manor, acquired Lockleys in 1624 from the Perient and Horsey families, m. Margaret, d. of Peter Taverner of Hexton and his wife Frances Docwra of Putteridge (see Taverner tree)

ROBERT WINGATE
1574-1603, m. Amy, d. of Roger Warre of Hestercombe in Somerset.

EDWARD WINGATE of Grays Inn, 1594-1656. m. (at Harlington) Elizabeth Button of Wootton, lived at Ampthill, a noted mathematician, went to France to teach the young princess Henrietta Maria (later queen of Charles I). In 1654 his name appears in the Ampthill registers attesting marriages as a Justice of the Peace.

FRANCES WINGATE
m. Eustace Nedham of Wymondley Priory.
(see Nedham tree)

EDWARD WINGATE
of Lockleys, m. Mary, d. of Ralph Alway of Cannons, Herts, d. 8 August 1685 age 79 years (tomb in Welwyn Church). Left 5 sons and 7 daughters.

JOHN WINGATE
b. 1601. Justice of the Peace. m. Alice, d. of Francis Smallman of Kinersley, Hereford

MARY NEDHAM
b. 1636 at Wymondley Priory, m. John Harmer of Weston.
(see Harmer Tree)

FRANCIS WINGATE of Biscot, 1628-75, m. Lettice, d. of Dr. Pierce. Francis was Justice of the Peace for Bedford and tried to persuade John Bunyan to give up his preaching because he was loth to send him to prison. He argued that John Bunyan could not possibly interpret the Scriptures since he knew no Greek,

GEORGE WINGATE
of Lewsey. d. 1670.
m. Elizabeth Pierce (sister of Lettice who m. his brother Francis)

POMFRETT TREE.
In 1592 John Harmer married Ann Pomfrett of Baldock, d. of Thomas Pomfrett of Baldock - almost certainly part of this family.

THOMAS POMFRETT Rector of Luton 1660-1705 ... m. Catherine ...

JOHN POMFRETT, baptised at Luton under the name Thomas Pomfrett on 12 March 1667. Died aged 35 in 1702. m. 1692 Elizabeth Wingate

JOHN POMFRETT, 'Rouge Croix', d.1751

SIR FRANCIS WINGATE
died 1691.
married Ann, daughter of Arthur, Earl of Anglesey

GEORGE WINGATE
born 1655.
married Katherine, daughter of John Griffith

WINGATE of Lockleys. *Sable a bend ermine cotised or between six martlets or.*

ELIZABETH WINGATE
m. 1692 (at Luton) John Pomfrett, poet and Rector of Maulden

ARTHUR WINGATE
Sold Biscot in 1718 to John Crawley of Stockwood Park.
(Related to the Hare family)

MARY WINGATE
married George Snagge of Maulden

Historical Notes
and extracts from documents

Names in this section are not included in the indexes.

Historical Note

Why certain 17th century clergy were turned out of their Livings.

During the 17th centuries there were many conflicts of loyalties both political and religious. Strong feelings on both sides led to heated arguments and much 'righteous' indignation.

The Puritans regarded the reformation of the church under Queen Elizabeth as incomplete. They were opposed to kneeling at the altar to receive Holy Communion, and many of the altar rails were removed. They also disapproved of the wearing of copes and surplices, and making the sign of the cross at baptisms. They insisted that 'all curious singing and playing of the organ should be stopped.'

Many clergy were turned out of their livings during this period, but the reasons seem to have varied. Much depended on the religious views of their patrons.

Charles Chauncy, who was removed from the church of Ware in 1630, later referred to the Book of Common Prayer as the 'English massbook', and strongly opposed the setting up of a rail around the communion table.

John Mountford of Tewin, on the other hand, (mentioned in Chapter 12) was removed from his rectory because he insisted on installing altar rails in Tewin Church, and refused to administer the sacrament to those who remained in their pews. After the benefice was sequestered, the Committee for Plundered Ministers ordered his successor to pay for the maintenance of Mountford's children.

But Clergy were not always removed because of their rituals. During the Commonwealth period it was sometimes because of their strongly expressed Royalist opinions. In some cases it was simply because they were not carrying out their church duties, spending all their time at the gaming tables or on the hunting field.

In the Walkern archives we come across the sad story of the Rev'd John Gorsuch, who was not only a High-Churchman, but also a strong supporter of the Royalist cause. The Humberstone family were Lords of the Manor of Walkern but at this time they were no longer Patrons of the Church, having sold the advowson in 1632 to David Gorsuch, a wealthy member of the Mercers Guild. He built a new rectory and proceeded to install his son John as Rector. Unfortunately the Humberstones strongly disapproved of John's religious views. In Chapter 8 we read that on Easter Sunday 1637 Thomas and

Elizabeth Humberstone insisted on kneeling in their pew in the Chancel, instead of coming up to the altar rail. The Rev'd Gorsuch refused to administer communion and a bitter dispute followed. The Walkern parish records give further details.

Letters to the Archdeacon, the Bishop and finally to Archbishop Laud (who supported the priest) failed to settle the dispute, and eventually Gorsuch was ejected by Parliament in 1642. The following year John White published his "First Century of Scandalous Malignant Priests" which included John Gorsuch, Rector of Walkern, "who hath published a wicked libell against Parliament, that some Lords whom he named were Fooles". It also states that Gorsuch had provided a horse and rider to serve under Prince Rupert against Parliament, and had also "denyed many of his Parishioners the sacrament of the Lord's Supper, without any cause shown, and refused to administer it to such as would not come up to the railes".

Having been turned out of his benefice, Gorsuch lived on in the parish, and continued to make himself a nuisance. Finally, in 1647 the authorities sent John Fairclough of Weston with a body of men to eject him. In order to escape he hid in a haystack and was smothered. Thus ended the life of this turbulent but probably well-meaning priest.

———————

Transcript of Inventory to John of Baldock's Will, 1613

A true and pfect Inventory of all and singuler the
goodes and chattelles of John Harmer late of Baldock
in the Countie of Hertford and dioces of Lincolne
deceased, made and praysed the xxiiii th daie of November
1613 by those whose names ar hereunder written
and in mannr and forme followinge vizt

In the Hall

Imprimis one table with a frame and sixe joyned stoles	xxviii s
Item one cubbard a pott shelfe one little table twoo chaires and one benchboarde	xxxv s
Item twoo spites twoo painted cloathes twoo Andirons and - of Iron a paire of bellowes certaine - twoo paire of potthookes twoo Cushines with othere small implemenmtes	xx s

In the plor nexte the hall

Item one beedsteed a bede a paire of curtaines a paire of valence a - table a pott shelfe a chayre a brasse pott and a truncke	x£
Item a table with a frame a forme a benchboard and three stooles and a wicker chaire a warme inge panne one window cushine and fower othere cushines	xl s

In the lofte over the hall

Item one bede and bedsteed a coverlett a materice a paire of curtaines a boulster twoo pillowes twoo blanketes and valence	viii£
Item a - table viii cushines two chaires fyve boxes a - table cloth	lii s
Item one table with a frame one forme a bench and benchboard twoo Coffers three stooles	xxxiii s iiii d
Item fower silver spones	xxiiii s
Item thirtie paire of sheeted	x£
Item nine paire of pillowbeares fower - cloathes and othere childbeed lynen	iiii£ x s ii d
Item fyve dossen of table napkins xi table cloathes three drinkinge cloathes	v£
Item ix -	vi s viii d
Item all his wearinge apparell	v£

In the lofte over the parlor

Item one bedstead and one feather bedde bolster and other furniture — vli

Item one other bedde and a trundle bedde with their furniture one chest and eight pounde of flax — xls

In the lofte over the hall house

Item a bedstead two chaires a trundle a little table [illegible] of woole and other implements — xxs

In the lofte over the kitchin

Item one bedde with other implements — xxxs

In the Seller

Item three barrells [illegible] and [illegible] and other implements — xxxs

In the kitchin

Item [illegible]

Item [illegible] brasse and [illegible] pannes [illegible]

two [illegible] pannes a table a paire of andirons a [illegible] and other small things — iijli

Item one brasse pot given to his daughter Anne

In the Brewe house

Item one leade or copper to brew in and the brewinge vessells with other small things — iiijli

In the yard

Item three hogges one horse one [illegible] of haye and [illegible] ladders — vli

Item the woode and timber in the yard — iiijli

Item all the corne and graine both threshed and unthreshed — xxxvjli xs

Item [illegible] a [illegible] and [illegible] — xxs

Item two [illegible] — iijli

Item graine sowen in the feilde and three acres of tilth lande — xxxs

debts owinge to the deceased

Item [illegible] — iijli xiijs

Item [illegible] — xvs iiijd

Transcript of Inventory to John of Baldock's Will, 1613

In the lofte over the plor

Item one fethere beed one Ionned beedsteed
Coverlett and othere furniture   v£

Item one othere beede and a truckle bede
with there furniture one cushine and eyght poundes of F--   xl s

In the lofte over the gate house

Item a cheste two chaires a cradle a litle
table one pcell of woole and othere   xxx s
implementes

In the lofte over the kitchin

Item one beede with othere implementes   xxx s

In the seller

Item three barrells ix firkins and
othere implementes   xxv s

In the kitchin

Item - pewter dishes and candel   -

Item - brasse and driping panns two pailes
twoo fryinge panns a table a paire of Andirons   iii£
a forme and othere smalle thinges

Item one brasse pot given to his daughter Annis   x s

In the Brewe house

Item one leade or copper to brewe in
and the brewinge velselles with   iiii£
othere smale thinges

In the yard

Item fower hogges one horse one pcell
of haye and a pcell of lathes   x£

Item the woode and strawe in the yard   iii£

Item all the corne and graine
boath threshed and unthreshed   lxxxvi£ x s

Item a - screne and a bushell   xx s

Item twoo cartes   iiii£

Item graine - in the feilde and
three acres of tilth lande debts owenge to the deceased   xx£

Item Michall Foster   iii£ xii s

Item Nicholas Phipp   xv s iiii d

The inventory ends with the names of the 'prayers':
Robert Yardley; ——; Thomas —, and James Slone.

Finally we have "Sum totalis ccv £ x s vi d" [£205 10s 6d]

Transcript of Inventory to Will of Leonard Fishe, 1668

An Inventory

of all And singular the goods and chattles of Leonard Fishe late of
Northmyms in the County of Hertford deied taken and appraized
by John Harte and ..... Addison the elder the twelfth day of
September in the yeare of his Lord 1668 as followeth:

In the hall

Imprimis one table and frame one	}	
little table two formes one little	}	xxiii ˢ iiii ᵈ
two chares	}	

In the parlor

Item one table and frame and eight	}
joyned stooles and three chaires and three	}
little stooles and two cushions one paire of	}
andirons one paire of tongs and one	}
and cupboard cloath.	}

In the kitchen

Item one table and one dresser and one	}	
forme foure chaires and foure stooles one	}	
rack three - one dripping panne one	}	
paire of racks one paire of andirons	}	iii £
foure paires of -	}	
- one - and other	}	
lumber.	}	

In the roome next the Hall

item five halfe - bedstedds foure	}	xi ˢ
flockbedds, eight blanketts foure bolsters	}	

In the little parlor

Item one - one halfe - bedstedd	}	
one table and frame, one forme two flock	}	xxxiiii ˢ
bedds foure blanketts two bolsters	}	

In the buttrey

item two trays three platters and other	}	vi ˢ viii ᵈ
lumber	}	
Item for the pewter		ii £
Item for all the brasse		iii £

In the chamber over the hall

One bedstedd with curtaines and	}	
vallence one feather bedd and bolster two	}	
blanketts and one rug one table and frame	}	x £ x ˢ
foure chaires and three stooles one paire	}	
of andirons one paire of tongs and one fire shovel	}	

Transcript of Inventory to Will of Leonard Fishe, 1668

In the chamber over the parlor

Item one bedstedd with curtaines and vallence	}	
one feather bedd and bolster two blanketts	}	vi £
one trundle bedd one table and frame	}	
one - cupboard two chaires five stooles	}	

In the roome over the little parlor

Item one bedstedd with one feather bedd	}	
and two pillowes one rugg one blankett	}	iiii £ x s
one court cupboatd one joyned stoole	}	

In the roome over the kitchen

Item one bedstedd with curtaines	}	
and vallence one trundle bedstedd two	}	
..... three chests one trunk three	}	iiii
boxes one forme ane joyned stoole	}	
two chaires with other lumber	}	

In the shovelboard Roome

One long table two side tables	}	
two ..... one court cupboard one	}	iii £ x s
chaire one desk five stooles one paire	}	
of andirons	}	

In the roome ove the Buttrey

Item one bedstedd one feather bedd one	}	iii £
bolster one trundle bedd two blanketts	}	

Item for linnen twenty paires of sheets	}	
six table cloaths two dozen and a halfe	}	vi £ x s
of napkins four paire of pillowcases	}	

Item for one gun or fowleing piece		xxi s

In the Garrett

Item one bedstedd one flockbedd one	}	xxi s
bolster two blanketts	}	
Item the wood in the yard		Liii s
Item for one hogge in the yard		xxviii s
Item for hay in the barnes		x iiii
Item for his wearing apparrell and	}	x
money in his purse	}	

Suma totalis

Pet Barrett

HERTFORDSHIRE

The NAMES of the NOBILITY, GENTRY, and others, of the County of HERTFORD, who contributed to the defence of this Country at the time of the SPANISH INVASION, in 1588

Marcii.	£		£
George Knighton, Armiger tercio die Marcii	25	Robert Wolley, gen. eodem	50
Raphe Ratcliffe, Gen. eodem	25	John Andrew, sen. 24 die Marcii	25
Elizabeth Chufie, vidua quarto die Marcii	25	John Binge, gen. 29 die Marcii	25
William Beswicke, Gen. eodem	25	William Ewer, eodem	25
William Sherwood, sexto die Marcii	25	Thomas Ewer, eodem	25
Edward Briscoe, jun. 10 die Marcii	25	Thomas Gardiner, eodem	25
Marie Browne, vidua eodem	25	Thomas Ansell, 31 daie of Marche	25
Thomas Parsons, Gen. eodem	25	April.	
John Gibbe, Gen. eodem	25	Thomas Dermer, quinto die Aprilis	25
Jane Bashe, vidua eodem	25	Foulke Onslowe, armiger, sexto die Aprilis	50
Thomas Turner, yeoman eodem	25	William Crawley, eodem	25
John Tarborowe, Armiger eodem	25	John Hurste, eodem	25
Henrie Sadler, Armiger eodem	50	Henrie Foster, 13 die Aprilis	25
Edward Fitz-John, 11 die Marcii	25	William Samme, eodem	25
Edward Bigge, Yeoman eodem	25	George Grave, 14 die Aprilis	25
William Grubbe, 12 die Marcii	25	Robert Garnett, 16 die Aprilis	25
Thomas Northe, Gen. 13 die Marcii	25	Jo. Sutton, gen. 18 die Aprilis	25
Roberte Hide, Armiger, eodem	50	Edward Briscoe, 28 die Aprilis	25
John Clerke, eodem die	25	John Rooley, 29 die Aprilis	25
Clement Manestyre, 14 die Marcii	25	Maye	
Henrie Mayne, 15 die Marcii	50	William Muffet, Gen. secundo die Maii	25
Robert Barber, 17 die Marcii	25	Edward Newport, Armiger, eodem	50
William Halsey, eodem die	25	Andrew Gray, Armiger, tercio die Maii	25
John Mitchell, sen. 18 die Marcii	25	George Chasey, Gen. eodem	25
Charles Nodes, Gen. eodem	25	Richard Canfeild, sexto die Maii	25
Michaell Meade, Gen. eodem	50	Richard Smithe, Armiger, 10 die Maii	50
George Clarke, eodem	25	William Godfrey, alias Cowper, Gen. eodem	25
William Clerk, eodem	25	Rowland Bafford, Gen. 26 die Maii	25
Thomas Harmer, eodem	25	William Mayne, eodem	25
George Graveley, gen. 19 die Marcii	25	Stephen Nobbes, 28 die Maii	25
Thomas Chapman, eodem	25	William Preston, Gen. 30 doe Maii	25
Henrie Spurlinge, yeoman, 20 die Marcii	25	John Okston, sen. eodem	25
Symonde Warren, 22 die Marcii	25	Julye	
George Field, 23 die Marcii	25	George Kimpton, Gen. 15 die Julii	25
Robert Spencer, armiger, eodem	25	John Kent, 29 die Julii	25

From a quarto Pamphlet printed for Messrs. Leigh and Sotheby, London, 1798.

HERTFORDSHIRE

The following inhabitants of this County were assessed at the sum of twenty pounds each towards a subsidy for the defence of the country in the year 1590. The list is preserved in the Record Office among the State Papers.

Ralph Gape of St Albans
Robert Fynche of Redbourne
Thomas Byscoe of Aldenham, sen
John Warener of Radlet
Ralph Heydon of Sarrett gent
Henry Baldwyn of Watford
John Redwood of Parke Street in Watford
William Wedon of Oxley hamlett
Richard Cubbage of Watford
Francis Palmer of Rickmansworth gent
George Baldwyn of the same
William Ethroppe of Wyndrich
William Cole of Parkwarde gent
Thomas Thrale of Sandrich
Thomas Penne of Coddicott gent
Thomas Hoo of Paleswalden gent
Lady Elizabeth Paulett of Ridge, vid*
John Halsey of Chipping Barnett
Arthur Hewett of Northall gent
David Hollyland of the same
John Bysouth of Corner Hall
Thomas Goold of Bovingdon
Thomas Welles of the Howe
John Emes of Gaddesden pva
Thomas Waterhose of Barkampstede gent
William Palmer of Wiggington gent
William Lake of Mylsterne
George Pace of Harpden
John Christian of Whethamsteed
John Brockett of the same
Henry Hickeman of Bushey
Thomas Barnard of Shenley

Leonard Fysh of Hatfield gent
Edward Smyth of the same
John Kitchen of Tatteridge
George Peryent of Ayett pva gent
William Sell of Munden magna
John Bigge of Knebworth
La: Julian Cotten of Wimley magna vid†
John Nedeham of Wimley pva Esqr†
Edward Lacon of Willien gent
Thomas Whittamore of Hitchin
John Campe of Ware
Richard Colly of the same gent
Thomas Mylles of Thundrich
John Hemming of Standon
Richard Fysher of the same
Richard Greene of Braughing gent
Andrew Calton of Starforde
George Marshall of Sabsforde [1]
Alexander Chauncey of the same
John Gardiner Doctor of the lawe
Robert Hemming of Benioy [2]
William Kimpton
John Harmer of Rusden
John Goodman of Clottall
John Haynes of Haddam magna gent
Phillip Allington of Burnt Pelham Esqr
Francys Delawood of Hormeade Magna
Thomas Brande of Hormeade pva gent
Thomas Chambers of Barkeway gent
John Crouche of Layston gent
Saunder Hammond of Buckland gent

The Clergy who were called upon to contribute were Marke Stubbyns of Whetham-steed, and Robert Abbott of Hatfeild Bushop, £20 each; and Theophilus Aelmer of Greate Hadham, and William Chapman of Therfield, £30 each.

* Assessed at fifty pounds   † Assessed at forty pounds

[1] Sawbridgeworth   [2] Bengeo

Sheriffs of Hertfordshire (Includes Essex until 1566)

HEN. V.

1412	Philip Englefield
1413	John Tyrell
1414	Sir John Howard, Kt.
1415	Sir Thomas Barre, Kt.
1416	Lewis Johan
1417	Reginald Malyns
1418	Sir John Howard, Kt.
1419	Robert Darcy of Danbury, Essex
1420	Lewis Johan (two years)

HEN. VI.

1422	John Tyrell
1423	Sir Maurice Brewyn of South Ockington, Kt.
1424	John Barley of Albury
1425	John Doreward of Bocking
1426	Conand Aske
1427	Thomas Tyrell of Heron
1428	John Hotoft of Knebworth
1429	Nicholas Rickhull
1430	Henry Langley of Rickling
1431	Sir Nic. Thorley, Kt.
1432	John Durward
1433	Robert Whytingham of Pendley
1434	Geoffrey Rockyll
1435	Sir Maurice Brewyn, Kt.
1436	Edward Tyrell
1437	Richard Alrede
1438	Richard Whytingham
1439	Richard Witherton
1440	Thomas Tyrell
1441	Ralph Asteley
1442	Nicholas Morley of Hollingbury
1443	John Hende
1444	Thomas Tyrell of Heron
1445	Thomas Pigot
1446	Thomas Baud of Hadham-hall
1447	John Hende the younger
1448	George Langham
1449	Geoffrey Rockhill
1450	Philip Boteler of Watton
1451	Thomas Barrington
1452	John Godmanston
1453	Sir Thomas Cobham, Kt.
1454	Humphrey Bohun
1455	Ralph Bothe, Esq.

1456	John Hende the younger
1457	Lewis John, Esq.
1458	Robert Darcy of Danbury, Esq.
1459	Thomas Tyrell of Heron

EDW. IV

1460	Thomas Juce
1461	Thomas Langley, Esq. (two years)
1463	Sir John Clay, Kt
1464	Roger Ree, Esq.
1465	Sir Lawrence Reynford, Kt.
1466	Henry Barley, Esq.
1467	Sir William Pirton, Kt.
1468	Walter Writell, Esq.
1469	Ralph Baud, Esq. of Hadham-hall
1470	Walter Writell, Esq.
1471	Sir Roger Ree, Kt.
1472	Alured Cornburgh, Esq.
1473	John Sturgeon, Esq. of Hitchin
1474	Richard Hance, Esq.
1475	Henry Langley, Esq.
1476	William Green. Esq.
1477	Alured Cornburgh
1478	John Wode
1479	John Sturgeon, Esq. of Hitchin
1480	Thomas Tyrell of Heron
1481	John Fortescue, Esq. of Hatfield

EDW. V and RICH. III

1483	William Say of Broxbourne
1484	Sir William Say, Kt. of Broxbourne
1485	John Sturgeon of Hitchin
1486	Sir Robert Percy, Kt.

HEN. VII.

1486	Sir John Fortescue, Kt. of Hatfield
1487	Henry Marney, Esq.
1488	Sir William Pyrton, Kt.
1489	Henry Tey, Esq.
1490	John Boteler, Esq. of Watton
1491	Robert Ter;;;vile, Esq.
1492	John Berfeild, Esq.
1493	Henry Marney, Esq.
1494	Sir Richard Fitz Lewis, Kt. of Thornton
1495	Robert Plomer
1496	William Pulter of Hitchin

1497	Robert Newport, Esq. of Pelham		1545	Anthony Cook, Esq.
1498	Thomas Peryent, Esq. of Digenswell		1546	Robert Lytton, Esq. of Knebworth
1499	Sir John Verney, Kt. of Pendley		1547	John Coningsby, Esq. of North-Mims
1500	Sir Roger Wentworth, Kt.			
1501	Sir Henry Tey, Kt.			**EDW. VI.**
1502	William Pyrton, Esq.		1547	Edward Brocket, Esq. of Hatfield
1503	Humphry Tyrell, Esq. of Heron		1548	John Cock, Esq. of Brokesborne
1504	William Skipwith, Esq. of St Albans (2 years)		1549	Sir John Gates, Kt. of Cheshunt
1506	Roger Darcy, Esq.		1550	Sir George Norton, Kt
1507	John Brocket, Esq. of Hatfield (2 years)		1551	Sir Henry Tyrell, Kt of Heron
1509	Humphry Tyrell, Esq. of Heron		1552	Sir Thomas Pope, Kt of Tittenhanger

HEN. VIII.

MARY

1510	John Leventhorpe, Esq. of Shingle Hall		1553	Sir John Wentworth, Kt
1511	William Lytton, Esq. of Knebworth			
1512	Anthony Darcy, Esq. of Danbury			**PHIL. and MARY**
1513	Edward Tyrell, Esq. of Heron		1554	Edward Brocket, Esq. of Hatfield
1514	John Seyntclere, Esq.		1555	William Harris, Esq.
1515	William Fitz Williams, Esq.		1556	Sir John Boteler, Kt of Watton
1516	Sir John Veere, Kt.		1557	Sir Thomas Pope, Kt of Tittenhanger
1517	Thomas Bonham, Esq.		1558	Thomas Mildmay, Esq.
1518	Sir Thomas Tyrell, Kt of Heron			
1519	Sir John Cutts, Kt.			**ELIZ**
1520	Sir John Veere, Kt.		1559	Ralph Rowlet, Esq. of St. Albans
1521	Thomas Bonham, Esq.		1560	Edward Capell, Esq. of Hadham
1522	Sir Thomas Tey, Kt.		1561	Sir Thomas Goldyng, Kt.
1523	Johm Christmass, Esq.		1562	Thomas Barrington, Esq.
1524	Henry Barley, Esq.		1563	Henry Fortescue, Esq.
1525	Sir John Veere, Kt.		1564	William Aloffe, Esq.
1526	Thomas Leventhorpe, Esq. of Shingle-hall		1565	Robert Chester, Esq. of Royston
1527	Thomas Bonham, Esq.		1566	John Brocket, Esq. of Hatfield
1528	Edward Tyrell, Esq. of Heron			
1529	Sir Gyles Capell, Kt of Hadham			**(Herts and Essex severed)**
1530	John Bollys, Esq. of Wallington			
1531	John Brocket, Esq. of Hatfield		1567	Sir George Penruddock, Kt
1532	John Smyth, Esq.		1568	Rowland Lytton, Esq. of Knebworth
1533	Sir Philip Boteler, Kt of Watton		1569	Henry Coningsby, Esq. of North-Mims
1534	Sir Brian Took, Kt. of Hatfield		1570	William Doddes, Esq.
1535	Sir William West, Kt.		1571	Edward Baesh, Esq. of Stansted
1536	Thomas Peryent the elder, Esq. of Digeswell		1572	George Horsey, Esq. of Digenswell
1537	Sir Henry Parker, Kt.		1573	Thomas Levensthorpe, Esq. of Shingle-hall
1538	Sir John Raynsford, Kt		1574	Henry Cock, Esq. of Brokesborne
1539	John Smyth, Esq.		1575	John Gill, Esq. of Widialll
1540	Sir Philip Boteler, Kt of Watton		1576	Thomas Bowles, Esq. of Wallington
1541	Sir John Mordant, Kt.		1577	Edmund Verney, Esq. of Pendley
1542	Ralph Rowlet, Esq. of St. Albans		1578	Philip Boteler, Esq. of Watton
1543	John Bowles of Wallington (½ year)		1579	Charles Morison, Esq. of Caishobury
	John Sewster, Esq. (½ year)		1580	Thomas Docwra, Esq. of Putteridge
1544	John Wentworth, Esq.		1581	Sir John Brocket, Kt of Hatfield

1582	Henry Coningsby, Esq. of North-Mims		1627	Sir Thomas Hide, Bart. of North-Mims
1583	Francis Heydon, Esq. of Watford		1628	Edward Gardiner, Esq. of Thunderidge
1584	Edward Baesh, Esq. of Stansted		1629	William Hoo, Esq. of Pauls Walden
1585	Henry Capell, Esq. of Hadhem		1630	Sir John Boteler, Knight of the Bath, of Watton
1586	Edward Pulter, Esq. of Bradfield		1631	Richard Hale, Esq. of Kings-Walden
1587	Thomas Leventhorpe, Esq.		1632	Henry Coghill, Esq. of Aldenham
1588	Sir John Cutts, Kt.		1633	William Plomer, Esq. of Radwell
1589	Edmund Verney, Esq. of Pendley		1634	William Priestley, Esq. of Esingdon
1590	Walter Mildmay, Esq. of Pishobury		1635	William Leman, Esq. of North-hall
1591	Thomas Hanchet, Esq.		1636	Ralph Freeman, Esq. of Aspenden
1592	Arthur Capell, Esq. of Hadhem		1637	Thomas Coningsby, Esq. of North-Mims
1593	John Leventhorpe, Esq. of Shingle Hall		1638	Thomas Hewyt, Esq. of Pishobury
1594	Rowlamd Lytton, Esq. of Knebworth		1639	John Gore, Esq. of Gilston
1595	Thomas Sadler, Esq. of Standon		1640	Richard Cole, Esq.
1596	Ralph Coningsby, Esq. of North-Mims		1641	Arthur Pulter, Esq. of Braudfeld
1597	Richard Spencer, Esq. of Offley		1642	*No Sheriff because of the Wars*
1598	Thomas Pope Blount, Esq. of Tittenhanger		1643	Sir John Garrard, Baronet, of Lammer
1599	Robert Cheater, Esq. of Royston		1644	Sir John Garrard, Baronet
1600	Thomas Hanchet, Esq.		1645	Sir John Garrard, Baronet and Sir
1601	Thomas Bowles, Esq. of Wallington			Robert Jocelin, Kt of Hide-hall
1602	Sir Edward Denny, Kt. of Waltham Abby		1646	Charles Nodes, Esq. of Sheephale
			1647	Rowland Hale, Esq. of Kings-Walden

JAM. I.

			1648	Francis Flyer, Esq. of Pelham
1603	Sir Henry Boteler, Kt. of Hatfield			
1604	Sir George Peryent, Kt of Digenswell		**CAR. II.**	
1605	Thomas Docwra, Esq. of Putteridge		1649	Roby Combe, Esq. of Hemel Hempsted
1606	Sir Leonard Hide, Kt. of Throcking		1650	John Rowley, Esq. of Berkway
1607	Sir John Leventhorpe, Kt. of Shingle-hall		1651	Thomas Keightley, Esq. of Hertingford
1608	Nicholas Trot, Esq. of Quickswood		1652	John Fotherley, Esq. of Rickmansworth
1609	Ralph Sadler, Esq. of Standon		1653	Humphry Shalcross, Esq. of Digenswell
1610	Sir Richard Anderson, Kt. of Pendley		1654	Sir John Gore, Kt. of Sacomb
1611	Sir Robert Boteler, Kt of Watton		1655	Sir John Read, Kt and Bart, of Hatfield
1612	John Wild, Esq.		1656	Edward Gardiner, Esq. of Thunderidge
1613	William Franklyn, Esq.		1657	John Berisford, Esq. of Rickmeresworth
1614	Sir Thomas Dacres, Kt of Cheshunt		1658	sir John Whitwrong, Kt. of Harpeden
1615	Sir Goddard Pemberton, Kt of St. Albans		1659	Robert Dycer, Esq. of Braughing
1616	Thomas Newes, Esq. of Hadham		1660	Sir Thomas Hewyt, Kt. of Pishobury
1617	Edward Brisco, Esq. of Aldenham		1661	Sir Henry Blount, Kt. of Tittenhanger
1618	Thomas Read, Esq. of Hatfield		1662	Sir Rowland Lytton, Kt. of Knebworth
1619	Sir Nicholas Hide, Kt of North-Mims		1663	Sir John Hale, Kt. of Stagenhoe
1620	Roger Pemberton, Esq. of St. Albans		1664	Sir Thomas Brograve, Bart of Hamels
1621	William Hale, Esq. of Kings-Walden		1665	Sir Jonathan Keate, Bart of Pauls Walden
1622	Edward Newport, Esq. of Pelham		1666	Edward Chester, Esq. of Berkway
1625	Sir Clement Scudamore, Kt. of North-Mims		1667	John Ellis, Esq. of St. Julians
1624	Richard Sidley, Esq. of Digenswell		1668	Israel Mayho, Esq. of Beyford
			1669	Sir Thomas Bide, Kt. of Ware

CAR. I.

			1670	Henry Baldwin, Esq. of Aldenham
1625	Sir William Lytton, Kt. of Knebworth		1671	Samuel Reeve, Esq. of Aston
1626	John Jenings, Esq. of St. Albans		1672	Thomas Priestley, Esq. of Esendon

Hertfordshire Sheriffs

Year	Sheriff	Year	Sheriff
1673	Henry Coghill, Esq. of Aldenham	1679	Thomas Halsey, Esq. of Great Gadesden
1674	Joshua Lomax, Esq. of St. Albans	1680	Sir John Boteler, Kt. of Watton
1675	Edward Chester, Esq. of Royston	1681	Sir Nicholas Miller, Kt. of Sandon
1676	Sir William Leman, Bart. of North-hall	1682	James Willymot, Esq. of Kelshall
1677	Sir Robert Jocelin, Bart. of Hide-hall	1683	Sir Thomas Field, Kt. of Stansted
1678	Sir William Lytton, Kt. of Knebworth	1684	James Goulston, Esq. of Widiall

---

List taken from Chauncy's "Historical Antiquities of
Hertfordshire" written in 1700.

Sheriffs of Bedfordshire. (Includes Buckinghamshire until 1574)

1501	John Seyntjohn, knt	1545	Lewis Dyve, esq (afterwards knt)
1502	Richard Blount, esq	1546	Robert Drurye, esq
1503	Edward Bulstrode, esq	1547	Francis Russell, knt
1504	Thomas Darell, esq	1548	Francis Pygott, esq
1505	John Cheyne, esq	1549	John Seyntjohn, knt
1506	William Gascoygn, esq	1550	Thomas Rotherham, knt
1507	John Longvile, knt	1551	Oliver Seyntjohn, esq
1508	George Hervy, or Harvy, esq	1552	Thomas Pigott, esq
1509	John Mordaunt, esq	1553	William Dormer, knt
1510	John Dyve, esq	1554	Arthur Longvile, esq
1511	Ralph Verney, esq	1555	Robert Drurye, knt
1512	Thomas Denham, or Dynham, esq	1556	Robert Peckham, knt
1513	William Gascoigne, esq	1557	Thomas Pygott of Stratton, esq
1514	Edmund Bray, knt	1558	Humphrey Rattclyff, knt
1515	John Seyntjohn, knt	1559	William Hawtrey, esq
1516	George Harvy, knt	1560	Thomas Teryngham, esq
1517	William Gascoigne, esq	1561	Robert Drury, knt
1518	Michael Fysscher, esq	1562	John Goodwyn, esq
1520	William Rede, knt	1563	Paul Darrell, or Dayrell, esq
1522	Robert Lee, knt	1564	Thomas Fletewood, esq
1522	Robert Dormer, esq	1565	Henry Cheyney, knt
1523	Thomas Langston, esq	1566	John Cheyney of Chesham Bois, esq
1524	Ralph Verney the younger, knt	1567	John Burlacy, esq
1525	Michael Fysscher	1568	William Dormer, knt
1526	Thomas Rotheram, esq	1569	Edmund Asshefeld, esq (afterwards knt)
1526	Edward Grevyle, knt	1570	Lewis Mordant, knt
1527	Francis Pygot, esq	1571	Thomas Leighe, esq
1528	John Hampden, knt	1571	Thomas Pigott, esq
1529	John Seyntjohn, knt	1572	Lewis Dyve, esq
1530	Michael Fysscher, knt	1573	George Peckham, knt
1531	Robert Dormer, esq	1574	Ralph Astrey, esq
1532	Edward Donne, knt		
1533	Robert Lee, knt		**Beds and Bucks severed**
1534	John Seyntjohn, knt		
1535	Roger Corbet, esq	1575	George Rotherham, esq. Luton
1536	Thomas Longvyle, esq	1576	John Barnardiston, esq. Northill
1537	William Wyndesore, knt	1577	George Kensham, esq. Tempsford
1538	Robert Dormer, knt	1578	John Spencer, esq. Cople
1539	Thomas Rotherham, knt	1579	Nicholas Luke, esq. Cople
1540	Ralph Verney, knt	1580	Henry Butler, esq. Higham Gobion
1541	John Gostwyk, knt	1581	John Thomson, esq. Husborne Crawley
1542	John Gascoign, knt	1582	Richard Conqueste, esq. Houghton Conquest
1543	Thomas Gifforde, esq	1583	Lewis Dyve, esq. Bromham
1544	Michael Fisssher, knt	1584	John Rowe, esq. Clapham

1586	Richard Charnock, esq. Holcote	1630	William Cater, or Cator, esq. Kempston
1585	Oliver Seyntjohn, esq. Bletsoe	1631	Edmund Anderson, esq. Eyworth
1586	Richard Charnock, esq. Holcote	1632	James Beverley, esq. Clophill
1587	William Boteler, or Butler, esq. Biddenham	1633	Onslow Winch, esq. Biggleswade
1588	Ralph Astrye, esq. Milton Ernest	1634	Humphrey Monnes, esq. Wootton
1589	Oliver Seintjohn of Stanfordburgh, esq. Bletsoe	1635	Richard Gearye, esq. Bushmead
1590	George Rotherham, esq. Luton	1636	Henry Chester, esq. Tilsworth
1591	Christopher Hoddesdon, esq. Leighton Buzzard	1637	John Charnock, esq. Holcot
1592	William Duncombe, esq. Battlesden	1637	William Butler, or Boteler, esq. Biddenham
1593	Nicholas Luke, esq. Cople	1638	William Plummer, or Plomer, esq. Warden
1594	John Dive, esq. Bromham	1639	Richard Child, esq. Toddington
1595	William Gostwick, esq. Willington	1640	John Burgoyne, esq. Sutton
1596	Richard Conquests, esq. Houghton Conquest	1641	Thomas Alston, knt. and bart. Odell
1597	Thomas Cheyney, esq. Toddington	1643	William Duncombe of Battlesden, Esq.
1598	Edward Ratcliffe, knt. Elstow	1644	Humphrey Fishe, esq. Northill
1599	William Butler of Biddenham, esq.	1644	Nicholas Denton, esq. Barton
1600	John Crofte, knt. Toddington	1647	Thomas Daniell, esq. Flitton
1601	Richard Charnock, esq. Holcote	1647	Matthias Tailor, esq. Clapham
1602	George Francklin, esq. Bolnhurst	1647	William Allen, esq. Gravenhurst
1603	John Dyve, knt. Bromham	1648	William Duncombe, esq. Battlesden
1604	John Leighe, or Lee, esq. Leighton Buzzard	1649	Robert Lovett, esq. Meppershall
1606	Edwin Sandys, knt. Eaton Bray	1650	William Bryers, knt. Pulloxhill
1606	Francis Anderson, knt. Eyworth	1651	Thomas Bromsall, esq. Biggleswade
1607	Thomas Snagge, knt. Marston	1652	John Huxley, esq. Eaton Bray
1608	Edmund Mordant, esq. Turvey	1653	Henry Pigott, esq. Biggleswade
1609	Thomas Austell, esq. Barford	1654	Robert Stanton, esq. Southill
1610	Francis Ventris, knt. Compton	1655	John Welles, esq. Leighton Buzzard
1611	Robert Sandy(s), knt and bart. Eaton Bray	1657	Owen Bromsall, esq. Biggleswade
1612	William Becher, esq. Renhold	1660	Edmund Wilde of Howton [Conquest], esq.
1613	Richard Saunders, esq. Leighton Buzzard	1661	Roger Burgoyne, knt. and bart. Sutton
1614	Edward Duncombe, knt. Battlesden	1662	Francis Wingate, esq. Harlington
1615	William Plomer, esq (knt 23 Sept 1616) Warden	1663	George Wyan, esq. Mogerhanger
1616	Roger Burgoine, esq. Sutton	1664	Edward Cater, knt. Kempston
1617	Oliver Luke, knt. Cople	1665	Thomas Snagg, esq. Marston
1618	Edmund Conquest, knt. Houghton Conquest	1666	John Huxley, knt. Eaton Bray
1619	George Keynsham, esq. Tempsford	1667	Henry Massingberd, nart. Potsgrove
1620	Francis Staunton, knt. Woburn	1668	Randolph Bovey, bart. Warden
1621	William Briars, esq. Pulloxhill	1668	Gideon De Lawney, esq. Roxton
1622	William Hawkins, esq. Tilbrook	1668	Thomas Bromsall, esq. Biggleswade
1623	Francis Clarke, knt. Houghton Conquest	1669	Ralph Bovey, bart. Warden
1624	Matthew Denton, esq. Barton	1670	Richard Wagstaffe, esq. Ravensden
1625	John Wingate, esq. Harlington	1671	Henry Brandreth, esq. Houghton Regis
1626	Edmund Gostwick, esq. Willington	1672	Thomas Bromsall, esq. Biggleswade
1627	John Moore of Layton, esq.	1673	Matthew Denis, or Dennes, esq. Kempston
1628	Anthony Chester, bart. Tilsworth	1674	Robert Bell, esq. Bedford
1629	Michaels Grigge, esq. Dunstable	1675	Samuel Reynardson, esq. Caddington

1675	Francis Dodworth, esq. Ridgmont		1712	Thomas Boswell of Dean, esq.
1676	Thomas Arnold of Ampthill, esq.		1712	John Vaux, esq. Whipsnade
1677	Samuel Reynardson, esq. Caddington		1713	Thomas Emerton, esq. Wootton
1678	Thomas Snagge, esq. Marston		1714	Thomas Bromsall, esq. Biggleswade
1679	William Gostwick, bart. Willington		1715	John Livesay, esq. Podington
1680	Villiers Charnoke, esq. (afterwards bart.) Holcot		1716	Theophilus Knapier, bart. Luton
1681	George Abbott, esq. Steppingley		1717	William Smith, esq. (knt Jul 1718) Warden
1682	James Astrey, esq. (knt 20 Nov 1683) Toddington		1718	Nicholas Luke, esq. Cople
1683	William Daniel, esq. Flitton		1720	Robert Hind, or Hinde, esq. Gravenhurst
1684	Humphrey Fish, esq. Northill		1721	Richard Orlebar, esq. Podington
1685	Thomas Halpenny, esq. Higham Gobion		1721	Henry Brandreth, esq. Houghton Regis
1686	John Crosse, esq. Luton		1722	Robert Abbott, esq. Steppingley
1687	John Wagstaffe, esq. Ravensden		1724	Thomas Aynscombe, esq. Dunstable
1688	Ralph Bromsall, esq. Biggleswade		1724	Thomas Garth, esq, Harrold
1689	Samuel Cater, esq. Kempston		1725	Joseph Johnson, esq. Milton Bryant
1690	William Boteler, or Butler, esq. Biddenham		1726	Theophilus Dillingham, esq. Dean
1691	John Neale, esq. Dean		1727	William Coleman of Cranfield, esq.
1692	John de la Fontaine, esq. Woburn		1728	Benjamin Rhodes, esq. Flitwick
1692	Samuel Tomson, knt. Husborne Crawley		1729	John Napier, bart. Luton
1693	John Eston, esq. Bedford		1730	William Lamb, esq. Totternhoe
1694	Stephen Anderson, bart. Eyworth		1731	George Blundell, esq. Cardington
1694	William Massingbeard, bart. Potsgrove		1732	Henry Southouse of Ravendon, esq.
1695	William Millard, esq. (afterwards knt) Flitton		1733	Edmund Morgan of Carrington, esq
1696	Robert Bell, esq. Bedford		1733	Hillersden Franks, esq. Heath & Reach
1697	John Burgoine, knt. Sutton		1734	Thomas Groome of Dunstable, esq.
1697	John Hinde, esq. Gravenhurst		1735	John Crawley, esq. Luton
1698	John Spencer, esq. Cople		1737	Francis Jessop of Bedford, esq.
1698	John de la Fontaine, esq. Woburn		1738	David Willaume, of Tingrith, esq.
1699	John Burgoyne, bart. Sutton		1738	Oliver Edwards of Carrington, esq.
1700	William Hillersden, esq. Elstow		1739	John Frankland of Gt Barford, esq.
1702	Maurice Abbott, esq. Steppingley		1741	John White of Ewe Green, esq. Ampthill
1702	Thomas Bromsall, esq		1741	John Lawson the younger of Barton, esq.
1702	Thomas Bromsall of Broxton, esq. Roxton		1743	John Coppin of Market Street, esq.
1702	Vincent Charnock, esq. Holcot		1743	John Miller the younger of Dunstable, esq.
1702	Thomas Johnson, esq. Milton Bryant		1744	Richard Browne of Egginton, esq.
1703	Samuel Ongley, esq. Warden		1744	Andrew Crosse of Westoning, esq.
1705	Edward Duncombe, esq. Battlesden		1744	Hammond Crosse, esq. Westoning
1705	Edward Snagg, esq. Marston		1745	Richard Bell of Bedford, esq
1706	John Huxley, esq. Eaton Bray		1746	Robert Ashwell of Leighton Buzzard, esq.
1707	Morgan Hinde, esq. Gravenhurst		1747	William Gary, or Gery, of Bushmead, esq.
1707	John Clarke, esq. Ridgmont		1748	John Hill of Bedford, esq.
1708	John Wright, esq. Bedford		1749	Thomas Crawley of Dunstable, esq.
1709	William Chew, esq. Dunstable		1750	Thomas Oave of Bedford, esq.
1710	Ralph Brumsell, esq. Biggleswade		1750	Harry Johnson of Milton Bryant, esq.
1711	William Nicholls, esq. Ampthill		1752	Thomas Gilpin, esq. Hockliffe
1711	John Harvey, esq. Northill		1753	Francis Herne of Luton, esq.

1754	David James of Ampthill, esq.	1786	Matthew Rugeley of Potton, esq.
1765	Thomas Vaux of Whipsnade, esq	1787	Joseph Partridge of Cranfield, esq
1756	James Smyth, or Smith, of Streatly, esq.	1788	William Lee Antonie of Colmworth, esq
1757	John Capon of Laighton Buzzard, esq.	1789	Samuel Boyden of Milton Ernest
1758	William Cole of Sundon, esq.	1790	James Metcalfe of Roxton House, esq.
1759	Dennis Farrer Hillersden of Helvestow, esq.	1791	Francis Pym of Hasell Hall, esq.
1760	Baker Coleman of Cranfield, esq.	1792	John Buchannan Riddell of Sundon, bart.
1761	Robert Burcher of Cople, esq.	1793	Thomas Crosse of Bramingham, esq.
1762	Simon Taylor of Wobourn, esq.	1794	Edward Nicoll of Studham, esq.
1763	Philip Monoux of Sandy, bart	1795	John Harvey of Ickwell, esq.
1764	William Pym of Hasell Hall, esq.	1796	George Brooks of Flitwick, esq.
1765	Richard Edwards of Ardesley, esq.	1797	John Higgins the elder of Turvey, esq.
1766	Philip Field of Barton, esq.	1798	John Fox of Dean, esq.
1767	Charles Chester of Tilsworth, esq.	1799	Robert Trevor of Flitwick, esq.
1768	John Cater of Kempston, esq.	1800	John Everett of Westoning, esq. (later knt)
1769	William Farrer of Kempston, esq.	1801	Stephen Raymond of Potton, esq.
1770	John Francklin of Northill, esq.	1802	John Higgins the younger of Turvey, esq.
1771	Charles Barnett of Stratton, esq.	1803	Godfrey Thornton of Moggerhanger, esq.
1772	Gillias Payne of Tempsford, bart.	1804	George Edwards of Henlow, esq.
1773	John Howard of Cardington, esq.	1805	John Polhill of Renholt, esq.
1774	John Crawley of Stockwood, esq.	1806	William Long of Kempston, esq.
1775	George Paunceforth of Ampthill, esq.	1807	Philip Monoux of Sandy, bart.
1776	Christopher Tower of Houghton Regis, esq.	1808	Richard Orlebar of Puddington, esq.
1777	John Sayer Weal Renal, of Egginton, esq.	1809	Robert Garston of Harrold, esq
1778	John Beecher of Hoobury, esq.	1810	Gregory O. Page Turner, Battlesden, bart.
1779	Rowland Alston of Odell, bart.	1811	Joseph Howell of Market Street, esq.
1780	William Thornton Astell of Everton, esq.	1812	John Cooper of Toddington, esq.
1781	John Harvey of Northill, esq.	1813	Richard Parkes of Luton, esq.
1782	Robert Thornton of Moggerhanger, esq.	1814	Stephen Thornton of Moggerhanger, esq.
1783	John Dilley of Southill, esq.	1815	Robert Hibbert of East Hide, esq.
1784	William Goldsmith of Streatly, esq.	1816	Henry Brandreth of Houghton Regis, esq.
1785	William Gibbard of Sharnbrook, esq.	1817	Samuel Crawley of Stockwood, esq.

Members of Parliament for Hertfordshire 1413 - 1694

HEN. V.

1413	John Hotoft and John Leventhorpe
1414	John Hotoft and William Fleete
1415	John de Leventhorpe and John Hotoft
1417	Philip Thornbery and John Hotoft
1419	Thomas Barre and William Parker
1420	John Barley and John Fray
1421	Philip Thornbery and John Kirkby

HEN. VI.

1422	John Leventhorpe and John Hotoft
1423	John Barley, Esq. and William Fleete
1424	Robert Leventhorpe, Esq. and John Kirkby
1427	John Terrell, Esq. and William Newport
1428	John Barley, Esq. and John Kirkby
1434	Thomas Brocket and Nicholas Morley
1441	John Troutbek and Nicholas Morley
1446	John Troutbek and Peter Paul
1448	Thomas Chivall and Bartholomew Halley, Esq.
1449	Sir Robert Wingfield and Sir Henry Barley, Kts
1450	Sir William Oldhall, Kt. and Philip Boteler, Esq.
1454	John Say and John Clay

EDW. IV

1467	Sir John Day and Sir Thomas Leventhorpe, Kts.
1473	John Sturgeon and John Forster

EDW. VI.

1547	Anthony Denny and Ralph Rowlet, Esquires
1552	Ralph Sadler and John Cock, Esquires

MAR.

1553	Sir John Boteler and Sir John Brocket, Kts
1554	Nath.

PHIL. and MAR.

1556	William Brocket and John Cobbys, Esquires
1557	John ... ...

ELIZ.

1558	Thomas Parrie and Sir Ralph Sadleir
1572	Sir Ralph Sadleir and John Brocket, Esq.
1584	Sir Ralph Sadleir and Henry Cock, Esq.

1586	Sir Ralph Sadleir, one of the Privy Council, and Henry Cock, Esq.
1592	Robert Cecil, Principal Secretary of State and Henry Cary, Esq.
1597	Robert Cecil, Secretary of State and Rowland Lytton, Esq.

JAC. I.

1603	Henry Cary and Rowland Lytton, Esquires
1623	Sir Charles Moryson, Kt and Bar. and William Lytton, Esq.

CAR. I.

1625	Sir John Boteler, Kt. and Bart. and John Boteler, Esq.
1627	Sir William Lytton and Sir Thomas Dacres, Kts
1640	Sir William Lytton, Kt and Arthur Capel, Esq.

CAR. II.

1660	Rowland Lytton and H. Caesar, Conventioners
1661	Thomas Lord Viscount Fanshaw, and Sir Richard Franklin, Bart. *Same Parliament* Sir Henry Caesar, Kt in the place of Thos. Lord Fanshaw deceased *Same Parliament*
1677	James Lord Viscount Cranbourne, Heir Apparent to William Earl of Salisbury, in the Place of Sir Henry Caesar, Kt. deceased *Same Parliament*
1678	William Hale, Esq. in the Place of James Lord Viscount Cranbourne, removed to the House of Lords upon the Decease of William Earl of Salisbury
1678	Sir Charles Caesar, Kt and Sir Jonathan Keate, Bart.
1679	William Hale and Silas Titus, Esquires

JAC. II.

1685	Ralph Freeman and Thomas Halsey, Esquires

W. and M.

1688	Sir Thos. Pope Blount, Bart. and Sir Chas. Caesar, Kt for a Convention
1689	Sir Thomas Pope Blount, Bart. and Ralph Freeman, Esq.

WILL. III.

1694	Sir Thomas Pope Blount, Bart. and Thomas Halsey, Esq.

List taken from Chauncy's "Historical Antiquities of
Hertfordshire" written in 1700.

Members of Parliament for Bedfordshire 1419 - 1767

1419	Thomas Wauton and John Enderby
1420	Roger Hunte and Robert Scot
1421	Robert Mordaunt and John de Goldington
1421	Thomas Mannyngham and Henry Cockayn
1422	Sir Thomas Wenlock and John Enderby
1423	Sir Thomas Wenlock and John Enderby
1425	Sir Thomas Wauton and Sir Thomas Wenlock
1426	Sir Thomas Wenlock and John Enderby
1427	John Enderby and William Ludsopp
1429	John Enderby and John Fitz Geffrey
1430	John Enderby and John Fitz Geffrey
1432	Sir Thomas Wauton and John Fitz Geffrey
1433	Thomas Sakevyle and William Whaplode
1435	John Enderby and John Fitz Geffrey
1436	John Ragoun and John Wenlok
1441	John Enderby and Thomas Reynes
1446	John Wenlock and William Gedney
1448	Sir John Wenlok and William Daubeny
1449	William Herteshorn and John Laurence
1450	William Herteshorn and John Laurence
1452	Sir Henry Norbury and Thomas Wychard
1467	William Lucy and Richard Godfrey
1472	William Lucy and John Harvey
1477	John Rotherham and Richard Carlile
1529	Sir William Gascoigne and George Ackworth
1542	John St. John and John Gascoigne
1547	Oliver St. John and Lewis Dyve
1553	Sir Humphrey Ratclyff and Lewis Dyve
1553	Sir John Mordaunt and Sir John Gascoigne
1554	Sir John Mordaunt and Sir John Ratclyff
1554	Sir John Mordaunt and Sir Humphrey Ratclyff
1557	Sir Humphrey Ratclyff and Sir John Gascoigne
1558	Thomas Pygott and John St. John
1562	John St. John and Lewis Mordaunt
1572	Sir Henry Cheney and George Rotherham
1572	John Thompson, vice Sir Henry Cheney, created a Peer.
1586	Thomas Snagg and George Rotherham
1588	Oliver St. John and Edward Ratclyff
1592	Oliver St. John and George Rotherham
1601	Oliver St. John and Sir Edward Ratclyff
1603	Oliver St. John and Sir Edward Ratclyff
1620	Sir Beauchamp St. John and Sir Oliver Luke
1623	Oliver Lord St. John and Sir Oliver Luke
1625	Oliver Lord St. John and Sir Oliver Luke

1626	Oliver Lord St. John and Sir Oliver Luke
1627	Oliver Lord St. John and Sir Oliver Luke
1640	Lord Wenworth and Sir Oliver Luke
1640	Lord Wenworth and Sir Oliver Luke
1640	Sir Roger Burgoyne, vice Lord Wenworth, created a Peer.
1658	John Okey and Richard Wagstaffe
1660	Lord Bruce and Samuel Browne
1661	Lord Bruce and Sir Humphrey Wynche
1664	Sir John Napier, vice Lord Bruce, created a Peer
1678	Lord William Russell and Sir Humphrey Monoux
1679	Lord William Russell and Sir Humphrey Monoux
1681	Lord William Russell and Sir Humphrey Monoux
1685	Sir Villiers Chernocke and William Boteler
1688	Edward Russell and William Duncombe
1689	Edward Russell and Thomas Browne
1695	Lord Edward Russell and William Duncombe
1698	Lord Edward Russell and Sir William Gostwick
1700	Lord Edward Russell and Sir William Gostwick
1701	Lord Edward Russell and Sir William Gostwick
1702	Lord Edward Russell and Sir William Gostwick
1705	Sir Pynsent Chernocke and Sir William Gostwick
1707	Sir Pynsent Chernocke and Sir William Gostwick
1708	Lord Edward Russell and Sir William Gostwick
1710	Lord Edward Russell and Sir William Gostwick
1713	Sir Pynsent Chernocke and John Harvey
1715	John Harvey and William Hillersden
1715	John Cater, vice John Harvey, unseated on petition.
1722	Hon. Charles Leigh and Sir Rowland Alston
1727	Hon. Pattee Byng and Sir Rowland Alston
1733	Hon. Charles Leigh, vice Hon. Pattee Byng, created a Peer.
1734	John Spencer and Sir Rowland Alston
1734	Sir Roger Burgoyne, vice John Spencer, returned for Woodstock.
1741	Sir John Chester and Sir Roger Burgoyne
1747	Sir Danvers Osborn and Thomas Alston
1753	Earl of Upper Ossory, vice Sir Danvers Osborn, on accepting Office
1754	Earl of Upper Ossory and Thomas Alston
1758	Henry Osborn, vice Earl of Upper Ossory, deceased
1761	Marquis of Tavistock and Robert Henley Ongley
1767	Earl of Upper Ossory, vice the Marquis of Tavistock, deceased

Local Gentlemen who served as Lord Mayor
of the City of London

1271 - 1272	Walter Hervey	1541	Michael Dormer
1337 - 1338	Henry Darci	1544	Sir Ralph Warren
1360	John Wroth	1556	Thomas Offley
1361	John Pecche	1560	Sir William Chester
1399	Thomas Knolles	1561	William Harpur
1410	Thomas Knolles	1581	James Harvye
1411	Robert Chichele	1583	Edward Osborne
1421	Robert Chichele	1588	Martin Calthorp
1435	Henry Frowyk	1594	John Spencer
1441	Robert Clopton	1598	Stephen Soame
1444	Henry Frowyk	1617	George Bolles
1457	Geoffrey Boleyn	1618	Sir Sebastian Harvey
1464	Ralph Josselyn	1619	Sir William Cokayne
1473	John Tate	1624	John Gore
1476	Sir Ralph Josselyn	1633	Ralph Freeman
1478	Richard Gardyner	1655	John Dethick
1482	Edmund Shaa	1660	Sir Richard Browne, Bt.
1486	Henry Colet	1688	Sir John Chapman
1488	Robert Tate	1693	Sir John Fleet
1491	Hugh Clopton	1696	Sir Edward Clarke
1493	Ralp Astry	1701	Sir William Gore
1495	Sir Henry Colet	1708	Sir Charles Duncombe
1496	John Tate	1710	Sir Gilbert Heathcote
1501	Sir John Shaa	1719	Sir George Thorold, Bt.
1503	Sir William Capel	1727	Sir Edward Becher
1510	Sir William Capel	1742	George Heathvote
1514	Sir John Tate	1750	Francis Cockayne
1515	William Boteler	1752	Crisp Gascoyne
1527	James Spencer	1773	Frederick Bull
1536	Ralph Warren	1781	William Plomer
1540	William Roche		

Index of People

Index of People

Index of People

Index of People

Shaw, George Bernard 34
Sheldon 81, 136
Sherwin 104, 139
Shipman 134, 136
Shoard 139
Shotbolt 121
Silvester 145
Sir Walter Raleigh 100
Skegg(s) 35, 91, 119, 146
Skipwith 12, 106, 122, 146
Slaney 137
Sloane 54
Smith 4
Smythe 130, 137
Snagge 35, 106
Soame 35, 43, 46, 73, 76, 118
Somerset 141
Spelman 126
Spencer 35, 48, 49, 121, 134
Spenser, Edmund 28
St George 41, 127
St John 3, 4, 5, 6, 8, 9, 10, 41, 44
    77, 112, 120, 127, 132, 137, 142
    143, 144, 147
Stafford 119
Stanton 65
Stevenson 14
Stone 43, 46, 127
Stuart, James Edward 46, 67
Stuteville 12, 134
Style 139
Sulyard 97

Swinburne 29
Talbot 100, 141
Tallebosc 142
Tarboys 3
Tate 5, 137
Taverner 43, 127, 139, 145, 147
Taylor 125
Thompson 130, 132
Thornbury 105
Thornton 106, 107, 146
Throckmorton 35, 100, 119
Thynne 143
Timpson, John 35, 73
Tooke 62, 131
Tresham 141
Trevelyan 52, 63
Trevor 81
Trevor Roper, Lord Dacre 17
Trollope 30
Tryce 134
Tudor 10, 144
Turnor 12
Tyler 26
Tyrrell 51, 97, 98, 121, 139
    141
Underhill 75, 122, 135
Vanderplank 104
Vaughan 135
Vaux 100
Vavosaur 118
Villiers 121
Vincent 146
Wadham 141

Wake 111, 142
Walcot 127
Waldegrave 141, 144
Walker 131
Wallace 121
Walsingham 118
Walter 135
Warburton 46
Warde 123
Warre 147
Warren 65, 91, 92, 103, 104
    105, 106, 107, 108, 112, 119
    131, 139, 146
Webbs 128
Welles 57, 144
Wentworth 97, 123
Weston Browne 123, 138
Whethill 126
Whettall 105
White 135
Williams 132
Willoughby 118
Wilson 15, 51
Wiltshire 133
Wingate 43, 45, 77, 103, 121
    132, 139, 144, 145, 147
Wintour 100, 141
Wiseman 112, 142
Wratting 13, 14
Wriothesley Russell 19
Wroth 89
Zouch 5

Index of Places

Index of Places

Index of Places

Index of Places

CHANGES IN OUR LANDSCAPE:
Aspects of Bedfordshire, Buckinghamshire and the Chilterns 1947–1992

Eric Meadows

In the post-War years, this once quiet rural backwater between Oxford and Cambridge has undergone growth and change – and the expert camera of Eric Meadows has captured it all . . .

An enormous variety of landscape, natural and man-made, from yesteryear and today – open downs and rolling farmland, woods and commons, ancient earthworks, lakes and moats, vanished elms. Quarries, nature reserves and landscape gardens. Many building styles – churches of all periods, stately homes and town dwellings, rural pubs, gatehouses and bridges. Secluded villages contrast their timeless lifestyle with the bustle of modern developing towns and their industries.

Distilled from a huge collection of 25,000 photographs, this book offers the author's personal selection of over 350 that best display the area's most attractive features and its notable changes over 50 years. The author's detailed captions and notes complete a valuable local history. The original hardback edition was in print for only 4 weeks in 1992. By popular demand now in a large format paperback.

EXPLORING HISTORY ALL AROUND

Vivienne Evans

A handbook of local history, arranged as a series of routes to cover Bedfordshire and adjoining parts of Hertfordshire and Buckinghamshire. It is organised as two books in one. There are seven thematic sections full of fascinating historical detail and anecdotes for armchair reading. Also it is a perfect source of family days out as the book is organised as circular motoring/cycling explorations, highlighting attractions and landmarks. Also included is a background history to all the major towns in the area, plus dozens of villages, which will enhance your appreciation and understanding of the history that is all around you!

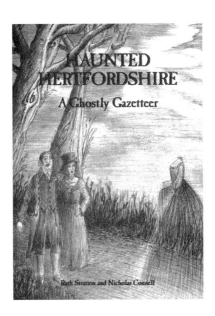

HAUNTED HERTFORDSHIRE

Nicholas Connell and Ruth Stratton

The most extensive collection of the county's ghosts ever written, with over 300 stories. Many are little-known and previously unpublished, having been hidden away in the vaults of Hertfordshire Archives and Local Studies. Others are up to the moment accounts of modern hauntings in the words of those who have experienced them. All supported by dozens of rare and evocative pictures, an outline of the latest theories and diary dates of regular apparition appearances.

Stories feature a feast of phantoms, including grey ladies, dashing cavaliers, spectral transport, headless horsemen and a gallery of Kings and Queens.

Locations include Bishops Stortford, Datchworth, Harpenden, Hertford, Hitchin, Hoddeson, St. Albans, Ware and Watford.

LEAFING THROUGH LITERATURE
Writers' Lives in Hertfordshire and Bedfordshire

David Carroll

The neighbouring counties of Hertfordshire and Bedfordshire have had close links, over the years, with some of the world's greatest writers. John Bunyan , of course, spent all his life in and around Bedford, and George Bernard Shaw lived for nearly half a century at Ayot St.Lawrence.

George Orwell, Beatrix Potter, Arnold Bennett and Charles Dickens are just some of the many famous names to be found in this lively and informative book. But there are some less familiar ones too: George Gascoigne of Cardington, for example and Edward Young at Welwyn. However, from Sir Thomas More in the sixteenth century to Graham Greene who died in 1991, they all have one thing in common: a connection, at some stage in their lives, with Hertfordshire or Bedfordshire.

THREADS OF TIME

Shela Porter

A pale-faced city child is evacuated from London during the Zeppelin raids of 1917. In Hitchin she takes a dressmaking apprenticeship and opens her own workshop with customers including the local gentry and the young Flora Robson.

Moving to Bedford on her marriage, her sewing skills help her rapidly growing family to survive the Depression; working long hours during the exigencies of war-time Britain, it is her re-designed battle-jacket that Glenn Miller is wearing when he disappears over the Channel in 1944, and entertainers Bing Crosby and Bob Hope leave comics and candy for her 'cute kids'. For five years after the war the family run a small café in the town but sewing then sees her through again as the business is sold, she is widowed with a nine-year-old son to raise, all her children gradually leave and she moves away to be wardrobe mistress to a big operatic society in High Wycombe. Finally she settles in a small cottage opposite the great airship sheds at Cardington from where she once watched the ill-fated R101 take off on its last journey in 1930.

A mirror of her times, this gripping biography tells the story of a remarkable lady, a talented dressmaker, mostly in Hitchin and Bedford – played out against the unfolding drama of the entire twentieth century.

JOURNEYS INTO BEDFORDSHIRE

JOURNEYS INTO HERTFORDSHIRE

Anthony Mackay

These two books of ink drawings reveal an intriguing historic heritage and capture the spirit of England's rural heartland, ranging widely over cottages and stately homes, over bridges, churches and mills, over sandy woods, chalk downs and watery river valleys.

Every corner of Bedfordshire and Hertfordshire has been explored in the search for material, and, although the choice of subjects is essentially a personal one, the resulting collection represents a unique record of the environment today.

The notes and maps, which accompany the drawings, lend depth to the books, and will assist others on their own journeys around the counties.

Anthony Mackay's pen-and-ink drawings are of outstanding quality. An architectural graduate, he is equally at home depicting landscapes and buildings. The medium he uses is better able to show both depth and detail than any photograph.